PENGUIN BOOKS

FUTURE STUFF

malcolm abrams is a magazine consultant and book author. He has worked with major publishing companies as a writer, editor, and editorial director. A native of Toronto, he lives in Manhattan, because that's where his stuff is.

harriet bernstein is a freelance reporter and a graduate of the Radcliffe Publishing Program. A recovering technophobe, Ms. Bernstein happened onto *Future Stuff* by accident. Although now quite taken by the subject, she still doesn't own a TV.

F U

ILLUSTRATIONS BY BOB JOHNSON

TURE
stuff

MALCOLM ABRAMS

HARRIET BERNSTEIN

PENGUIN
BOOKS

PENGUIN BOOKS
Published by the Penguin Group
Viking Penguin, a division of Penguin Books USA Inc.,
375 Hudson Street, New York, New York 10014, U.S.A.
Penguin Books Ltd, 27 Wrights Lane,
London W8 5TZ, England
Penguin Books Australia Ltd, Ringwood,
Victoria, Australia
Penguin Books Canada Ltd, 2801 John Street,
Markham, Ontario, Canada L3R 1B4
Penguin Books (N.Z.) Ltd, 182–190 Wairau Road,
Auckland 10, New Zealand

Penguin Books Ltd, Registered Offices:
Harmondsworth, Middlesex, England

First published in Penguin Books 1989

10 9 8 7 6 5 4

Copyright © Malcolm Abrams and Harriet Bernstein, 1989
Illustrations copyright © Viking Penguin, a division of Penguin Books USA Inc., 1989
All rights reserved

Many of the trade names in this book are registered trademarks; they are protected by
United States and international trademark laws.

LIBRARY OF CONGRESS CATALOGING IN PUBLICATION DATA
Abrams, Malcolm.
    Future stuff / Malcolm Abrams and Harriet Bernstein.
        p.   cm.
    Includes index.
    ISBN 0 14 01.2639 2
    1. New products—United States.   I. Bernstein, Harriet.
II. Title.
HF5415.153.A27   1989
338'.02'0973—dc20   89-3892

Printed in the United States of America
Set in Bodoni Book
Designed by Beth Tondreau Design/Jane Treuhaft
Illustrations by Bob Johnson

for

Paul and Aaron,

Gabrielle and Max

• • • • •

May the Future Be

as Good and Bright

INTRODUCTION

Future Stuff is a book for consumers. Everything in this book should be in your supermarket, hardware store, pharmacy, department store, or otherwise available by the year 2000. Many of the technologies behind the products in *Future Stuff* are new and developing. So it's doubtful that any one reader is going to be knowledgeable about all of them. For that reason, we have made the book light on scientific and technical talk and heavy on lightness and clarity.

It's our hope that as you read along you get a good idea of what each product does, some idea of how it works, and a clear idea of the need each fulfills. We also hope that you are inspired by the imagination and creativity of the people responsible for the stuff in this book. We were. From an eight-year-old girl in Belmont, Massachusetts, who invented a puddle detector so that blind people won't get their feet wet to scientists at the Massachusetts Institute of Technology who are developing a holograph telephone, there's something innately noble about each person's search for new ideas.

As you read along—about flying cars and round refrigerators, sonic painkillers and painless dental drills, smart cards and smart houses— something else is likely to happen. The products, like pieces in a jigsaw puzzle, start to form pictures. And suddenly, in your mind's eye, you have a vision of what life will be like in the final decade of the twentieth century.

This is exciting stuff.

A few words about the products in this book: Not every one will be new to you. From newspapers, magazines, and television, you'll know about some of them. There may even be the occasional item that's being test-marketed in your area or has arrived sooner than expected. Mostly, though, you'll be surprised at all the new stuff that's coming.

There's serious stuff, like cholesterol- and fat-free foods, voice-activated computers, home tests for infectious diseases, and new lenses that will let blind people see. And there's fun stuff, too: a robot dog, a kiss moisturizer, potato ice cream, and a bathing suit that changes color with your mood.

In between the fun and the serious are hundreds of useful, entertaining, delicious, invigorating, stimulating, self-improving, time-, energy-, and money-saving products that will make life better.

Think of this book as a kind of window-shopping expedition into the future.

Enjoy picking out what you'll buy tomorrow.

Malcolm Abrams

Harriet Bernstein

viii

THE HEADINGS EXPLAINED

Below the title of each product, there are three headings: *Odds*, *ETA*, *Price*. A few words of explanation are needed for each.

ODDS: This is the probability, measured as a percentage, that the product will actually be on sale by the year 2000. When the odds are listed as 100%, that means the product exists in a form that can be marketed and sold. For example, the *mini-portable oven* (Odds: 100%) has a manufacturer who is ready to bring the product to market.

On the other hand, *no-calorie sugar* (Odds: 85%) exists in natural form and has been synthesized. However, it has not yet been manufactured in sufficient quantities or at a feasible cost. It has also not been approved by the Food and Drug Administration.

In most cases, the odds of a product reaching the market have been projected by the inventor or manufacturer. In some cases, though, the authors have made this projection based on the available information.

ETA: This is the Estimated Time of Availability—the year that the product is expected to arrive in stores nationwide. In many cases, when the ETA is listed as 1990 the product is already being sold in a limited fashion, usually from the manufacturer or through mail-order houses. We have listed addresses when possible.

In most instances, the ETA has been supplied by the inventor or the manufacturer. However, in some cases, the authors have made the projection.

PRICE: This is what the inventor or manufacturer believes the product will sell for in today's dollars when it arrives on the market. When the price is listed as N/A, that means it is not available either because it has not yet been determined, or because it is not applicable, as the product will not be sold directly to consumers but will be incorporated into other products.

ACKNOWLEDGMENTS

A book that covers this much material could never be done without the help of a strong body of researchers. We were exceptionally fortunate to receive help from friends, colleagues, and new faces that came to us through a healthy grapevine. Our deepest thanks go to Fritz Bernstein, Grace Bennett, Jane Berryman, Diane Burley, Suzanne Carmick, Peter Cerbone, Wendy Cole, Chris Collins, Sue Crystal, Jennie Danowski, Kris DiLorenzo, Fonda Duvanel, Sarasue French, Annette Foglino, Tom Garafola, Diane Giles, Ira Hellman, Roger Jennings, Easy Klein, Miriam Leuchter, Matthew Levine, Chris Levite, Elizabeth MacDonald, Chris Markle, Ann Whipple Marr, Julie

xi

Moline, Lisa Murray, Didi Pershouse, Judy Sandra, George Schaub, Chris Secrest, Jacqueline Smith, Pam Supplee, Divya Symmers, Linn Varney, Valerie Vaz, Monte Williams, Brooke Zern. Very special thanks to Norman Meyersohn, our automobile expert, and to Lisa Towle, our most prolific reporter. Thanks also to our agent, Madeleine Morel, our editor, Mindy Werner, her assistant, Janine Steel, as well as to Gina Holloman and Amy Renson, who helped us out at office central.

We are also indebted to the many people in organizations whose purpose is to present the marketplace with the great ideas and inventions discovered in their worlds. There was Pam Michaelson of the *International New Product Newsletter*, Al Kaff and Yong Kim of the Cornell News Service, Mark Seitman of NASA, Professor Patrick Purcell of the Massachusetts Institute of Technology Media Lab, Joe Durocher of the University of New Hampshire, Marilyn Miller of Princeton Dental Resources, Judy Sawyer of *Video Magazine*, Peter Moore of *Modern Photography*, Eric Schrier of *Hippocrates*, Tom Duretsky of *Omni*, Roger Dooley of *Electronic House*, Elaine Stern of Rohla DiClerico, Chuck Wicksome of Food Technology Institute, Deborah Dallinger of the Rochester Institute of Technology, Charles Downs of Michigan State University, Jack Losse of the University of Alabama, Joe Kepneck at Stanford University Tech Transfer, and the many inventors' organizations from Invent America, which runs a contest every year for the best kid's invention, to the National Congress of Inventors' Organizations and all the folks in between: Richard Wantz of the Kessler Corporation, Steve Gnass of the Invention Convention, John Cronin of DirecTech, who publishes *Tech Trans International Technology Transfer Directory*, John Pike of International Business Development, Alan Tratnor of Inventors' Workshop, Intellectual Property Owners, the Small Business Administration, the U.S. Patent Office, Industrial Innovation Service of Canada, Lomar Associates, and others who connected to our grapevine but whose names got lost in the twine. A special appreciation to Blair Newman and Jerome Svigals for making us a little less technophobic and for clarifying all our technology research, and to Susan Sanders of Hammacher Schlemmer, who not only helped us locate terrific inventions around the world but had the graciousness not to laugh at us when we told her what we were going to do.

And where would we be without the cooperation and warm enthusiasm of the many inventors, researchers, public-relations agents, professors, scientists, and corporate executives who spoke to us—many of whom have become new friends—and the consistently amazing support of personal friends and family, particularly Seena Harris-Parker, Nancy and Mildred Abrams, Seymour Bernstein, Bob Swerdling, and Eileen Fisher.

We thank you all from the bottom of our hearts.

C O N T E N T S

XV

CONTENTS

xvi

FUTURE STUFF

1

stuff you wouldn't believe!

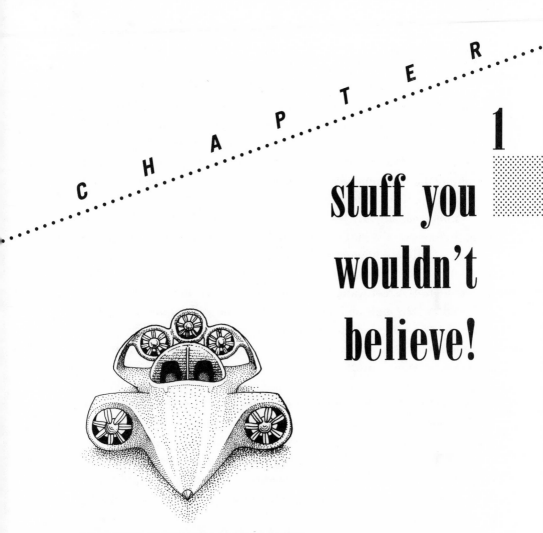

LEVITATION VEHICLE

This is the stuff of comic books, sci-fi magazines, and the dreams of generations of little boys who loved machines. It's called the Moller 400. In appearance, it's a sleek cross between a Corvette and a rocket ship. In function, it's a car, helicopter, and airplane, all in one.

• • • • •
ODDS: 100%
ETA: 1991
PRICE: $100,000
• • • • •

It seats four, takes off vertically, can do 400 miles an hour, hover low, land softly, and park in your garage. And it's almost as easy to operate as a video game.

1

The inventor of Moller 400 is Paul Moller, one of those boys from the 1940s who held on to his dream. While earning his doctorate at Montreal's McGill University and through fifteen years of teaching at the University of California at Davis, he worked to develop new types of aircraft. Now head of his own firm, Moller International, he is putting the final touches on his masterpiece, which he modestly calls "an alternative to the family car."

Moller has already tested the technology for the Moller 400 in his earlier model, the 200X, which looks like a flying saucer. It operated successfully on numerous flights—both by remote control and with a pilot aboard. Now the Moller 400 is about ready for takeoff. It's 6 feet high, 9½ feet wide, and 18 feet long. It has an economy cruising speed of 225 mph and gets 15 miles to the gallon, and is powered by eight 65-pound, 528-cubic-centimeter rotary engines. Each engine generates 150 horsepower, or over 2 horsepower per pound, four times that of a typical aircraft engine.

These eight compact engines are encased in 4 ducts. With no exposed blades, the craft is much safer to maneuver on the ground than either a helicopter or a small plane.

Moller has built the Moller 400 with safety in mind. Three on-board computers check each other's work and can back one another up. These computers will also provide the aircraft with a sophisticated collision-avoidance system expected to aid air traffic safety by the year 2000.

At speeds above 125 mph, altitude can be maintained even if six of the eight engines should fail. And if all the engines should die, the Moller 400 will land with the aid of an emergency parachute. Also, its 5-foot stiletto nose will crumple to absorb shock.

While it may seem like the fulfillment of every commuter's fantasy to leave bumper-to-bumper traffic below, Moller believes that the craft's first application will be performing search-and-rescue missions in isolated areas. Still, there are a lot of childhood dreamers already lining up for the fully certified craft. According to Jack Allison, marketing director for Moller International, forty-seven people have already reserved a Moller 400 by paying a fully refundable $5,000 deposit.

THE WATER BATTERY

A battery that runs on water, or juice, or Coca-Cola, or even beer and wine sounds too bizarre, right? Roger Hummel, director of VentuResearch in El Paso, Texas, says he has one and it can last up to fifty years.

ODDS: 85%
ETA: 1991
PRICE: $5

VentuResearch, a small firm of engineers and computer programmers, specializes in product development. Clients have included IBM, ITT, AT&T, General Motors, and General Electric. A few years ago they made Ripley's *Believe It or Not* with a watch that was powered by liquid. The "water watch" was a moderate success with consumers; the water battery is an extension of the technology.

Hummel explains it this way: Conventional batteries run on a chemical mix and last up to three years. They "die" when the chemicals corrode the battery's innards. Also, conventional batteries begin to discharge from the moment they're manufactured, wearing down even as they sit on store shelves. "Our battery presents none of these problems," claims Hummel, "because it runs on liquids instead of toxic chemicals."

To use a water battery, just unscrew the cap, pour in the liquid of choice, screw the cap back on, and you're ready to go. When you're finished, just rinse out the battery and store it dry. The inside won't corrode because the "juice" is drained. And the battery doesn't die because it discharges only when there's liquid inside.

VentuResearch hopes to go into head-on competition with conventional dry-cell batteries by 1991. The first commercial versions will be offered in the same size, shape, and form as the industry standards: AA, C, and D.

3

SMART HOUSE

A few years ago, it took a bit of a conceptual stretch to imagine a VCR that could record a program while you weren't at home. But just imagine a Smart House, which can operate *all* appliances from anywhere. And that's just the beginning.

•••••
ODDS: 90%
ETA: 1997
PRICE: $7,000–$10,000, INCLUDING INSTALLATION
•••••

The National Association of Home Builders, along with a consortium of manufacturers, research organizations, and utility companies, are working on the final stages of bringing the concept of a totally responsive habitat to the American public. The group has given their project the obvious name, Smart House, and is preparing to launch the world's most all-inclusive system for home automation.

Once your home is wired, your wish is its command. It will turn the lights on for you as you come up the walkway, and shut off the burglar alarm to allow you to enter in silence. You can flash the lights in the whole house to alert people that dinner is ready. Or you can tell your oven to make the TV flash when the roast is done. Before you go to bed at night, a control panel will let you know the temperature of each room in the house, and whether or not any appliances need to be turned off. The washing machine will be alerted by the utility company as to what hours of the day it can take advantage of lower rates for water and electricity. And your stereo speakers, your phone, your television will work with any socket in the house regardless of where the stereo receiver, the phone jack, or the VCR are installed—all without additional wiring.

Everything will be controlled by a panel on the wall, a video touch screen, a remote control device, a voice recognition system, automatic sensors, and/or by telephone from anywhere in the world. Take your choice of any or all combinations, although voice recognition will cost you a bit more. Old appliances will work with the system, but eventually appliances will be built with their own "smarts." Some will even be able to diagnose themselves. A repair person will call the machine on the telephone to see what's wrong, or will come to the house and read it on the control panel.

Beyond convenience, Smart Houses will offer the ultimate in safety. If there is a gas leak, an electrical shortage, or any malfunction in the system, the energy flow will be shut down. Fires will be visible on screens before they spread. And when the plug of any appliance is inserted into a socket, a microchip in the plug will tell the socket how much and what kind of energy is needed. So if a child inserts a paper clip or a finger into the socket, no electricity will be activated.

"Oh, and what if the power goes out?" you say in disbelief. Don't worry. You will not lose all your intricate programming. A backup power unit that constantly recharges itself will keep the basics of the system—clocks, instructions for timing, security system, and the spark for the gas—all operative. If you have set the coffeepot to start percolating by 7 A.M. and the power goes off in the middle of the night, the backup can be counted on to produce your wake-up cup right on schedule if the power comes back on.

According to Ken Geremia, who handles communications for the project, "More than a hundred folks are working together to establish the common denominator for all these services."

Several millions of dollars have been invested so far, with several more to come, and twenty new homes are scheduled to be built with "smarts" by the beginning of the decade. Retrofitting old homes will be possible a few years later.

DEODORANT UNDERWEAR

O kay, here's one for the Gipper: a T-shirt that permanently prevents body odor. Or maybe the Gipper would like a pair of Jockey shorts that "just say no" to jock itch, or a pair of socks that help fight athlete's foot?

ODDS: 85%

ETA: 1999

PRICE: SLIGHTLY MORE THAN REGULAR UNDERWEAR

The old football hero himself would've loved to know that a company in Atlanta, where textiles are king, has cooked up an antimicrobial agent that reduces the buildup of bacteria and fungus—the main causes of body odor. And as if that wasn't enough, they found a way to add it to fabrics. And if even that wasn't enough, they knew that the chemical, called Intersept, is not hazardous to human health. Now they are starting to add it to undergarments and diapers and the insoles of shoes.

Walter Ivkovich, spokesman for Interface, Inc., the company responsible for all this niceness, says, "The neat thing about this product is that it is effective but has about the same amount of oral toxicity as table salt."

But don't fling your roll-on down the incinerator yet. The Environmental Protection Agency needs to take a long, hard look at this stuff before it goes to market. It may not be toxic to human beings, but it could still prove to be a skin irritant or harmful to some one-celled organism at the bottom of the food chain. Many industry sources, however, are convinced that underwear with built-in deodorant will definitely make it to your locker.

6

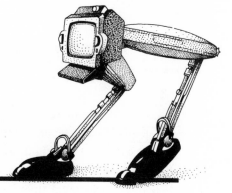

THE WALKING TV

A television on two legs is robotic design at its most amusing. That's what
Brian Elliot intended when he invented
the Animan. This television of the future
will be able to walk freely from room to
room without human help, boogie to MTV,
and add drama to action-packed chase scenes by leaning into the
curves.

· · · · ·
ODDS: 50%
ETA: 1995
PRICE: $5,000
· · · · ·

Elliot, a student at the Art Center College of Design in Pasadena,
California, also equipped his prototype television with a security
camera. When night falls, the Animan becomes the Aniscout as it
patrols the home and sounds an alarm if a burglar is on the premises.

Martin Smith, associate chairman of industrial design at the school,
states, "I don't know why it couldn't be a product in the nineties. If
done today, it would probably have an umbilical cord running to a
powerful computer bank, but it will probably be untethered in the
future."

Sony hopes to develop the television and plans to add voice recognition as one of its features.

7

· · · · ·

THE MOST INTELLIGENT TOILET

A nd here's the answer for all those hypochondriacs on your Christmas list. It will help put their medical fears aside by providing instant readouts of their health whenever they feel the urge.

ODDS: 80%
ETA: 1996
PRICE: N/A

A company called TOTO, Ltd., is the largest manufacturer of toilets in Japan. They are interested in marketing an "intelligent" toilet that takes your temperature and your blood pressure, analyzes your urine and stool, and weighs you whenever you use it. Their representative in France, where bidets have long been essential to bathroom sophistication, says the product is *"en teste"* for now. The Japanese office is all hush-hush about any specifics, but the great advantage of this new bathroom fixture will be that a patient's health condition can be monitored by a doctor without the patient having to leave home, or even the bathroom!

The most intelligent toilet will be able to transmit its readings by telecommunications to a physician's office. NIT, the Japanese telephone and telegraph company, is in on the development of this product, as is Japan's largest manufacturer of electronic clinical thermometers, Omron Tateisi, which also manufactures electronic systems for transferring money.

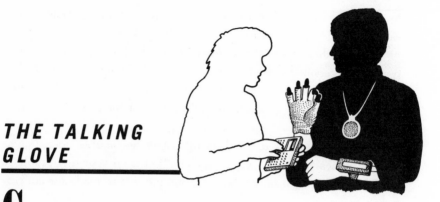

THE TALKING
GLOVE

Communicating with non-vocal deaf people can make your heart sink if you don't know their sign language. Not only do you regret not being able to understand them, but you usually feel that you are insulting them in some unforgivable way.

••••
ODDS: 95%
ETA: 1993
PRICE: $1,000
••••

Well, thank you, Jim Kramer, for an invaluable contribution not only to those of us who want to interface with deaf people but also to the two million Americans who live in silence and the half million of those who cannot speak intelligibly.

Kramer, a Ph.D. candidate in electrical engineering at Stanford University, has applied for a patent on what he calls a Talking Glove. How does he describe the need for his invention? "If I were a non-vocal deaf person," he says, "this is what I would build for myself."

There are sensors in the flesh-colored "glove" that read the positions of the fingers as they spell out words using the American Manual Alphabet, also known as fingerspelling. The glove is wired to a Walkman-size processor unit, worn on the belt, that recognizes the fingerspelling of each letter, combines the letters into complete words, and translates them into synthesized speech. A speaker pendant about the size of a half dollar is worn around the neck and projects the speech. Kramer says "the speaker can be worn unobtrusively under the shirt, and the sound will emerge from in front of you, as if you were speaking."

The device also comes with a wristwatch that has an LCD screen which displays what the glove is spelling. As soon as a letter is formed

9

by the gloved hand, it will show up on the wristwatch. When a full word is spelled, the word is immediately spoken.

There is also a pocket-size keypad on which hearing people can type their responses. Whatever is typed onto the miniature keyboard is displayed on the wristwatch for the deaf person to read. The watch can be replaced by a mechanical braille unit for a deaf and blind person.

"I would like to see the Talking Glove become as accepted as glasses or hearing aids," says Kramer. "Put it on your night table at bedtime, then put it on in the morning and you're ready for conversation."

ULTRASONIC 3-D CLOTHES

C lothes manufacturers have seen the future and it looks like this: garments molded—not stitched—into three-dimensional shapes and produced in a mere forty-five seconds. That's where the industry should be by 1993. By the end

• • • • •
ODDS: 75%
ETA: 1993
PRICE: COMPETITIVE
• • • • •

of the year 2000, customers will choose colors, fabrics, and details by computer, have body scans, and get the finished outfit, all in a matter of minutes.

Spearheading this new technology is Brett Stern, president of New York–based Symagery Inc. Says Stern, "I realized that there had been no improvement in the manufacturing process since the invention of the sewing machine." But now, using the same technology that brought us "the plastic cottage cheese container and molded brassiere cups," he has invented a machine—already accepted by the National Bureau of Standards—which "takes a bolt of fabric and creates a garment in forty-five seconds without any human intervention."

The cloth, made of at least 50 percent synthetic fiber, is molded into a three-dimensional shape, cut, and ultrasonically sealed and

10

finished along the seams, according to Stern. Exact size is guaranteed and "by being made in a three-dimensional way, the clothing inherently fits the body better." The garment will lie flat when finished, "but will have a memory of the 3-D shape in which it was created."

By the end of the century, Stern expects that designers will develop "looks" in clothes, but it will be the customer, using a computer, who picks the colors, fabrics, and details. By means of a video body scan, the final product will be individually manufactured to fit each person perfectly. *En garde*, Ungaro and Calvin Klein!

THE WALKING DESK

Whether you work at home or in an office, sitting at a desk for long periods of time is bound to get you down. Nathan Edelson, inventor of the Walking Desk, calls it "postural fixity," a condition that may cause aches, pains, fatigue, stress, and eventual illness.

His solution is a computer work station that stands higher than a regular desk and has a treadmill, stationary bike, and stair climber installed underneath. On a good day, a worker should be able to walk four to five miles and burn as many as 1,500 calories while maintaining a normal workload.

ODDS: 90%

ETA: 1992

PRICE: $10,000

Edelson heads a company called Environments for Health in Missoula, Montana, which produces the Walking Desk and other "active" ergonomic office products. "Over the next ten years," he maintains, "ninety percent of us will be doing some form of computerized office work. Unless we bring some new ideas to bear on the way this work is performed, it's going to continue to make us very sick."

11

In addition to the exercise features, the Walking Desk comes with a compact disc player for listening to calming music and a color monitor for viewing relaxing nature scenes. "When you have a client screaming at you on the phone," reasons Edelson, "turning up the speed on the treadmill and gazing at scenes of foaming surf on the 'video window' makes a lot more sense than returning your caller's hostility."

It may also help you maintain a trimmer waistline. Edelson estimates that the calories expended over a few hours a day can add up to an appreciable weight loss as well as improved muscle tone. His tests have indicated that the exercise function does not impair job efficiency, and appears to enhance creativity. "Best of all," he says, "people say it makes them feel better, and that it's fun to walk at work."

MOOD SUIT

Bathing suits may be more "revealing" than ever in the 1990s if Donald Spector's new invention becomes the rage. His swimming togs will do more than reveal parts of the body. They will reveal the temperature of some of the parts the suits are concealing.

· · · · ·
ODDS: 100%
ETA: 1991
PRICE: UNDER $100
· · · · ·

Spector, a New York inventor who gave the world hydraulically operated exercise equipment, has developed a thermally sensitive fabric that changes color in concert with the wearer's temperature. So if something embarrasses you, your suit may blush even if you don't.

As Spector explains it, the suits will turn dark blue or even black around an area that is heating up, or where the blood is collecting. It will turn brown over an area that is cooled down and doesn't have much blood flowing. But stand by for the veritable light show that will happen in-between. As the suit goes from hot to cold it will pass through versions of black, blue, yellow, and green before cooling off at moderate brown.

This fun-in-the-sun gear was originally made entirely of the magic mood material. But when it hits the boutique market, expect to see only parts—that is, upper parts—of the suits made from the special cloth. "Some people don't want it on all areas of their body," explains Spector. "They're embarrassed."

So far Spector is working on marketing the Mood Suit to women only. A tank-style one-piece is already developed, but different styles are on the drawing board.

VIRTUAL WORLD

Virtual World is a little hard to grasp, so hang on! What we're talking about is the ability to visit faraway places or even different eras without leaving your living room.

• • • • •
ODDS: 75%
ETA: 1995
PRICE: $5,000–$10,000
• • • • •

You will need special equipment and clothing. But the effect will be out of this world.

Suppose you want to visit a tropical island. First, you'll put on a headset that replicates the sound of the surf, the wind, and the wildlife. Next, you'll put on special goggles with mini-TV-like visual displays. Not only will you get a three-dimensional look at the island, but as you turn your head, the scenery will change, giving you a panoramic view of your surroundings. Finally, put on your Virtual World suit and gloves, which let you feel the heat, the breeze, the sand, the textures of anything you might touch on the island. All of this equipment is hooked up to the "home reality engine," an egg-shaped unit that plugs into an ordinary phone jack.

For the final bit of magic, any friend also wearing a Virtual World

13

outfit can join you from any location around the globe on this tropical adventure.

This is the future of home entertainment. You are in the "Virtual World." You are experiencing "Virtual Reality."

You can experience many sensations and visit many environments in the Virtual World. Once suited up, "previews" will appear in your special goggles. All the possible worlds you can visit appear before you like aquariums lined up in a pet shop. There might be a Prehistoric World, a Western World, a Future World. You place your Virtual World glove in the aquarium of your choice and you are instantly transported to that time and place.

But you're not finished yet. At the Virtual World "makeup mirror" you get to choose the life-form you wish to be when you visit these Virtual Worlds. Come back in prehistoric times as a dinosaur, if you like. Your movements will be dinosaur-like. A friend visiting the same world will see you as a dinosaur. Or, want to go back to the Old West looking just like John Wayne? It can be done, pardner.

The inventor of Virtual World is Jaron Lanier, a high school dropout (naturally) who became a computer scientist and is now CEO of VPL Research in Redwood, California. "It feels like being in a computer-generated dream," says Lanier.

The pieces of this dream are already past the "drawing board" stage. The Virtual World glove exists. Lanier expects a total version of Virtual World to be available at amusement parks and museums as early as 1991. By 1995, he expects a high-priced home version to be on the market, and by 1999 a more affordable one for the mass market.

If you have it in your home, you'll pay a once-a-month "reality bill" for the amount of time you spend in Virtual World. It's also possible that the equipment could be leased or that you will be able to buy and use one piece of the Virtual World wardrobe at a time, though you won't get the full effect.

14

A bit hard to grasp, isn't it? But then imagine trying to explain the present array of computer games to a child in the 1960s.

. . . . .

FROZEN BEVERAGE MUG

A lover of hot summer days, beautiful beaches, and frosty brews, Saul Freedman is the creator of the frozen beverage mug—an all-ice container that keeps the drink cold until the mug melts.

ODDS: 50%

ETA: 1991

PRICE: $1

Freedman, a Vineland, New Jersey, inventor, intends to mass-produce his mugs and market them as "perfect for the beach." His brainstorm—putting the liquid into ice rather than the ice into liquid—was born out of frustration. He was tired of drinking warm beer and cola at the Jersey shore, and he was tired of paper cups and cans littering the sand.

The frozen mug melts from the outside in, and except for the wooden stick that serves as its handle, it disappears without a trace. On a hot day at the beach, the mug is good for almost forty-five minutes. "It's a trash-free, self-disposing drinking container, and with the environmental problems we have today, the mug will help decrease the litter," Freedman says. Some seaside towns ban the sale of drink containers at the beach, but he thinks the ice mug could swim around this rule.

Although the frozen mug will stay solid for up to two hours indoors, Freedman sees as his greatest market potential people who want fast refreshment in the hot sun. And he doesn't view the summer meltdown time of forty-five minutes as a negative. "With ice cream, if you don't eat it in five minutes, it will be all over your lap. Besides, how long do you hold a paper cup that's filled with soda?"

15

The ice mug is produced by a patented process that first takes the impurities out of the water (thus making the ice freeze quickly and melt slowly) and then chills the molds in super-cold storage.

Assuming he finds investors who share his belief that ice is nice, Freedman will manufacture his mugs in New Jersey, near his potential customers. Franchising is a possibility, too.

HOT/COOL FABRIC

Imagine a lightweight jacket that keeps you as warm as a fur coat, and living-room drapes that keep the air cool in the summer. Now imagine that both are made from the same fabric. What you'll have in mind is a new patent from the U.S. Department of Agriculture. The process gives fabric the ability to store, absorb, and release heat.

ODDS: 90%
ETA: 1992
PRICE: N/A

A chemical called polyethylene glycol—the same polymer used for temperature control in spacecraft—is applied to fabric. When the mercury rises, the molecules of the chemical absorb the heat and lock it in the cloth to keep you cool. When the temperature goes down, the fabric will warm you up by releasing the heat molecules it's been storing. The process is similar to the forming and melting of ice; at a certain point, the molecules take on different properties.

The treatment is being successfully applied in various ways to cotton, wool, and synthetics. A limitation is that the fabric runs hot or cold for only a half hour at a time, so scientists are busy trying to extend the staying power of the process. But the treated material has proved to be more durable and wear-resistant than untreated fabric. And the chemical compound won't wash out.

16

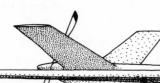

THE FLYING CAR

Of all the wacky, crazy, and wonderful inventions in this book, the Aerocar may be the wackiest, craziest, and wonderfulest of all.

ODDS: 50%
ETA: 1999
PRICE: $150,000

Start with a standard Honda CRX; add wings, a tail, another engine; make a few modifications; and you have it. A car that actually flies! And when you're on the ground, the 34-foot wings fold up to form a 20-by-8-foot trailer that's hauled behind the car.

The Aerocar is the dream of one man: Molt Taylor, a World War II Navy pilot and aeronautical engineer who's been hammering away at his invention for more than thirty years. Taylor is now working on Model 4, which in 1988 received the Federal Aviation Administration's approval as an experimental aircraft. That means it can be sold in kits to do-it-yourself pilots, who must then actually construct more than half of the Aerocar. (Taylor's earlier model, number 3, the one that has actually flown, is now in Seattle's Museum of Flight.)

As if a flying car isn't incredible enough, the thing uses most of its regular car equipment when airborne. Explains Taylor, "The same controls fly and drive it, but the steering wheel moves back and forth to operate the elevators. And there're rubber pedals that lie on the floor when you drive and come into position when you're ready to fly."

The airplane's turbine engine uses jet fuel, while the car engine uses regular gasoline. The Aerocar meets all the requirements of

17

standard automobiles, including those for fireproofing, pollution control, and safety.

Taylor, now in his seventies, still puts in a full day at his Aerocar Inc. office in Longview, Washington. In need of more financing, he doesn't yet know when Aerocars will be available for distributors, and he admits that the government is hoping it's not too soon. "The problem," he explained, "is how anyone is going to control thousands or even millions of flying cars."

So why did he spend more than three decades developing his dream? "I just figured if I didn't do this, some other son of a gun would!"

2

good stuff in small packages

WEATHER CUBE

What's the weather like? In the future we won't have to check the newspaper, catch the TV weather report, or even look out the window. We'll simply glance at our weather cubes.

Currently the hottest gadget in Japan, Toshiba's 4-inch cube is a battery-powered device that predicts the weather eight hours in advance. The cube's LCD screen displays its forecast with an appropriate symbol—sun, clouds, rain, or snow— or, for a mixed review, like partly cloudy, half sun and half clouds.

• • • • •
ODDS: 20%
ETA: 1999
PRICE: $100
• • • • •

19

The device is actually a microcomputer with a program that's based on forty years of weather patterns. Unlike a barometer, with its old-fashioned mechanical system dependent on air pressure and humidity readings, the weather cube uses a semiconductor for readings of current weather conditions and comparisons with past weather data.

Although Toshiba had hoped to produce a U.S. version of its popular product, they saw clouds on the horizon, according to a company spokesperson. Japan's size allows it to have uniform weather conditions, so it's relatively easy to program from past climatic conditions. Not so in the States. Different versions of the cube would have to be made for each region of the country—a Bostonian would need one model; a Houstonian, another. So Toshiba would have to collect complete weather data for all regions of the country spanning the last forty years—a daunting job request for the U.S. Weather Bureau, and hardly a cost-effective proposition. Still, chances are that while Toshiba has no plans to enter the American market in the near future, it's such a good idea that someone else might.

The weather cube has become a popular travel accessory within Japan—at picnics, it warns of rain; on the ski slopes, it hails the next snowstorm.

But if the cube becomes standard equipment in U.S. households, Americans who venture cross-country would do well to leave their cubes at home. Looking out the window will still be a better way to predict the weather.

· · · · ·

POCKET COMPUTER

From calculators to television sets, everything electronic is going petite. But how do you miniaturize a computer screen without losing most of the image or making the text so tiny that it's unreadable? Well, keep reading and use your imagination.

· · · · ·
ODDS: 100%
ETA: 1992
PRICE: $300
· · · · ·

Picture a home computer with a full screen of graphics and text displayed. Now lose the computer box and the keyboard. Picture only that full image of graphics and text floating by itself two feet in front of you. Now come back close to reality and imagine the physical screen shrunk to half the size of a cigarette box.

And there you have the solution to the pocket computer problem. The small screen has a 1-inch-square window. When you look into it, you will see the equivalent of what you would see on a full 12-inch screen; only the information will appear to be floating in space two feet in front of your eyes. The mini-screen could be clipped onto a pair of glasses, or hang down over your eye from a headset. The whole operation will work much the same as a Walkman: the visual display screen will be wired to a mini computer—with a keyboard—that will be carried in your pocket.

Steve Lipsey, who spends his time explaining this technology to electronic companies who will eventually be using it, is vice president of Reflection Technology. This Massachusetts company is marketing the visual part of the pocket computer under the name Private Eye. "We've freed up the electronics industry to make their products in a very different way," says Lipsey. "They no longer have to restrict themselves to putting their products in boxes large enough to read."

The technology will someday be used for all sorts of miniaturizations, from fax machines to pagers that can receive road maps. Surgeons will use the Private Eye to check on a patient's vital signs while performing surgery at the same time.

21

THE ELECTRIC TRAIN ATTACHÉ

You're sitting in an airplane—business class—when the well-dressed executive in the next seat suddenly snaps open his attaché case. Only it's not filled with papers and reports. Inside is a miniaturized electric train set.

ODDS: 100%

ETA: 1990

PRICE: $585

It's complete with an engine and freight cars (2 to 4 inches long), a quarter-inch track, a Bavarian landscape, trees, houses, cows, and sheep—all housed in a 14-by-19-inch briefcase and powered by a 9-volt battery. The inside top of the case holds the executive railroad yard.

Marklin Inc. of New Berlin, Wisconsin, a longtime manufacturer of model trains, is responsible for this little fantasy. It's available in a few specialty shops and from the catalogue of that Rolls-Royce of toy stores, F.A.O. Schwarz. By the early nineties, its availability should be widespread.

"The train-in-a-case is the perfect accoutrement for the business person who wants to make an impression," says Fred Gates, president of Marklin. One of his customers, an attorney, took his attaché case out during a tense negotiating session. "He opened it up and started the train and everyone laughed—just when there was need for relief."

Clear your desk of those perpetual-motion contrivances, boys and girls. This is the next executive status toy.

FLAT SATELLITE ANTENNA

The days of huge satellite dishes perched atop buildings, in back-yards, and outside taverns may soon be numbered. And the ability to receive scores of TV channels may soon be within reach of even the most humble apartment dweller.

ODDS: 100%
ETA: 1992
PRICE: $600

A flat mini-antenna, 1 inch thick and measuring 2 feet by 1 foot, has been developed in a joint venture between Matsushita Electric of Japan and America's Comsat.

Despite a diminutive size, it can receive signals from special new high-powered satellites orbiting thousands of miles above. The mini-antenna can be easily mounted on a roof, porch, or even a wall, and in a color to match your decor.

These antennas are already being marketed in Japan in connection with the beginning of their direct broadcast satellite service. Comsat is just waiting for the launch of the required higher-powered satellites before marketing in the United States.

BINOCULAR GLASSES

Dr. William Beecher, an ornithologist and director emeritus of the Chicago Academy of Sciences, set out more than forty years ago to design the perfect bird-watching binoculars. He wanted his in-strument to have all the power, field of

ODDS: 100%
ETA: 1990
PRICE: $295

23

vision, brightness, and resolution of the best-made binoculars in the world, but with only a fraction of the weight.

The Beecher Mirage 7 × 30 binoculars are the result of that quest. A shock- and waterproof body encloses an optical system of fourteen lenses—including four made from rare earth glass—and eight super-thin mirrors. Multicoating allows 99 percent of the light to pass through each lens and reflect from each mirror. The more expensive earth glass creates greater depth of focus. And the mirrors replace the weightier prisms found in most binoculars.

But the best part, according to Dr. Beecher, is that the binoculars weigh only 3 ounces and can be worn like eyeglasses. In fact, says Dr. Beecher, the Mirage "disappears before your eyes," because the mass of the binoculars is in a blind spot.

The Beecher Mirage should also be a boon to sports and opera fans and anyone who needs binoculars. Currently the Mirage can be purchased only from the Beecher Research Company in Chicago. Dr. Beecher, who donates his sales profits to charity, has so far resisted the idea of using dealers, because "that would at least double the price to buyers."

FREEZE-DRIED COMPRESSED FOOD

I t's compact, it's nutritious, and it's tasty, too. It's freeze-dried compressed food, a unique food preparation originally devised by the U.S. military for attack submarine and space missions.

24

ODDS: 100%

ETA: 1992

PRICE: VARIES BY PRODUCT

"On submarines and in space capsules, you've got a big problem, and it's called space," says Joseph Durocher, Ph.D., professor of hotel administration at the Whittemore School of Business and Economics, University of New Hampshire. "The military needed a product that would provide the most amount of food in the least amount of space."

Freeze-dried compressed food is dehydrated food that can be re-constituted by adding water, like a sponge that swells when wet. "Instead of throwing something in the microwave, you just pop hot water on and—whammo—you have a whole meal," says Durocher.

The resultant bulk is what is important. With a compressed ratio of 16 to 1, a pound of freeze-dried compressed carrots, for instance, would yield 16 pounds of edible vegetables. "You can take a chunk of beef stew the size of my thumb and it will yield one and a half cups of stew," says Durocher. However, only certain foods take well to the process. "Veggies are great," says Durocher, "but you can't freeze-dry anything with a large mass, like a prime rib."

What does the food taste like? "It's actually quite good," says Durocher. As for nutrition: "It's not the same as buying fresh, but it's better than canned." It also has a very long shelf life.

Durocher envisions freeze-dried compressed products someday being used by people living on space platforms and moon colonies. He also sees applications in big cities, where apartment dwellers already are pressed for space. For now, it is being used on a limited basis in the camping world.

SMART PILL BOTTLE

Let's face it, nobody likes taking medicine. In fact, many people don't take it or they don't take it according to their doctor's instructions.

. . . . .
ODDS: 85%
ETA: 1994
PRICE: $40
. . . . .

25

"Nearly one in every three patients misuses his drugs in a way that impacts on his effectiveness," says Keith Mullowney, president of Aprex Corporation, a company that's developed a solution to this critical problem. (It can be so critical that if a patient on a drug regimen designed to lower the risk of a heart attack stops taking his medicine, the sudden interruption of drug therapy caused by this non-compliance may actually trigger a heart attack.)

Aprex's remedy is the "smart" drug container. Initially introduced to monitor participants in FDA tests of new drugs, the product is a cap designed to fit a standard pill bottle. What it does is record the time and date every time the container is opened and closed. When the subject is finished with his medication, the cap is turned in to the tester, who sends it to Aprex. Retrieving the data in the cap by computer, Aprex prepares a report on when and how often the patient took his medication.

Obviously if this product were available to doctors treating patients on medication, the physicians would be in a much better position to monitor treatment. Aprex sees a future in which doctors would prescribe the cap along with a prescription and both would be dispensed at a pharmacy. Patients would return the caps to their doctors, who would read the records directly from a monitor on their desks.

Better yet, Aprex foresees caps with "buzzers and alarms" and LCD displays. Such caps would signal patients who have neglected their medication and display instructions, including what to do if a dosage has been missed. Such caps, says Mullowney, will function for about two years.

WATCH PAGER

Your answering machine or answering service can't deliver messages to you instantly, and a thick, black-box pager around your belt is not your idea of slick. Soon one product will alleviate both problems. It's a digital wristwatch that serves as a sophisticated miniature paging system.

• • • • •
ODDS: 95%

ETA: 1991

PRICE: $150–$200 FOR THE WATCH; $12 PER MONTH FOR THE SERVICE
• • • • •

When someone calls, your watch won't embarrass you by beeping loudly at a bad time. Instead, it will gently flash one of several messages: Call home, call the office, call the following number, or it will flash a code from 0 to 9 for best friends and other frequent callers.

Philip Gugel, vice president of financial services for AT&E, the San Francisco company that will handle the service, says it could take as little as fifteen seconds from the time a message is initiated until it gets to your watch.

The watch, to be made by Seiko, contains a receiver designed to function in all countries without modification. Plans call for initial introduction of the service in the continental United States with international service to be introduced shortly thereafter. The retail price of the watch is expected to decline significantly as production increases.

As for the possibility of leaving more than simple codes? "Since the technology can send letters and numerals," says Gugel, "you could eventually have longer messages scrolling across the face of the watch."

PUDDLE DETECTOR

The need for an invention is sometimes so obvious only a child can see it. This was the case with eight-year-old Lillian Ruth Lukas of Belmont, Massachusetts. One winter day, while shopping with her mother, she noticed a blind man walking near the local mall. He was walking through puddles. What the world needed, Lillian decided, was a puddle detector for canes.

ODDS: 100%

ETA: 1991

PRICE: $12

With the help of her father, Scott, Lillian came up with a small (2-by-½-inch) battery-operated device that will snap on to any cane, collapsible or solid, and emit a beep when the end touches water.

Lillian's idea was welcomed by the American Foundation for the

27

Blind. It's also made her a celebrity: she was a national finalist in the Invent America contest for schoolchildren, and has appeared on a half dozen television shows, including "Sesame Street."

Although there have been overtures, Lillian and her parents decided not to cash in on her invention. Rather than manufacture the puddle detector, they send a diagram and instructions to workshops for the blind. The device is easily made for about $12. "We decided not to sell it," Scott Lukas explained. "Lillian gets satisfaction just from helping people."

THE POCKET PRINTER Digital Writer

The folks at Casio have come up with a combination calculator, word processor, and printer that's small enough to fit in your pocket, yet big enough to store 5,300 characters, 3 character styles and 8 character sizes.

ODDS: 95%
ETA: 1991
PRICE: $300

The device, called a Digital Writer, comes in two pieces. The base unit has a miniature keyboard and a multiline display, so that you can edit text before printing. A wand, which connects by a small cable to the keyboard, contains the printing heads and an inked ribbon. Two small wheels on either side of the wand allow the printing head to be rolled straight and smooth over the paper. The Digital Writer prints 13 characters per second. Dennis Reer, a spokesman for Casio, has dubbed it "the first electronic rubber stamp." And that it is.

Reer claims that the Digital Writer will be the "most cost-effective lettering system" available when it hits the market. The pocket printer will never replace a standard printer, but for small jobs and people on the go, it should be ideal.

COMPUTER ALARMCARD

To hear inventor D'Arcy Dawe talk about the computer industry, you would never guess he is in the insurance business. Of course, if his computer alarm does as well on the market as he hopes, he may not stay in the insurance business for long.

• • • • •
ODDS: 85%
ETA: 1991
PRICE: $120
• • • • •

Dawe's product is the Alarmcard, a 4-by-6-inch motion-sensitive board that plugs into personal computers and sounds a loud alarm if the machine is moved. Running on a 9-volt battery, the Alarmcard plugs snugly into the PC's interior, where it can't be seen.

Dawe would like to see the Alarmcard become a standard feature in personal computers. "My immediate goal," he says, "is to lobby insurance companies in order to gain support for security items in computers." However, Dawe has higher hopes for the technology behind Alarmcard than computer security alone. He hopes to develop the Alarmcard further, so that it can be reduced to a chip that would theft-proof any device containing a microprocessor. Any item that can be programmed could then be wired to sound an alarm easily and cheaply.

The Alarmcard can conveniently be monitored by a central security post, making it a worthwhile security investment for corporations, schools, or government installations.

29

• • • • •

MINI PORTABLE OVEN

A portable "heating pad" for food? That's one way of describing the Porta-Oven, a lightweight heater-upper that can be used in car, truck, boat, home—anywhere you can plug it in. The Porta-Oven weighs less than 1 pound, is slightly larger than a TV dinner, and heats to 280 degrees Fahrenheit. It stays cool on the outside and can handle anything from a small pizza to a baby bottle.

ODDS: 100%
ETA: 1990
PRICE: $30

The envelope-like device is covered in a bright blue cloth and sealed with Velcro on the outside, and "there's a state-of-the-art heating element inside," according to Donavan Harpool, vice president of marketing at Watkins Inc., the Kansas company that designed Porta-Oven. The inner lining of the oven is FDA-approved, so food can be slipped right in without a wrapping.

The Porta-Oven is available in two models: AC for home and office use, and DC for use in cars, trucks, and boats.

30

PERSONAL BETTING MACHINE

A n American invention in Hong Kong has revolutionized that colony's horse-racing industry. Odds are good that by the time China reclaims Hong Kong, it will change the way Americans wager as well.

ODDS: 75%

ETA: 1997

PRICE: $200

The Portabet is a hand-held betting terminal, 5 by 3 by ³/₄ inches, that lets you place your wagers anywhere, anytime. Your fingers do the betting on the device's LCD screen. For example, the screen will ask the bettor if he wants to wager. Press YES or NO. The races of the day are listed. Press one. The horses are listed. Select. How much money is to be bet? A keypad appears. Press the amount. And finally, what kind of wager is to be placed: win, place, show, quinella, exacta, double? When you win, money is credited to your account. When you lose, money is deducted.

Fantastic! That's what the 360,000 members of the Royal Hong Kong Jockey Club have been saying since the service was introduced in the spring of 1988.

Portabet was developed by the Murata Link Corporation of Amherst, New Hampshire, in association with Varitronix Ltd. of Hong Kong.

31

HAND-HELD SPORTS MONITOR

F or sports nuts with money and a need to know, this portable paging device is a must. It's pocket size, weighs 4 ounces, and delivers up-to-date sports news twenty-four hours a day wherever you are.

• • • • •
ODDS: 100%
ETA: 1990
PRICE: $350
• • • • •

The Sports Page is a microprocessor-controlled receiver. Its dot-matrix display screen gives you updated information every five minutes from three wire services via satellite transmission. The information includes current and final scores, weather conditions, and point spreads on every major professional and college football and basketball game, baseball, and hockey. The data also includes game times, pitching match-ups, injury reports, and horse-racing results, scratches, and payoffs.

The actual sports monitor is manufactured for Beeper Plus by Motorola and costs about $350. There's an additional monthly charge of $45–$65 for the information service and an option for personal paging.

Right now the service is available in 16 locations, including New York, Chicago, Philadelphia, Boston, San Francisco, St. Louis, and, of course, Las Vegas. According to Beeper Plus, more cities will be added soon and the cost should go down.

Available through Beeper Plus, Inc., 3900 Paradise Road, Suite 110, Las Vegas, NV 89109.

• • • • •

THE WORLD'S SMALLEST WEATHER STATION

With the World's Smallest Weather Station, you can have the latest forecast in the palm of your hand. Weather enthusiasts, sailors, and budding meteorologists can use this battery-operated, computerized gadget to measure wind speed, wind direction, and air temperature.

ODDS: 100%
ETA: 1990
PRICE: $160

The wind assembly mounts easily on a home antenna or sailboat mast and transmits data to a hand-held station. Its computerized memory allows the user to record readings over an extended period of time. And for another $50, you can add the option of a rainfall monitor, which measures rainfall to within a tenth of an inch.

The World's Smallest Weather Station is available through the Digitar catalogue (800-678-3669) and at a few electronic equipment and marine specialty stores.

PORTABLE VOICE-ACTIVATED TRANSLATOR

For the American in Paris . . . or anywhere, for that matter, the language barrier is about to come down with this voice-operated portable computer translator.

ODDS: 100%
ETA: 1991
PRICE: $2,000

Voice—that's what it's called—is a hand-held computer with software that can recognize over 35,000 sentences. You simply speak to it in English—for example, "Waiter,

33

another bottle of your best champagne, please"—and it will electronically speak the words in French—"Garçon, une autre bouteille de votre meilleur champagne, s'il vous plaît"—or in German, Spanish, or Italian.

On an LCD screen, you will see what you said in English, to make sure that Voice got it right. And by pressing a button, Voice will repeat the phrase in the foreign language and display it, so you can be sure everyone heard it right.

"Voice makes a laptop computer with a keyboard look like a dinosaur," says Steve Rondel, president of Advanced Products and Technologies, Inc., the Redmond, Washington, company that makes the revolutionary computer. "It fits in the palm of your hand and listens to and acts on your spoken command." Voice weighs 2.8 pounds, is about the size of two VHS cassettes stacked together, and runs three hours on a charge.

Voice is speaker dependent. That means it has to be trained and that it will respond only to your voice. In about an hour, Voice will lead you through an interview in which it memorizes the way you talk. This information is stored on your cartridge. Others can use the machine by training their own cartridges.

Cartridges—a different one for each foreign language—will cost $200 to $300 each. And functions other than translating are also available.

It took six years and millions of dollars to develop Voice, and researchers aren't finished yet. Its vocabulary will expand with more languages, specifically Japanese, Chinese, and Russian, on the drawing board.

Rondel sees Voice's first applications in the business community and tourist industry. (Imagine Voice in every taxi, helping drivers and visitors to *comprendre*.) And despite its high cost, Americans abroad will probably be carrying Voice, along with guidebooks and camera, by the early nineties.

34

PRAYER WRISTWATCH

If you're a frequent traveler and a Muslim, getting to the mosque on time can be a real problem. Now, however, life on the road for Islamic travelers is much easier. David Kohler, an Englishman who worked in Saudi Arabia, has invented a watch so that even the fastest-moving businessman can keep track of the five daily prayer calls and holidays while flitting through time zones.

ODDS: 100%
ETA: 1990
PRICE: $95–$139

Powered by two tiny microprocessors and a 12K memory, this amazing timepiece points to Mecca, chimes ten minutes before prayer calls, and flashes the date according to the Muslim calendar (which began with the Prophet's flight to Medina in A.D. 622).

This is not an easy task when one considers all the variables. To set the watch, the wearer must program in the time, date, and his position on earth. Two hundred locations are set in the watch's memory, so if you're in one of those places, it's automatic. If not, the watch will help you determine your coordinates by triangulation. Since prayer times are calculated differently in different parts of the world, the watch has five programs from which to choose in determining the correct time for the wearer's location.

The chime gives ten minutes' notice, so that worshippers can wash before praying, as mandated in the Koran.

Though not widely distributed, the watch is presently available through ASR Inc. in Mountain View, California. The chrome model sells for $95. A gold-plated watch costs $139.

35

3

stuff for
the house

COMPUTERIZED HOME DECORATING

By the beginning of the decade, a new service will be available that should take the guesswork out of redecorating your home. It's called Design and Decorate, a computer system that will actually let you see 3-D pictures of what your room will look like with different furniture, colors, wallpaper, upholstery, and arrangements.

• • • • •
ODDS: 100%
ETA: 1990
PRICE: N/A
• • • • •

37

A cooperative effort of Intel and Videodisc Publishing Inc., the system will be capable of storing the equivalent of 200,000 pages of text from a catalogue. Using a technology called Digital Video Interactive, various room components can be placed on a screen that eventually could show up to 16 million colors. According to Richard Stauffer, manager of DVI technology, "the customer will be able to view the new layout from any perspective in the theoretical room."

It's expected that some retailers will charge for the service, but with the fees deductible if a purchase is made.

ROUND REFRIGERATOR

Anyone who has seen Woody Allen's *Sleeper* may be a little surprised by the "kitchen of the '90s" as designed by Electrolux of Sweden. If you have seen the futuristic movie, you may wonder, "What's an Orgasmatron doing in the

· · · · ·
ODDS: 50%
ETA: 1997
PRICE: N/A
· · · · ·

kitchen?" Well, that large round appliance with the sliding door has every right to be where it is—it's a refrigerator.

Electrolux has rounded the refrigerator to create "a more friendly form in the kitchen," says Jan Van Rooy of their design department. "Instead of opening the door and taking up a lot of space in the kitchen, it's a sliding door like on a van," explains Van Rooy. The door slides in between the insulation and the outside of the refrigerator. Inside, there are layers of shelves that turn, like lazy Susans, "so you can have a good view of what's inside and never have to reach over goods in front." The top level is a refrigerator and the lower level is a freezer, both operating in the same way.

The refrigerator is currently shown for display purposes only, with production plans set for the mid-1990s.

38

MICROWAVE CLOTHES DRYER

T he microwave dryer will save energy and time, and may also kill harmful bacteria while it dries your clothes. Research on the dryer has been ongoing at the University of Tulsa, funded by Micro Dry Inc., an Oklahoma-based company. The first model is expected to be on sale in 1990.

ODDS: 95%
ETA: 1991
PRICE: $300

Those first units will be portable and small (about the size of a microwave oven) because, unlike standard dryers, they don't require vents. The dryer could be used in a closet, under the kitchen sink, or practically any place you desire. A small load would take only about five minutes to dry.

According to Mary Ellen O'Connor, a spokeswoman for Micro Dry, the microwave dryer should not only be faster but much easier on fabrics. "In a regular dryer you heat the air, which heats the clothes. Then the water evaporates and you have to get rid of it. But microwave radiation eliminates one whole step of the process. You heat the water, not the air, directly. Clothes will come out much cooler."

The research-and-development team has recently discovered that microwave drying also kills basic bacteria. So far it has been shown that seventeen different strains of bacteria are eliminated. The hope, according to Micro Dry president Paul Kantor, is that the microwave clothes dryer will also kill staph infections, making the dryers useful in hospitals. Kantor believes that the dryer will also destroy viruses. "Liquids are attractive to microwave energy and viruses are liquids. This could be a major breakthrough."

When full-size microwave dryer units come on the market, drying time should be reduced by at least 30 percent, the developers claim. Another breakthrough.

39

SOLAR ROOFING MATERIAL

Photovoltaic roofing should not be confused with solar heating. These are
not panels installed on the roof to collect
sunlight and convert it into heat. What we
have here is a roofing material that is actually used in place of shingles. It keeps

· · · · ·

ODDS: 80%

ETA: 1995

PRICE: $8 to $10 PER
SQUARE FOOT

· · · · ·

your roof from leaking at the same time as it provides free, clean
electricity for the whole house.

Photovoltaic energy is a form of solar energy, but the key difference
is that these layered semiconductor devices turn sunlight directly into
electricity. Unlike solar water heaters, these solar cells have no moving parts, use no fuel except sunlight, and produce neither smoke
nor noise. Sounds like a major breakthrough, doesn't it?

Well, photovoltaic energy has been around since 1969, when it
was used to charge batteries on a satellite in outer space. Prohibitively
expensive then, the cost has been cut to one-tenth of 1 percent of
what it was. It's now affordable. The roofing material would sell for
$8 to $10 per square foot compared with $2 to $8 for normal waterproof
shingles.

Dr. Heshmat Laaly, a California analytical chemist, is the developer of this wonder roofing. He's made it flexible, so that it can be
rolled up and transported to remote areas where electricity isn't available. It's easily installed and produces a minimum of 12 volts per
square foot. The electricity runs down two wires into the house, where
it enters a converter. Excess electricity generated during the day is
stored in the equivalent of about 8 car batteries.

Dr. Laaly is looking for a few "sincere millionaires" to get his
product off the ground. (*Note to sincere millionaires:* Dr. Laaly's invention won the Most Commercial Potential Award at the 1988 International Invention Convention.)

40

· · · · ·

REFRIGERATOR COLD SAVER

You've seen them in supermarket freezers—those plastic strips you part to get to the ice cream. Someday soon you may be parting them at home to get at the leftovers. Those inch-wide plastic strips, though a bit of a nuisance, do serve a useful function: they keep the cold in and the electric bills down.

ODDS: 90%

ETA: 1991

PRICE: $15

Mike Gordon, president of Micro Products in Stickney, Illinois, is the man who's marketing Arctic Shields for home use. But it was his nine-year-old daughter, Elizabeth, who gave him the idea. Scolded for gazing too long into the open refrigerator, she suggested doing what the supermarkets do.

The hanging strips of clear vinyl come in three models "guaranteed to fit any refrigerator." Gordon is now negotiating to sell Arctic Shields through appliance and hardware chain stores. In the meantime, he says, he's selling them directly to everybody but his mother. The address: Miro Products, P.O. Box 268, Riverside, IL 60546.

THE INTELLIGENT TOILET

The Orient only recently discovered the Western toilet, and—true to form—is already improving on it. Consider the workings of the Taiwanese Eletto toilet:

ODDS: 95%

ETA: 1992

PRICE: N/A

1. The lid remains closed when not in use and opens up at the touch of a button. (A separate button lifts the seat for men.)
2. The temperature of the seat is maintained between 82 and 100 degrees Fahrenheit.
3. When the user gets up to leave, an infrared ray detector activates the seat cover to close and the toilet is automatically flushed.
4. An ultraviolet-ray lamp in the seat cover then goes to work sterilizing the seat and the bowl for the benefit of the next user.
5. And to further enhance your experience, a push of a button activates the Eletto deodorizer, which uses organic charcoal to rid the bowl of odors. A freshener for the bathroom is also provided.

The Eletto comes in four colors and three option packages.

THE MORE INTELLIGENT TOILET

W hat's beyond toilets that sterilize themselves? Bottoms that wipe themselves! Well, not exactly, but several companies in the Orient are marketing some version of a toilet that cleans you up automatically without toilet paper.

. . . . .
ODDS: 80%
ETA: 1992
PRICE: AS MUCH AS
$3,600
. . . . .

Besides the now "ordinary" function of sterilizing and preheating, these paperless toilets have a mechanical arm that appears underneath you after you have completed your business. The arm shoots up a stream of warm water, and follows it with a blast of dry air that can gust for sixty seconds at a time. The full treatment is complete with a perfumed misting of your underparts. Some of these automated geniuses even play gentle music!

One advertisement in Japan claims that to clean the bottoms of a family of four the toilet uses one half the amount of electricity needed to run the refrigerator. Who could ask for anything more?

HAND-SCANNING LOCK

F orget your key? No-o problem. In the future, the front door will unlock automatically by reading your handprint with a digital scanner.

. . . . .
ODDS: 50%
ETA: 1995
PRICE: $200
. . . . .

The product, which should be in commercial use in three years, is being developed for high-security offices and for banks, which can apply the scanning device to automated teller machines. Instead of punching in a secret code, you'll place your palm on the machine's screen, the computer will compare your hand to a digital description of your one-of-a-kind print, and the teller machine will verify that you are who you say you are.

Applying this same concept to house locks will be the next step for this technology, says Tom Kelley, marketing executive with David Kelley Designs, the Palo Alto company that is creating the model scanner for the manufacturer, Biometrics Inc. "You could have your front door programmed so that only certain people could come right in," says Kelley.

The prototype hand scanner is a rectangular box with a red plate on top, and an outline showing the proper position for the palm. Smaller than a cigar box, the mechanism could be mounted into the wall of an entryway or near a garage door.

Initially, the product will be expensive, Kelley says, estimating that such a home scanner might sell for two to three times the cost of a combination door lock. And while the general public might not throw away lock and key immediately in favor of this handy device, Kelley sees a market for the·unit, predicting that the hand scanners will appear first in prestigious new housing developments that tout their state-of-the-art accoutrements.

As an extra security benefit, the scanner should be a winner—hands down.

PRIVACY WINDOWS

Drapes, blinds, and curtains could all be window coverings of the past if a new product catches on. Called Varilite Vision Panels, they work like this: Sandwiched between two panes of glass is a liquid crystal layer, similar to the LCD

44

. . . . .

ODDS: 100%

ETA: 1990

PRICE: $125 PER
SQUARE FOOT

. . . . .

displays in digital watches. The glass is smoky until a switch is flicked on and the glass becomes clear.

The Varilite windows are run by electricity and are controlled by any standard lighting switch, timer, or computer.

Manufactured by the Taliq Corporation of Sunnyvale, California, Varilite windows are already being used in some conference rooms, limousines, and hospitals. They should be available to everyone early in the next decade. They'll even come in colors: clear, bronze, and gray.

WINDOW SHATTER PROTECTOR

A group of Dutch researchers has invented a transparent covering that allows a window to withstand the blast of a hand grenade without shattering. The product, called Profilon Plus, is a transparent sheet made of polyester fibers that sticks to the inside of glass windows.

ODDS: 100%

ETA: 1991

PRICE: $5 PER SQUARE FOOT

During World War II, scientists remembered, people would tape their windows during air raids to prevent shattering. Well, Profilon Plus is a lot tougher than tape. Its American distributor claims it will increase the strength of glass by 300 percent. A promotional video shows a stick of dynamite exploding while fastened to a window; the blast fails to shatter the glass. "The consensus of government officials who have tested Profilon Plus is that the wall will fall before the glass shatters," says Peter Hotjes of American Armatura, the U.S. distributor.

Profilon Plus, he adds, could dramatically reduce the number of injuries caused by flying shards of glass. He estimates that nearly a quarter of a million Americans are treated annually for such accidents. In parts of the country where hurricanes and tornadoes are prevalent, Profilon Plus could become a household name.

45

SOLAR WINDOWS

The windows in your home through which you see out and the sun sees in will someday also capture the sun's energy and convert it to electrical power.

ODDS: 90%

ETA: 1992

PRICE: N/A

Transparent amorphous solar cells have been developed by researchers at Sanyo Electric in Osaka, Japan. They collect solar power in the same way as the bulky solar roof panels with which we are familiar. The difference—and it's substantial—is that these new cells have been constructed with an exclusive technology that delicately etches microscopic holes throughout each cell, which render them transparent. Natural light can pass through the window cells to light up your living room while, simultaneously, the rays are being tapped to run your television set.

Sanyo plans to market transparent solar cells for skylights, car sunroofs, and greenhouses, as well as for windows in the home. Somewhere down the road, the cells may also be used as a power source for yachts.

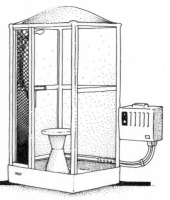

EXPANDABLE
HOME STEAM ROOM

F or those who like to do their per-
spiring in private, the home steam
room could be the Jacuzzi of the nineties.
It's easy to install, takes up little room,
costs less than a whirlpool, and is even
expandable, for those times when you're
feeling a bit more sociable.

ODDS: 100%

ETA: 1990

PRICE: $1,150

The basic one-person unit is the size of a shower stall (3 by 3 by
7 feet high) and can fit into even the tiniest apartment. But if you
have the space and want to share your new toy, the steam room can
expand to accommodate up to eighteen people.

Invented in Sweden and now manufactured in New York, the Expandable Home Steam Room uses standard household current, has
its own mini-generator, and produces temperatures from 90 to 130
degrees Fahrenheit. Steam can be produced for up to one hour at a
sitting. The unit is made of tempered glass with a transparent acrylic
dome.

"Steam has a cleansing effect on the lungs and it also cleans the
skin," says Alex Urban, sales manager for Calgym New York Fitness
International, the manufacturer. "It's also soothing and great for relaxing the muscles." Right now, the Expandable Home Steam Room
is available from the manufacturer or from Hammacher Schlemmer
at 1-800-543-3366.

47

4

. . . and stuff for around the house

SOLAR AIR CONDITIONER

New Breeze is an air conditioner that uses the elements—water, air, and sun—to keep a home cool.

The brainchild of the Independent Power Company of North San Juan, California, New Breeze is mounted on a wall,

· · · · ·
ODDS: 100%
ETA: 1991
PRICE: $830
· · · · ·

49

will cool a 100-square-foot room, and requires no electric power. Instead, during the day, it gets its energy from a 4-by-1-foot rooftop panel which harnesses the energy of the sun to generate the power that runs the unit. Inside the cooler is a fan which draws cold water from your water supply and then mists it out into the air stream. In the evening, if cooling is still needed, New Breeze can be run on regular AC current.

While New Breeze may come with a price tag that's almost twice as large as conventional air conditioners, that money is easily recovered, says company spokesman Christopher Freitas. "Owners can save at least $30 a month with New Breeze. They supply the water; nature does the rest."

EMBALMED HOUSE PLANTS

T he idea of an embalmed house plant may sound a little morbid, but for people without the time to care for plants, it makes sense.

• • • • •
ODDS: 100%
ETA: 1990
PRICE: 3 TIMES REGULAR PLANT
• • • • •

These "eternal" plants never have to be watered, fertilized, pruned or exposed to sunlight. All they require is an occasional dusting. Yet, according to Steve Barger, general manager of Weyerhaeuser Co., the Washington State manufacturer, "the process can capture the natural look of the living plant—even the fragrance."

The plants are preserved with nontoxic chemicals that are absorbed by the cells. The process, developed in Europe a decade ago by Broadike, a Dutch company, has been used to preserve about forty different kinds of plants, including several that do not thrive indoors, such as eucalyptus, palm trees, beech trees, junipers, cedar and statice.

Embalmed or "interiorized" plants will be sold through florists, garden centers, department stores, and mail-order catalogues.

50

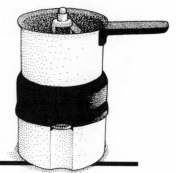

SELF-STIRRING SAUCEPAN

Leave it to the French to find a way to de-lump good ol' American gravy. They've come up with an electric saucepan that, besides straightening out our gravy situation, gradually warms sauces, stirs puddings, and can even scramble eggs.

ODDS: 100%

ETA: 1990

PRICE: $69

Whatever you wanted stirred on a burner can easily be taken care of by this electric *saucier*. The non-stick, dishwasher-safe COOK 'N STIR from the Tefal Appliance Company, based in France, is a lightweight (3¾ pounds) kitchen appliance that can hold 36 ounces. A small motor in the base of the unit controls the stirring device, gently mixing ingredients and heating them. "In effect," says Walter Nachtigall, vice president of sales and marketing for Tefal's U.S. operation, "the *saucier*'s little paddle is an extra hand. But it's a hand that knows exactly how long and how hard to cook and stir."

"*Le saucier* COOK 'N STIR," the full name on its passport, comes with a recipe book that includes instructions on how to adjust the temperature. Nachtigall reports that sales in Europe are doing well. In the United States, the no-hands sauce maker will soon be a popular item in gourmet specialty shops. Right now it's available through Hammacher Schlemmer (1-800-543-3366).

51

BREAD FRESHER

A delicious bite of "fresh" bread that is really two weeks old? The chef didn't perform the miracle; the earth's magnetic field did.

ODDS: 90%

ETA: 1992

PRICE: $50

A bread box that retards the normal aging process in bread, keeping it moist and mold-free for a couple of weeks or more without refrigeration, has been developed by John Hastie, a former electronics professor turned product designer. After six years of developing his product, Hastie has now applied for patent protection on his food fresher concept. Various models have been tested by several of his friends, who report that "it works like magic."

"It isn't magic," Hastie explains. "It's a spin-off from my earlier invention, the Acusharpe Razor Conditioner, which is based on the ability of the earth's magnetic field to twist or bend metal and polarize matter to prevent oxidation."

According to Hastie, magnetic energy can also be used to extend the shelf life of eggs, vegetables, and other food products, even bananas!

He sees major applications for an entire line of food freshers, including long-distance transportation in the United States and for use in Third World countries, where refrigeration is not readily available. Having worked earlier in his career for a support contractor on the space shuttle program, he also sees applications for food freshers in space exploration and travel.

SUPER LAUNDRY DETERGENT

I t seems that everybody who gets laundry done in Mexico comes back talking about it. Americans marvel at how stains that never came out in washing machines at home disappeared when Mexican women scrubbed a batch of laundry on stones by the riverbank.

ODDS: 80%

ETA: 1991

PRICE: N/A

Well, as it turns out, it's not the hard work of the señoritas. The swamps of Mexico are ripe with a powerful enzyme that does the job on "those tough laundry stains" that, judging from TV commercials, have been causing trouble in laundry land for years.

Discovered by researchers at Cornell University, the highly potent enzyme cleans stains from animal protein—like blood—as well as stains from plant proteins—like grass. It also works up to thirteen times faster than the leading enzyme used in today's detergent formulations.

Todd Gusek, a Ph.D. candidate at Cornell, has worked extensively with this enzyme. He explains that it's a protease, which is something that breaks down protein. Gusek is attempting to clone the enzyme through genetic engineering in order to make commercial quantities available. He expects the enzyme to be made into granules as well as liquid detergent, to be used just like Tide and other laundry detergents.

XEROGRAPHIC BEDSHEETS

Imagine searching for bedsheets that not only match the floral pattern of a Laura Ashley chintz-covered chair but also highlight the sea-green background of an heirloom rug. Unless you're lucky, you could be searching a long time in a lot of stores.

ODDS: 80%

ETA: 1995

PRICE: COMPETITIVE WITH INEXPENSIVE FABRICS

But the shopper of the future could find those sheets in minutes. She—or he—would simply scan a computer display of patterns, press a few buttons, and instantly an electrostatic printing system would begin printing the sheets. In a few more minutes, the customer would be out of the store, bedsheets and pillowcases in hand.

The technology is called xerographic textile printing. A group of engineers sponsored by the Department of Energy are working at the Georgia Institute of Technology developing ways to adapt modern xerography (such as your office copier) to fabric printing. So far, so good. Xerography works quickly and uses less energy than the traditional water-based dye process. Another advantage is that it eliminates the dye-filled, polluted water that's left over.

"The American textile industry is anxious to get into this," says John Toon, spokesman for the research project. "It could cut costs and give them a competitive edge over the Asian textile explosion."

54

THE SNORE-REDUCING PILLOW

S ince she couldn't sleep, Australian grandmother Judy Challen used to sketch her husband's sleeping postures as he snored the night away. By day, she would use a kitchen knife to shape foam pillows based on her sketches, hoping that

• • • • •
ODDS: 100%
ETA: 1990
PRICE: $60
• • • • •

she could create a pillow that would alleviate the problem. Her work finally yielded a shape that tilted her husband's head back, instead of forward, and allowed him to breathe more quietly. With the rudimentary pillow in hand, Challen approached an Australian company that manufactures foam cushions and pillows, and they agreed to produce her invention.

The Snore-Reducing Pillow is geared for people with "positional" snoring problems, rather than those with physical breathing difficulties. It differs from an ordinary pillow because its center-ridge construction supports the head from any sleeping position and eliminates air blockage in the larynx and the upper airway—the most common cause of snoring. The pillow is made of a flame-retardant and non-allergic material that retains its shape. The price includes a zippered stretch cover and a fitted pillowcase.

The Snore-Reducing Pillow is distributed to a few retail bedding and specialty stores by Hollander Home Fashions and is also available in some catalogues.

By the way, Judy Challen—and her husband—both sleep soundly now.

55

• • • • •

COOL PILLOW

I f you're a pillow flipper—one who's always looking for the cool side—Hitachi Inc. could help you sleep better. But first the Japanese company will have to export its head-cooling pillows to the United States.

ODDS: 50%

ETA: 1995

PRICE: $37

The 12-by-20-inch pillow is plugged in an hour before bedtime and ensures a cool surface all night. In Japan it sells for 5,000 yen (about $37 U.S.) and costs less than a dollar a month in electricity when run on a standard home current. More expensive models are available with small lights, a timer, and temperature control.

The pillow is popular in Japan, but so far, according to a Hitachi spokesman in Los Angeles, there's no plan to bring it to the United States. Still, Americans like their sleep as much as the Japanese, so it's likely that cool pillows will be a hot Christmas present sometime in the next decade.

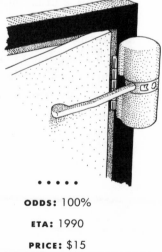

THE DOORBUTLER

W hen you were a child, how many times did some adult admonish you to "close the door behind you and don't let it slam!" But that wasn't just a way of keeping the coolness or warmth inside the home; it was a matter of safety.

ODDS: 100%

ETA: 1990

PRICE: $15

"Hazardous situations can develop when a door is inadvertently left open in the home or office. Stairwells, working areas, and furnace rooms are just a few of the places where an open door may lead to accidents," states Joel Meyers of Canada's Molvan Enterprises, Inc., a firm which is marketing a solution to the open-door problem.

The Doorbutler, made of a tough engineering plastic from Dupont, weighs about 5 ounces but is capable of repeatedly closing a 60-pound door 355,000 times, explains inventor Fred Vandergeest, who came up with the idea some thirteen years ago while toying with heavier and costlier versions of the device.

The life expectancy of the Doorbutler, which has a three-step, five-minute assembly process, is approximately twenty years of normal indoor use. There is also an outdoor version, which is resistant to heat, corrosion, and repeated impact.

Both Doorbutlers, which can be painted to match a decor, are currently available only through selected outlets in Canada and the United States.

SQUEEZE SCREWDRIVER

The SqueezeDriver, invented by a young engineer in the garage of his parents' California home, is manually operated and requires no electrical cords or batteries, yet it does many of the same things sophisticated motor and battery-driven screwdrivers do.

ODDS: 100%
ETA: 1990
PRICE: $25

57

Shaped for comfort like a ray gun out of *Star Wars*, the SqueezeDriver is a cinch to operate: The user holds the gun in his hand and squeezes the elongated trigger to make the screwdriver turn.

The screwdriver can rotate in either direction to tighten or loosen a screw or bolt.

A key feature of the SqueezeDriver is its three automatic speed modes. "During the course of the squeeze, the tool speeds up and slows down according to what's necessary to drive the screw," says Michael Marks, a partner in WorkTools Inc., a Los Angeles company which manufactures and markets the SqueezeDriver. (Marks's brother Joel, also a partner, invented the tool.) This feature eliminates the risk of stripping bolts and screw heads. Also, because the tool is mechanical, "you get to feel what you are doing: you have more control," says Marks. "This is a modern tool, but it's not high-tech. It's a very human tool: it keeps you close to your work."

Marks maintains that the SqueezeDriver is better than battery-operated screwdrivers because it is lighter weight (1 pound) and never has to be charged. "You can store them and use them anywhere," he says.

SqueezeDriver is already being used by some industrial and construction workers. It's available from WorkTools, Inc., 1748 Westwood Blvd., Los Angeles, CA 90024.

DIGITAL MEASURING TAPE

Peter Hsing, a jewelry caster in Long Island City, New York, tried to market his digital measuring tape to Stanley Tools, but Stanley was already selling its sonar measuring tape. Still, Hsing claims his device is more efficient.

• • • • •
ODDS: 50%
ETA: 1994
PRICE: N/A
• • • • •

58

It is small, like a watch, and you wear it on your wrist. A string 25 feet long is rolled up inside. The string has 2,500 digital marks that count space for you. When you pull out the string to measure the width of your chair, an internal counter records the amount of markers passed on the string. Each marker represents a certain distance, about an eighth of an inch. The number of markers is transformed into the number of inches and then displayed on the "watch" screen.

Sonar devices from Stanley and other companies bounce a signal off a wall to tell you how large a room is. But according to Hsing, you need a large wall to get the signal to bounce back to you. And it can measure only a large wall, not something small like a chair.

Does Hsing have a chance with his tape? If not, maybe he will be successful with his patented shoes with suction cups for walking on ice or oil.

ROTARY BLADE PAPER CUTTER

Move over, scissors; watch out, X-acto knives; beware, bulky paper cutters, there's a new kid on the cutting block. This cutter, designed by Glenn Polinsky of San Francisco, is cheaper than big professional cutting boards, easier to use, and small enough to fit on a desk or in a drawer.

• • • • •
ODDS: 75%
ETA: 1992
PRICE: $80
• • • • •

The new paper cutter uses a small round steel blade that rolls along an 18-inch flat blade for straight cutting. The round blade cuts as it is pushed. It is attached to a top bar that lifts to allow you to position the blade over the paper wherever you wish to cut. The cutter can hold ten to fifteen sheets of paper at a time. Polinsky was looking for a design that would be small, easy to use, and affordable. "What's new about this is that it reduces the cost," compared to other large paper cutters, Polinsky explains. It also puts the blade in a more visible position so it's easier to see what you're cutting.

The cutter is currently in the prototype stage. Polinsky is approaching manufacturers with the hope of selling the design for retail production.

59

PLASTIC NAILS

The world is changing in fundamental ways—right down to the nails that bolt our home and furniture together and hold our pictures on the wall. The future, as Dustin Hoffman was so prophetically told in *The Graduate*, is one word, "plastics." So, watch for plastic nails . . . coming soon . . . to a hardware store near you.

ODDS: 100%

ETA: 1990

PRICE: $7–$17 PER 1,000 NAILS. GUN, $540

The new-age nails are surprisingly strong and offer a number of advantages over the metal ones we've been crookedly hammering for the past several centuries. Plastic nails won't rust, they're not magnetic, and they have three times the pull-out resistance of metal nails. Further, they won't tear your sandpaper or break your blade if you accidentally run over one with a saw.

What makes plastic nails so strong is that they melt slightly as they penetrate, thus bonding the nail's surface to the wood. The downside, unfortunately, is that they have a greater tendency to snap in two. So there may be some jobs for which they're not appropriate.

The nails are the product of the Kotoko Company of Japan and will be distributed in this country by Marukyo U.S.A. under the brand name Kowa. "We're not trying to compete directly with metal-fastener manufacturers," says Marukyo spokesman Todd Drake. "We've tried to come up with a new product." This new product has already attracted the attention of NASA, the Ford Motor Company, McDonnell Douglas, and forward-looking handymen.

The air-driven Kowa fasteners come in all the standard sizes of T-nails (large-headed), finishing nails, and staples. You need an air gun made by Kotoko or by one of the other companies that make similar models. Because they don't rust, the nails are perfect for any outdoor or underwater job. They accept most paints, come in a variety of colors, and can even be custom-tinted.

60

BIODEGRADABLE PLASTIC BAGS

Plastic garbage put in the ground today will last four hundred years. Burning it results in acid rain and damage to the ozone layer. "And we're running out of places to put it," says Mike Gould, a researcher trying to come up with a way to get the stuff to biodegrade. "We'd be better off with plastic that bacteria in the soil would eat." But as we all know, plastic was designed specifically to resist that!

· · · · ·
ODDS: 95%
ETA: 1993
PRICE: N/A
· · · · ·

Gould is working with a team of researchers and a $2.5-million annual government budget to come up with an answer. He's proud to report that they've got something that will at least half-biodegrade within three weeks, but it may not be 100 percent biodegradable. The trick is to determine how to measure for biodegradability, which no one has yet been able to do.

The group's early version is now being studied at the Northern Regional Research Center in Peoria, Illinois, where Gould works. He says the plastics industry, environmental groups, and state legislatures are all eagerly awaiting the results. He's confident that his team is close.

61

· · · · ·

SOLAR-POWERED COOKER

Forget about gathering firewood or messing around with charcoal briquets and lighter fluid; now all you need is the sun to fuel your backyard barbecue.

ODDS: 100%

ETA: 1991

PRICE: $1,200

Alvin Marks, president of Advanced Research Development, Inc., in Athol, Massachusetts, has invented the SunCooker, a versatile, solar-powered cooker that can be used indoors or out, as a conventional oven or a backyard grill.

It works like this: An optical system that resembles a small satellite dish collects sunlight and sends it through a glass pipe into a cavity inside the oven. There, the energy is stored in phase-change material, which, like an ice cube in reverse, turns from a solid to a liquid as it stores heat, and resolidifies as it gives up heat. When the top of the cooker is raised, this stored heat comes from below, like a grill; with the top down, it works like an oven. The temperature is adjustable and can reach as high as 630 degrees Fahrenheit, approximately frying temperature, for up to twenty-four hours before additional sunlight is required. For use indoors, the solar disc, which has sensors that let it automatically follow the sun's direction, is placed on the roof and the light energy is piped down to the stove through longer glass tubes, like thick optical fibers.

The SunCooker couldn't come along at a better time, as the need for cleaner, less expensive, and more efficient energy sources becomes crucial. Indeed, Marks believes use of the SunCooker in developing countries could reduce deforestation by reducing the need for wood as a cooking fuel.

62

LETTER SLEDDER

Diane Powers was forever driving on the lawn—leaving ruts behind—when she stopped to pick up the mail at her country mailbox. She also had developed the habit of knocking the car door into the post, doing damage to both, plus the sideview mirror. Her husband, Todd, noticed while walking the dog every morning that lots of their neighbors were having the same trouble.

• • • • •
ODDS: 100%
ETA: 1991
PRICE: $325 WITHOUT POST; $420 WITH POST
• • • • •

So, to save the lawn and the car door, Powers invented a simple remote device that brings the mailbox into your car. He calls it the Letter Sledder, because it slides out 30 inches on two runners. A remote-control device (a bit smaller than the ones used for automatic garage doors) has two buttons. If you press one, the letterbox will extend into your car, stopping whenever you pick up your finger. If you hit the other button, the unit will retract all the way back to the post.

There's a model that runs on electricity (you need to run a wire from the house) and a solar model that recharges itself. Hammacher Schlemmer (1-800-543-3366) carries the solar version, while the electronic one is available from Powers directly.

63

• • • • •

SELF-WEEDING LAWN

Grass that weeds itself: It's a home-
owner's dream come true.

A geneticist in Canada has unearthed
a grass that emits its own natural herbi-
cide, an agent that destroys or inhibits
plant growth. Not only is the grass self-
weeding, it's lovely to look at. "It makes

ODDS: 100%

ETA: 1992

PRICE: SAME AS
CONVENTIONAL LAWN

for a beautiful lawn," says Dr. Jan Weijer, a scientist at the University
of Alberta, who first discovered the grass in the eastern Rockies in
the seventies while looking for grasses to battle erosion. "The texture
is rich and the color is a very lush jade green," he says, warning,
however, that a dandelion may "creep in every now and then."

Because the grass originated in the dry, hostile soil of the Rockies,
it is virtually maintenance-free. Apart from being self-weeding, it can
grow in nearly any soil and climate, and it needs no fertilizer or
watering. Also, "the grass grows just four inches annually, so you
only have to mow it about three times a year," says Weijer. "That
leaves a lot of free time for the suburbanite on Saturdays and Sun-
days."

Weijer says the principle of self-weeding is not new: "There are
thousands of plants that weed themselves," he says. There are also
plenty of North American grasses that are self-weeding. However,
historically, non-self-weeding European grasses have been used for
American lawns. "I think people made the mistake that something
grown in foreign lands would be better for our American climates,
but homegrown grasses are better adapted to our environment and
ecology," says Weijer.

Weijer is patenting the product in the United States. Super Grass
U.S. has been chosen to represent the lawn grass here. Marketing of
the product should begin in 1992.

64

POLKA-DOT GERANIUMS

We're all familiar with the common geranium, that old standby for Mother's Day. Well, geraniums are getting a shot in the stem, so to speak, from researchers at Penn State University. They've created some geraniums in wild new colors and others with the ability to resist insects and disease.

• • • • •
ODDS: 100%
ETA: 1990
PRICE: SLIGHTLY HIGHER THAN REGULAR GERANIUMS
• • • • •

Dr. Richard Craig, professor of plant breeding, has developed new garden varieties in magenta and lavender, as well as in subtle shades of red, coral, and pink. One plant has variegated green-and-white leaves, while others have flowers that appear to be polka-dot—pink with red dots or white dots. "By analyzing the pigments in the flowers, we are able to plot new color directions," says Craig. "Red, for example, is a combination of many pigments. The combinations are endless."

A second group for indoor potting, called Regals, was bred to flower more predictably and to keep better in the home. These come in white, lavender, salmon, orange, red, or pink, with "blotches" or "feathers" of darker color. While some of these new geraniums are already available, newer ones will be coming on the market every spring for the next few years.

Dr. Craig has developed a third group of zonal geraniums that is highly resistant to rust, a plant disease that is widespread in California and Europe. And studies are revealing how some geraniums immobilize insects with a sticky substance produced on leaf hairs. "These findings are the result of two decades of work here at Penn State," says Craig. "Developing disease- and insect-resistant plants is the way of the future."

65

• • • • •

NEW, IMPROVED CHRISTMAS TREE

I t was poet Joyce Kilmer who decreed that "only God can make a tree." Not anymore. Now James Hanover, a professor of forest genetics at Michigan State University, also holds that distinction.

ODDS: 100%
ETA: 1995
PRICE: $5–$50

Soon the Christian world will be opening presents around the Spartan Spruce, a hybrid which combines the best qualities of the blue and white spruce trees.

The Spartan, which took Hanover twenty years to develop, is as blue as its Colorado ancestor and just as hardy in cold or drought. It also has the soft needles and rapid growth rate (eight to nine years) of the white spruce. As a result, the Spartan Spruce won't prick your fingers or shed all over the living-room floor.

The tree is unique and as such has been granted a Certificate of Plant Variety Protection, similar to a patent, by the U.S. Department of Agriculture. Right now, the Spartan Spruce can be found in only two nurseries, which have licensing agreements with M.S.U.

However, Hanover says it will be commercially available as potted seedlings nationwide by Christmas 1989 and as full grown trees by 1995, at a price of "just a few dollars more than similar varieties."

5

tvs, videos, cameras

SMART TV

Your taste in television leans to the soaps, the talk shows, anything about music from the fifties, and "Wild Kingdom." But you don't seem to be able to catch all those shows when they're on, and who can keep up with TV schedules to record them on the VCR?

ODDS: 100%

ETA: 1993

PRICE: $1,200

Relax! When you feel like watching the tube, just pick up your SmarTV remote control and press ON. The SmarTV knows just what you like and has been recording your favorites all week—up to 250

67

shows at a time. Just select which one you want to see from the jukebox-like menu that comes up on the screen. Another button will give you a brief description of the show. If you think you're interested, press PLAY SHOW. You never have to touch a tape, or figure out how to program the VCR. You can always stop the show (when the phone rings), rewind (if you miss a joke), and, best of all, you can fast-forward at twenty-seven times regular speed past the commercials. Or press STOP and check the menu again.

Blair Newman, of Metaview Corporation in San Francisco, originated the idea for SmarTV some time ago. "I came up with the idea, and when several years later no one was doing it, I decided I'd just go ahead and do it."

The "genius VCR," as Newman calls this baby, is a black box about the size of a 19-inch TV set. After you program your TV preferences, it monitors all channels, twenty-four hours a day, and records every show it thinks you might like to see.

HIGH-DEFINITION TV

T elevision makers have brought us from black-and-white sets to color, from furniture-size cabinet models to miniatures worn on the wrist, and from unruly rabbit-ear antennas to cable. Now they are finally going to improve the picture.

• • • • •
ODDS: 100%
ETA: 1994
PRICE: $3,000
• • • • •

The goal for High-Definition TV (HDTV) is to look like 35mm film—rich tones, clarity, and all. That means no more fuzzy edges and shallow saturation for the tube of tomorrow. But Alec Shapiro, who coordinates a group of manufacturers who make the production equipment for high-definition programs, claims that while HDTV delivers 35mm film quality, "HDTV has its own distinct look. It does for the eyes what CDs did for the ears."

In order to get this next phase in TV viewing, you will have to purchase a new television set. As a result, the change from old to new will be handled similarly to the transition from black-and-white to color—slowly. HDTV will be available, at first, only from cable and satellite companies. The networks will have to wait until their governing body, the FCC, decides which of the nineteen viable proposals they're studying will best serve the public. That could take a while. The decision rests on various aspects, from band width to lines of resolution, and the all-important compatibility issue of whether or not your old set will still be able to receive any broadcasts at all if broadcasters turn to HDTV signals en masse.

The sets will be wider—just like in the movies—with a 16:9 ratio. They also will be bigger: HDTV can be viewed only on screens of 25 inches and larger. And since conventional broadcasting is totally different from the HDTV signal, the new sets will have a way to switch back to the "old" signal, at least at first, like AM/FM radio.

Shapiro is busy promoting one production format called the HDTV 1125/60. Meanwhile, he's hoping the FCC will decide soon what transmission format it wants. "That will allow HDTV to happen on a widespread basis."

INTERACTIVE GAME NETWORK

This is what game-show nuts and sports fanatics have been waiting for: the chance to second-guess quarterbacks or participate in crazy games without fear of humiliation. The Interactive Game Network will allow viewers to play along and win prizes without ever leaving their living rooms.

The Game Network will be available over cable and network TV. Participants will purchase a control box, allowing them to choose answers or options by pressing buttons. An

• • • • •

ODDS: 100%

ETA: 1990

PRICE: TERMINAL: $300–$500
ANNUAL FEE: $120
PER EVENT: $1–$2

• • • • •

69

LCD display on the box will feed viewers all the information they need to know. "What we send is the equivalent of a *TV Guide* with the current week's list of programs which are interactive," explains Kevin Randolph, Interactive Game Network marketing vice president.

Once you make your selection, the fun begins. For example, you can play along with a regularly scheduled live football game. The Interactive Game Network signal will be broadcast parallel to the actual game. Using your control box, you will try to predict upcoming plays. If you guess right enough times, you'll win a prize. The same applies for game shows. You can play along with Monty Hall . . . and not have to dress like a chicken.

There'll be no limit to the number of home viewers who can participate in any program. But in addition to the cost of the box, there'll be a monthly fee plus a small charge for every program you play.

FLAT TV

A TV so slim that it can hang on your wall like a picture? Don't be surprised if one is adorning your living room sometime in the 1990s.

· · · · ·
ODDS: 90%
ETA: 1994
PRICE: N/A
· · · · ·

"We haven't become so overcrowded that if a TV isn't flat we won't buy one," says *Video Magazine* editor Lance Braithwaite. "Nonetheless, there is an aesthetic push for flat TVs. In fact, flat television could be available now," he adds. "But for what price?" That is indeed the question. Manufacturers have been exploring the feasibility of a "full-size" flat TV which will most likely be based on LCD technology.

Currently, Sony markets a hand-held, color, LCD-based, 2.7-inch screen, with tuner and battery pack, for $650. The next step is to make larger LCD panels. But the larger the panel, the higher the rejection rate due to imperfections. Until Sony or some other company finds a solution, we'll have to wait for affordably priced flat television sets to hang on our walls.

VIDEO-ON-THE-GO

A tiny revolution has just begun.
    With the introduction of Sony's GV-8 Video Walkman, we can expect a barrage of new entertainment and instructional 8mm videocassettes.

ODDS: 100%

ETA: 1990

PRICE: $1,300

But first, the Sony Video Walkman. It's a TV and a VCR. It's hand-held, about the size of a paperback book, weighs 2½ pounds, is battery-operated, and has a 3-inch color LCD screen. The VCR uses tiny 8mm videocassettes, which can play or record for four hours in the "extended play mode."

The Video Walkman can be used virtually anywhere. "In the car, while taking public transportation, readying a meal in the kitchen, or lying in a hammock in the back yard" are a few suggestions from Shinichi Takagi, president of Sony's consumer video products division.

Business applications abound as well. Sales-training tapes could be viewed minutes before an appointment and product demonstration videos could be shown to clients over lunch.

"It probably won't be long," says Sony spokesperson Steve Hoechster, "before magazine publishers in the United States do what the Japanese publishers have done. That is, begin marketing video versions of their publications for Video Walkman use."

71

DIAL "M" FOR MOVIES

Those video-rental stores that seem to have sprung up at every corner and mall in America could be out of business by the year 2000. On the way is a system called Advanced Broadcatching, which replaces the video store with a home shop-

ODDS: 20%

ETA: 1999

PRICE: N/A

ping service that delivers movies right into your computer. All you do is pick up the phone and order up to thirty films at a time. That night, they will be entered into a computer that doubles as a TV for viewing at your leisure.

Well, probably not completely at your leisure. It's a subscription service and you will either have to pay a fee for every film you want to keep permanently or the films will self-erase after one use.

Stephen Benton of the M.I.T. Media Lab predicts that in the future, "free broadcasting as we know it will cease to exist and everything will become pay TV" on systems similar to Advanced Broadcatching.

The movies available will include golden oldies, those just-seen-at-a-theater-near-you, and quite possibly brand-new films—even pre-mieres. You could have the opening-night festivities right in your living room. "Should be great for champagne sales," says Benton.

72

DESKTOP VIDEO

Soon after desktop publishing became a buzz word in the computer world, desktop video rolled itself onto the list of the new and amazing.

• • • • •
ODDS: 100%
ETA: 1990
PRICE: $1,500
• • • • •

The professionals who do the computer graphics on your nightly news hour were astonished at first, but for basic video enhancing many of them now have the same system in their studios that you can buy for your home use. So it's your turn to make the clouds speed by under images or words that you create.

Commodore has the computer system, and they call it the Amiga 500. With one of those hooked up to your VCR, you can take those tapes of your graduation, your wedding, Christmas at Dad's, or baby Jane's first birthday and add sound, graphics, titles, and other touches for a professional broadcast flavor. It won't look like "The CBS Evening News" with this lower-priced model, but it will look as good as most cable productions, with the same rolling, twisting, and turning of images, as well as dissolves, fades, 3-D animation, and chromakey used in both cable and network TV.

For a few hundred dollars more, you can upgrade the Amiga's genlock, the gizmo that synchronizes the videotape signal with the computer-generated graphics. The better genlocks give your home production a sharper image with higher resolution.

As with all computer systems, a lot depends on your software. But fear not, plenty exists that will enable you to create wipes, squeezes, page flips, animation of all sorts, and the full range of computer graphics in various typefaces and colors.

73

• • • • •

3-D HOME VIDEO

F or over thirty years, 3-D has been little more than a fad and a lot less than a major entertainment technology. Now Toshiba is about to try it again with a camcorder that makes jump-off-the-screen videos.

. . . . .
ODDS: 100%
ETA: 1991
PRICE: $3,800
. . . . .

According to David Shoults, Toshiba America's national sales-promotion manager, the camera works on the same principle as your eyes: two lenses viewing the world each from a slightly different angle. When the videotape is played back through your TV via a special adapter, the images appear combined on the screen.

But 3-D wouldn't be 3-D without the special glasses. These are actually goggles that are hooked up to the adapter. During playback, the lenses in the glasses shut off and on, allowing your left eye to see the left recorded image, and the right, the right recorded image. The adapter synchronizes these two fields so fast that the human brain combines them to create a single 3-D image.

The camcorder, adapter, and glasses are sold as a unit. From *House of Wax* in the fifties to your house in the nineties, 3-D is still trying to catch on.

DUAL DECK VCR

A small Arizona video company has come up with a big idea. Go-Video of Scottsdale will soon market a twin deck videocassette recorder that lets you watch one tape while recording on another. Both decks can be operated from the same remote-control unit and both play stereo sound.

ODDS: 90%

ETA: 1990

PRICE: $650

Terren Dunlap, Go-Video's CEO and chairman, says that his VCR-2 represents the "new generation" of videocassette recorders. "It provides an answer to a screaming need for a VCR that is simple to operate yet lets the consumer do two things at one time."

VCR-2 will be available directly from Go-Video and through a few selected catalogues, and may also be distributed through electronics stores.

Assuming your mind is almost as devious as ours, you may be wondering whether you'll be able to rent a movie and conveniently copy it on your VCR-2. Well, that depends on you and the movie. By agreement with the Motion Picture Association of America, the VCR-2 incorporates a circuit that prevents illicit copying of films that have been specially encoded to guard against the practice. But that still leaves some 150 million copies of movies out there that are protected only by your regard for the copyright laws.

75

• • • • •

TALKING VCR REMOTE CONTROL

V CRs are great. The pain is in programming them. To take the frustration out of all that time setting and button pushing, Sharp Electronic Corp. has come up with a remote control unit that verbally guides you through the programming process.

ODDS: 100%

ETA: 1990

PRICE: WITH VCR, $450–$650

The Optonica Voice Coach by Sharp has a 50-phrase, 500-word vocabulary. Even if you're phobic about machines, you'll be able to handle the step-by-step spoken instructions. The Voice Coach also allows you to record the program you're watching while simultaneously recording the audio from another source, such as an FM simulcast on the radio. The remote unit doubles as a timer, alerting you when your favorite TV show is playing. "Alarm time is 8 p.m.," it will tell you.

Initially, the Voice Coach will be available only with Optonica VCRs. But with the increasing sophistication of video equipment, talking controls should become widespread.

76

HAL:
TELEPHONE-ACTIVATED VCR

N amed HAL, after the computer in the science fiction classic *2001: A Space Odyssey*, this device lets you program your VCR from any Touch Tone phone anywhere in the world. It works with any VHS or BETA VCR equipped with infrared wireless remote control.

• • • • •
ODDS: 100%
ETA: 1990
PRICE: $190
• • • • •

The process is simple because HAL, using an electronically synthesized voice, actually gets on the line and patiently leads you through the programming steps. HAL can store a program you want to see up to a year in advance, without interfering with your answering machine's normal functions.

HAL is available from Advanced Video Dynamics, 705 General Washington Ave., Norristown, PA 19043, and in some electronic specialty stores.

ELECTRONIC STILL PHOTOGRAPHY

P hotography is going digital. It's called electronic still photography. It will change the way you take, view, select, develop, edit, and feel about pictures. The technology is here now and so is the first generation of cameras, playback drives, and printers. But the quality isn't great and the price is high.

• • • • •
ODDS: 100%
ETA: 1990
PRICE: CAMERA: $2,500
PLAYBACK: $3,000
PRINTER: $3,000
• • • • •

77

How does it work? Instead of exposing film to light (the way it's been done since 1839), a chip, similar to that in your camcorder, receives the information framed in your camera lens and records it on a miniature video floppy disk. For the time being, the disk can be used only with the electronic photography hardware.

The main advantage is instantaneous feedback. Film has to be printed before you can view the results of your creativity—or lack thereof—but with these floppies, you can hook up a special playback device to your television set, pop in the disk, and instantly preview your pictures before committing to a print. You can decide which photos you want to keep and which you want to forget about.

Preview the pictures any time, whether you've shot one frame or the whole 25–30 available on the disk. With the help of a pricey machine you can print your own photos right at home. Otherwise, send your disk off to the photo developer and mark the frames you want returned.

Right now the quality of electronic stills leaves a lot to be desired, according to Mike Stensvold, an editor at *Petersen's Photographic* magazine. "The image definition is just not as sharp as film." Stensvold likens it to the quality of a color Xerox. But the picture will improve as researchers develop better chips.

The next breakthrough in electronic still photography—digital editing—is expected to arrive by 1993. By interconnecting with a computer, you should be able to digitally alter any portion of your picture. For example, you'll be able to make that telephone pole disappear or add a beautiful sunset to pictures of your rained-out trip to the Caribbean.

MEMORY CARD CAMERA

Forget about film. Who needs video floppy disks? We may be bypassing all of these still picture systems in favor of a memory card image-making system.

ODDS: 80%

ETA: 1995

PRICE: $250

Shown in prototype by Fuji, the card camera is a palm-size basic point-and-shoot unit that contains a charged couple device (CCD), which converts light photons to electrons (electrical energy). The pictures are recorded on a credit-card-size 16-megabit "memory card." At present, the card can hold ten "fields" (pictures). In the future, it should be able to hold forty. However, a key feature of the card is that it carries its own tiny battery, which can be recharged and used over and over again. So there's no need to buy new cards (or film or disks). After you take your pictures, you can preview and edit them on a special playback device. Next, you transfer the images to your personal computer disk or onto digital tape. From the tape, you can make prints using a special printer.

When you're finished with that batch of pictures, just go out shooting again. The advantage over electronic still photography (see page 77) is that there is no loss of quality as you go from tape to player to printer.

Fuji is hoping to price its system so that it will appeal to the snapshot market.

79

CAMERA STABILIZATION LENS

N ew lenses that take the shake out of the pictures you shoot should help professional photographers and amateurs alike. Canon has already shown a prototype of the system in their L series 300mm lens. Demonstrated on a vibrating platform, it produced rock-steady pictures. The lens is about 10 percent heavier and about 25 percent longer than normal.

· · · · ·

ODDS: 100%

ETA: 1991

PRICE: 2 TO 3 TIMES MORE THAN REGULAR LENSES

· · · · ·

Inside the new lens, highly sensitive meters detect camera vibration and respond with an optical compensator that actually displaces the image so that it appears shake-free.

Though Canon anticipates that the system will be used first in long telephoto lenses (the longer and heavier the lens, the harder to hold steady), it should eventually find its way to even the simplest snapshot camera.

Image-stabilization lenses will also make it easier to get sharp pictures at low speeds, when even the slightest movement can blur a photo.

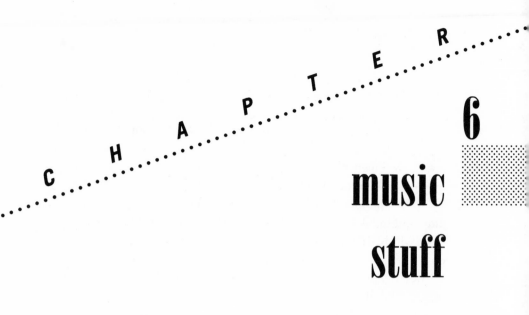

music stuff

DIGITAL AUDIOTAPES AND DECKS

Popular Science magazine has called digital audiotape (DAT) recorders "the finest home tape recorders ever invented." Yet for years there's been a battle to keep this technology out of the United States.

The issue is being argued in Congress, where major record companies are fighting for legislation that would require DAT tape decks to be equipped with anticopy circuitry. Otherwise, the record industry claims, it will lose a billion dollars a year as home audio enthusiasts make duplicates of compact discs and prerecorded tapes. But no matter who wins the battle, digital audiotapes and decks are coming . . . and soon . . . with or without the capacity to erase and record. And that's good news for everyone who

• • • • •

ODDS: 95%

ETA: 1991

PRICE: $1,300 FOR TAPE DECK
$13 PER TAPE

• • • • •

81

loves music. For DAT quality is outstanding. Many audio experts claim that every tape is as good as the master made in the recording studio.

What's more, DATs hold more music. Each tape, a bit larger than a match box, can store up to two hours of sound. And you can scan a tape in a mere forty-five seconds, so you don't have to wait forever for the deck to locate your favorite song. Part of the secret to DATs' speed and performance is the way information is arranged on the tape. Standard tapes record along their length, whereas DATs record along their width. It's more efficient, like stacking books the normal way on a shelf, instead of laying them end to end.

DAT decks are a cross between a VCR and a standard audiotape player. All the advanced functions, such as auto search and programmable playback, are exactly the same as in the old players, but the tape loads like a VCR. Also, like a VCR, DAT recorders require a few seconds to wrap the tape around its record/play drum.

Another major advantage of DATs is that they are not nearly as sensitive to bouncing and jarring as compact discs. The slightest bump while driving or jogging will cause a CD to skip. Not so with DATs, making them ideal for pocket-size portables and cars. In fact, some experts believe that the first DAT decks in the United States will be for your car stereo system.

DIGITAL SPEAKERS

N ow that digital audiotapes and decks are on their way, you'll need to be more discriminating when selecting loudspeakers. How good your system sounds has always been highly dependent on the quality of its speakers. After all, it's the speakers' responsibility to convert elec-

82

· · · · ·
ODDS: 100%
ETA: 1991
PRICE: $900–$5,000/ PAIR
· · · · ·

tronic signals from the amplifiers into the sound waves that eventually enter your ears.

Digital recordings capture a wider range of frequencies and a greater dynamic range—the difference between loud and soft passages—than do conventional analog recordings. But the overall effect is lost on speakers incapable of reproducing the sounds accurately and duplicating musical peaks (especially loud bass passages) without distortion or audible vibration. This is the challenge facing loudspeaker manufacturers.

"In order for speakers to be ready for digital sound, they have to be able to handle more power and respond more quickly," says Hector Martinez of Northridge, California's JBL Inc., one of several companies pushing for better speakers. JBL is using titanium—an ultrastrong, lightweight metal—to jump some of the hurdles. The metal's strength-to-weight ratio allows the speakers to react more quickly and accurately to the electronic signals. "It provides more clarity and acoustic articulation," says Martinez. In other words, it sounds terrific.

England's KEF Electronics is likewise working to eliminate cabinet rattle caused by digital's increased power. The company is connecting the two woofers in each cabinet—the larger speakers responsible for bass and lower-frequency sound—with a stiff metal bar to help cancel out vibration. Another British firm, B&W Loudspeakers, is testing a "cabinetless" speaker whose design incorporates a honeycomb-like housing filled with an acoustic foam.

By the early 1990s your stereo store will be stocking these and other innovative speakers. Although they've been called more "evolutionary" than revolutionary, when it comes to great sound quality, their importance can't be denied.

83

COMPACT DISC RECORDER

Compact discs may sound better and last longer than audiocassette tapes, but they still have one disadvantage. You can't erase and record on a CD.

ODDS: 100%
ETA: 1991
PRICE: $600

That's going to change soon. Tandy Corporation, the parent company of Radio Shack, has applied for several patents on a compact disc record and play technology that is similar to a VCR. You will be able to erase, record, play, and even edit your discs.

Simply explained, a CD is pressed just like an old-fashioned record. If you look closely you can see the grooves. Those grooves have pits and bumps that contain information. A laser scans the disc and converts the information to sound. Now Tandy has created a new disc called THOR-CD, comprised of several different types of layers, one of which is heat-sensitive. When heated by the laser, the pits and bumps literally melt away.

Another layer is reflective and lets you create new pits and bumps when you want to record. There is also a layer that protects against fingerprints and dust.

This new recorder will be "completely backward compatible," according to Robert McClure, president of Tandy Electronics. This means that the CDs you already own will play on the new machine— but you won't be able to erase or record over them. That can be done only with a new CD on the new machine.

3-D SOUND

"It's been studied for more than a hundred years," says the IBM veteran. "It's called psychoacoustics, the scientific discipline that studies how human beings tell where sounds are coming from."

● ● ● ● ●
ODDS: 100%
ETA: 1993
PRICE: SAME AS
REGULAR RECORDINGS
● ● ● ● ●

Ralph Schaefer is president of American Natural Sound Development, the company that will revolutionize how we hear our entertainment. His seventeen years at IBM fit well with the background of his partner, Peter Myers, who at eighteen was already a consultant to NASA. Myers was investigating how information gets to the brain. He recognized that the most overloaded entry is through the eyes. But he thought auditory channels were very promising as a complement to the eyes. With the eyes, after all, you can see only what's in front of you. But with sound, you can hear what's all around you. "Melodies also can have three dimensions," says Schaefer. "The sugar-plum fairies will not only dance in front of you; if you close your eyes and listen, you'll think they are swarming all around you."

Schaefer goes on to explain that current stereo audio is delivered in a lateral wall of sound. But with 3-D sound, it will be all around you, just as in real life. It's different from quadriphonic and Surround Sound. Those techniques require multiple channels of sound recorded from lots of microphones and transmit them through many speakers. With 3-D, only one piece of recording equipment is necessary for production, and the usual two channels of sound for reproduction. Since the difference is in how the sound is recorded, there's no need to buy any new playback equipment.

Myers and Schaefer at first will market the technology for use in simulators. Then their march into the recording industry will begin, followed shortly, they hope, by a penetration of Hollywood.

85

● ● ● ● ●

BODY MUSIC

Bobby McFerrin can sing his hit "Don't Worry, Be Happy" for now. McFerrin, known for terrific rhythm and blues performed by using parts of his body and no musical accompaniment, will have some competition from Ben Knapp, who's also using parts of his body to make music.

ODDS: 90%

ETA: 1993

PRICE: $2,400, INCLUDING SYNTHESIZER

Knapp, in conjunction with a Stanford physiologist, put together a box called a Biomuse that can receive electrical signals from nerve or muscle tissue and translate them into predetermined sounds. Where normally you would have a keyboard or an electrical instrument doing the work, a thigh muscle, your heart muscle, your little finger muscle, even that oft-forgotten muscle the brain can now be heard practicing scales. "We just made the body into a keyboard," says Knapp.

A Velcro band with a disposable electrode is wrapped around a muscle and wired into the system. Flex your bicep slowly and, depending on how your Biomuse is programmed, a note could get higher or lower, could repeat faster or slower, could get louder or softer, or it might move from one side of the room to another and back again when you relax your arm. The larger the muscle, the more signal that is available, but Knapp's working on amplifying weaker muscles and balancing them with the stronger ones.

What on earth prompted this invention? Knapp, a graduate student in electrical engineering at Stanford University, plays an electronic keyboard in his spare time. When he plays, he's forever having to flip switches to get different sounds. He thought it would be convenient if he could just control the switches with his eyes or with his brain. "You wouldn't have to interrupt your playing that way," he says.

The current model is able to monitor only eight "channels"—or muscles—at a time. Each muscle is attached to an electrode that relays the impulses over a wire to a dispatcher unit small enough to be worn on the hip. The dispatcher is attached by a cable to the Biomuse box.

For now, the easy-to-locate alpha wave is the only brainwave wired for sound. As research gets more sophisticated, however, chances are good that you'll be able to play "Moonlight Sonata" just by thinking.

COMPUTER SONGWRITER

With a computer program called Personal Composer, anyone— whether he or she can even read music— can now write it!

. . . . .
ODDS: 100%
ETA: 1990
PRICE: $495
. . . . .

"It's great," says Jim Miller, the inventor of Personal Composer. "You don't even have to know what an eighth note is to print your own sheet music."

The floppy disk works with a standard IBM compatible computer that has the ability to plug into any MIDI instrument plug—the standard plug for the music industry.

A MIDI Mic is available from MEI Incorporated, the company marketing the Personal Composer, if you wish to use non-electrical instruments or record your own voice.

The music computer was introduced in limited supply in 1988. Already there are professionals using it, including Jack Marek, who composes the sound tracks for "Sesame Street" cartoons.

"By the year 2000," MEI president Bill Theis predicts, "at least 50 percent of grade schools will have this. It can be used as an evaluation tool. A student can play his trumpet music into the computer and get the sheet music back, along with the correct version that has been programmed by the teacher. The teacher or the student can then compare both versions. The student's version will even compare dynamics and expression."

87

The Personal Composer software sells for $495 and the MIDI Mic for $695. The total package, including computer, sells for $2,550, and is available through MEI Incorporated, P.O. Box 599, Chesterton, IN 46304.

CONCERT HALLS AT HOME

I f you missed Sinatra at Carnegie Hall or the Beatles at the Royal Albert, the technology is now here to re-create such magical experiences.

ODDS: 100%
ETA: 1990
PRICE: $699

Yamaha Electronics, applying digital technology, has come up with the DSP-100U, a device that can re-create dozens of actual acoustic environments. Controlled by a remote keypad, the DSP-100U requires a stereo system with a minimum of four channels of amplification and four speakers. It works with a CD player, a turntable, a tape deck, or even a radio. The DSP-100U includes highly sophisticated integrated circuits that reproduce the way sound waves react within a particular environment. Included are jazz clubs, discos, outdoor arenas, churches, and concert halls.

The DSP-100U is already available at many audio specialty dealers.

PRIVATE LISTENING AT HOME

J ust when you thought there could not possibly be another small portable listening device, along comes Private Waves, a new type of wireless headphone. Happily, it does something none of the others can do.

odds: 100%

eta: 1990

price: $80

The sounds you hear over Private Waves can originate from your stereo, VCR, CD player, or TV. So you can be making beds upstairs, doing laundry downstairs, or gardening in the backyard and still listen to your favorite music or TV shows. Like a Walkman or mini-cassette player, here's a miniature receiver that clips onto your belt or goes into your pocket. Lightweight bud-style headphones connect to this receiver.

There are other so-called wireless headphones, but they are restricted to line-of-sight use. That's because they use infrared technology. Private Waves relies on RF (radio frequency) transmission. Since RF signals can travel through walls, which infrared cannot, you can use these headphones anywhere. Well, anywhere within 75 feet of the source.

The Private Waves system is easy to set up. A compact transmitter is connected to the audio-out or headphone jack of your TV, VCR, stereo, or CD player. You just clip on a 3½-ounce mini-receiver, put the headphones on your ears, and you're in business.

Private Waves, incidentally, is the product of Datawave, Inc., of Van Nuys, California.

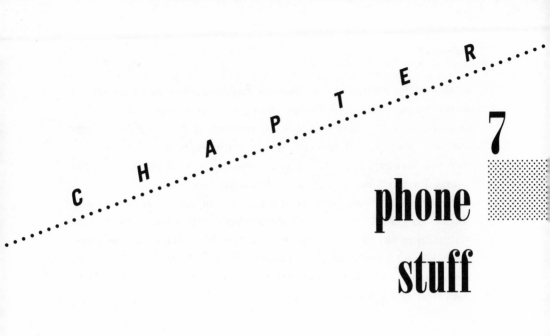

phone stuff

TELEPHONE SMART CARDS

This is cool. If you're a college kid, you won't have to collect gobs of change to call your sweetie from the dorm pay phone. Just go to the newsstand and load up on these telephone cards.

ODDS: 99%

ETA: 1994

PRICE: N/A

They are easy to work and could save you precious dimes and nickels—to say nothing of quarters for laundry. Just insert one in the special phone slot and you and your honey can start breathing heavy over the wires. There are a certain amount of calling units, say $10 worth, on each card. When your time is up, you have ten seconds to replace the card with another one.

Jerome Svigals, author of the book *Smart Cards*, says that telephone cards are in use in France, and being tested in Switzerland, Germany, Japan, and in five airports in the United States. He predicts that the

91

cards—often referred to as Memory Smart Cards—will save money in two ways. The cards charge you by the penny—no rounding out to nickels, dimes, and quarters. At present, if you want to say just one more good-bye, it may cost you an additional dime. In the future, with the Memory Smart Card, you might pay only 3 cents, the exact charge for the time you are actually on the line.

Better yet, Svigals tells us that the cost of operating pay phones should go down, because telephone cards will reduce the cost of maintaining pay phones by as much as two-thirds. How? For starters, phones won't have to be able to differentiate between dimes, nickels, and quarters, which will make the equipment less expensive. Also, both coin collection and vandalism will be eliminated.

PICTURE PHONE

Picture-transmitting phones have been on the drawing board for years, and in fact the technology has been around since the 1960s. The problem has been the high cost of the units and the special phone lines. Now there is a picture phone that's reasonably priced, but it doesn't do all that we might have anticipated.

• • • • •
ODDS: 100%
ETA: 1990
PRICE: $800 FOR SET OF TWO
• • • • •

Developed in the United States by Mitsubishi Electric Sales America, Inc., in California, VisiTel can send black-and-white still pictures across regular telephone lines onto a 4½-inch screen. Just plug the VisiTel unit into a phone jack with one wire and into an electric socket with the other wire. Then plug your regular phone into VisiTel. Now you're ready to sit pretty for the camera!

"You'll see yourself on your screen, so you can smile and center yourself in front of it, push SEND, and the person at the other end will see a picture of you," says Kozu Tsuya from Mitsubishi's Visual Telecom Division. But don't worry about getting caught just out of the shower. VisiTel will transmit a picture only when you push the SEND button.

You can send as many pictures as you want, but each time you do, expect 5½ seconds of silence on the wire. Each transmission occupies the whole line so there's no room for sound.

The price is $800 for a set of two monitors. A wide-angle lens (to send pictures of the whole wedding party) and a close-up lens (to transmit a picture of the ring) are available options.

VIDEO TELEPHONE

Twenty-five years ago AT&T showed a "picture phone" at the New York World's Fair. Now a video phone is about to arrive on the telecommunications scene. The U.V. Communicator may well be the first marketable video phone of its

ODDS: 90%

ETA: 1995

PRICE: $14,900

kind. Developed by U.V.C. Corporation of Irvine, California, the phone should lead the way for enhanced telecommunications between households, offices, and businesses.

The system is comprised of a color video camera, a 13-inch color video monitor, a transceiver (an apparatus that alternately transmits and receives) with software for recording and transmitting video images over ordinary telephone lines, and a telephone for transmission of audio signals over a second telephone line. The audio quality is similar to a standard telephone, while the video resolution approaches a regular television screen.

The video phone also comes equipped with an electronic "blackboard," through which images drawn on the screen with a light pen can be sent to a recipient's screen. It can also capture and store permanent records of visual images on a 3½-inch floppy disk at the touch of a button.

The phone transmits only the part of the picture that moves. Back-

93

ground images remain static and software irons out any jerkiness. A typical video picture contains 100 million bits of information, but only 15,000 bits of information can be transmitted at a time through an ordinary telephone line. The Communicator compresses the first 30,000 bits per second, and then records only the information in a picture frame that changes, such as hand or head movements. Background objects become painted onto the screen, leaving the telephone lines open for motion only.

"We are convinced," states John Looney, president of U.V.C. Corporation, "that in time, every home and office that currently uses a telephone will one day use the video phone."

He does not boast in vain. Since the video phone can be linked to ordinary phone lines via the common jack found in every home or office, the product has virtually unlimited potential for consumers and industries alike. Looney foresees the Communicator benefiting industries such as finance, real estate, and medicine. Boardrooms can reduce the time and expense of out-of-town meetings with face-to-face meetings over the phone, real-estate agents can show property to residential or commercial customers without unnecessary travel, and doctors, especially, can consult around the globe about patients, providing for life-saving decisions. Families across the country or even in different parts of the world can "welcome their first grandchild, be part of the reunion they couldn't work into their vacation, or watch the baby take her first steps," Looney explains.

HOLOGRAPH PHONE

Imagine looking into a 4-inch cube at a three-dimensional image of the person you are speaking to on the phone. Sounds like a peep show! But Professor Stephen Benton of M.I.T.'s famous Media Lab says this is not too far off.

• • • • •
ODDS: 5%
ETA: 1999
PRICE: $2,000
• • • • •

The phone Benton's talking about would use a holographic image, and he is renowned for having developed the best of these 3-D images. The phone would make use of a camera with two lenses installed in your home and would need to be hooked up by a fiber-optic line to a super-computer, presumably operated by the phone company. The super-computer would take the images of both camera lenses, analyze them, and transmit a fully holographic image to the person on the other end of your line. The problem with the technology is that the phone needs a "dedicated" fiber optic, meaning it would have to use every last hair's width of the line, not allowing for any other use. It is expected that every home in the future will have a fiber-optic line, but the 3-D phone would require households to have two lines if they wanted any service other than this one.

Benton, who teaches physics as well as computer science and electrical engineering, says that holography seems to be on a commercial back burner at present. "The scientific and technical applications are driving this now, not use by consumers, so it's not getting a whole lot of attention."

When asked about holographic TV, Benton reports it would take several fiber-optic channels to get into your home and could be twenty years away. So for now, Benton is thinking only about the 3-D phone when he says, "I hope it happens!"

95

• • • • •

SELECTION TELEPHONE

For those who desperately "vant to be alone," Sanyo's Incoming Calls Selection Telephone is just the ticket . . . and much less expensive than a private secretary for screening calls.

• • • • •
ODDS: 50%
ETA: 1995
PRICE: $208
• • • • •

When a caller dials your number, they will hear three rings (though you won't hear a thing) after which a prerecorded voice will come on the wire and ask for a four-digit, predetermined secret code that you have assigned. If these numbers have been registered with your machine beforehand, the call will be accepted and the numbers will be displayed so you can tell who is calling.

If callers don't have a code, they can forget it. As long as you have your selection phone on, they won't be able to get through. Their call will automatically be disconnected unless an acceptable code is offered within fifteen seconds of the third ring.

The device, invented by Sanyo's Japanese Research and Development Center, comes equipped with an on/off function so you don't have to use it all the time. Unlike an answering machine, it will not take messages—and will not lose them either. It will simply disconnect any call that doesn't respond with the proper code, and leave you uninterrupted.

The Selection Phone stores up to thirty codes. It is equipped with an automatic dial that stores up to ten outgoing numbers, and onhook dialing. It even has line-hold Muzak-like versions of "Hey Jude" and "Yesterday."

Unfortunately, the device has been available only in Japan, since its premiere in 1987. Currently it sells for 28,000 yen—about $208. A Sanyo spokesperson claims the company has no plans yet to expand into other markets, but it does seem inevitable that like so many other Japanese innovations, the Selection Telephone will be here in the not-too-distant future.

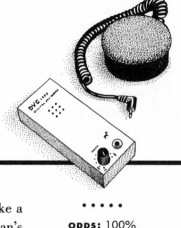

TELEPHONE VOICE CHANGER

The digital voice changer can make a
man's voice sound like a woman's
voice, a woman's voice sound like a man's
voice, or any voice sound like another
voice.

ODDS: 100%

ETA: 1990

PRICE: $995

Now, the big question is, why would
anyone want to do any of the above? Well, if you're a spy, a private
detective, or a cheating husband or wife, one can imagine scenarios
where a change of voice might come in handy. Also, if you're elderly
and/or female and getting harassing telephone calls, a deeper, more
threatening voice wouldn't hurt. To help things along, the digital voice
changer also comes with background noises, such as a barking dog
(to discourage would-be harassers) or construction site sounds (to give
the illusion you're someplace you're not).

If all this sounds a bit James Bondish, well, it is. The voice changer
is made by CCS Communications Control, a Portchester, New York,
company that makes a whole line of security devices. Called the DVC-
1000, it comes in two compact pieces. There's a hand-held mike and
master control with a dial to adjust your voice from very low to very
high, and another dial for background sounds. Attached by cord is
a cup-like device that fits over the mouthpiece of your telephone.

The DVC-1000 is for sale through CCS distributors in a few cities.
In 1990 it should be available wherever this kind of stuff is sold.

97

MESSAGE STOPPER

Message Stopper is a little gadget that won't change the world, but for people who live and die by their answering machines, it will be worth $15 in annoyance relief.

ODDS: 100%
ETA: 1990
PRICE: $15

If you forget to turn off your machine or if you are simply screening calls, you won't have to shout over your recorded message should you decide to pick up the phone. Message Stopper stops the message and allows you to talk. It also automatically resets the machine so it's ready to go again when you hang up. Message Stopper works by assigning priorities. When you pick up the receiver, it gives you priority over the recording on your answering machine.

Message Stopper is available from DesignTech International, Inc., 941-B 25th St. NW, Washington, DC 20037. By 1990, it should be widely available.

SOUND WEDGE

Getting rid of one more of life's little annoyances is the *raison d'être* for the Sound Wedge. What it does is automatically turn off your stereo when the phone rings. No more sprinting across the room to lower the volume or trying to hear over U2.

ODDS: 100%
ETA: 1990
PRICE: $30

The wedge is a small box that interfaces between your stereo amplifier and your phone. At the first ring, the speaker volume is cut off.

The sound wedge is available now in a few specialty catalogues.

TWO-RECEIVER PHONE

H ello, hello! Here's something for the teenagers. NTT, the Japanese equivalent of old Ma Bell, may she rest in peace, will be pumping up the rumor mill with this product launch. It's a telephone built for two—or four, if you will. Two fully equipped receivers on each phone allow you and your best friend to giggle and gossip with two other friends on the wire. The four-way conversations don't guarantee any better communication, but they do guarantee more of it.

· · · · ·
ODDS: 50%
ETA: 1995
PRICE: $95
· · · · ·

Plus One, as it's called, takes its cue from the successful Duet public phone that was set up in 450 Japanese teenage haunts to further the use of the native tongue. The Duet, with its slightly enlarged phone booth, has Japanese teenagers setting records for cramming people into phone booths. One American company sold several thousand Plus One home units in the United States, although they stopped when they ran out. Some other company may soon offer Plus One if they see a market for it. What do you say, parents?

"No, no."

99

· · · · ·

MOVABLE PHONE JACK

Have you ever wished you could just plug in your telephone anywhere you wanted? Well, soon you'll have that wish, providing you have a phone, phone service—and electricity! All you'll need is a two-part unit called a Phonex adapter.

ODDS: 90%
ETA: 1990
PRICE: $125

The basic part of the unit connects your phone line to your electrical wiring. The other part is an extension unit that can be directly inserted into any electrical socket in the house in order to receive your phone at that location. All of your electrical outlets become potential phone jacks once the base unit is in place. You can move your phone to wherever you need it.

Furthermore, the base unit serves as its own phone jack, so you can leave your primary phone right where it is. And though the extension unit is easily movable, if you would rather leave it in a particular place, additional extensions are available for $65.

Says Ron Spence, sales vice president for Phonex, "We feel confident that most everyone will have an adapter in the future, as will many small businesses." Rod Mansfield, chairman of Phonex and the product's inventor, first displayed the prototype at a recent National Consumer Electronics Show in Chicago. "Since then," he says, "our telephones have not stopped ringing with inquiries."

This convenience will initially be available from retail, drug, and phone outlets in most sections of the United States. Phonex will also be made available via direct sales such as mail-order, TV, and door-to-door. "That's because," says Spence, "if the product were just sitting on a retail shelf, a potential customer might not recognize its purpose."

8

for those who have everything

SELF-IMPROVEMENT CHAMBER

Wouldn't it be wonderful if you could merely step into a phone booth and be converted from a nervous, insecure Clark Kent to a calm, self-assured Superman? Frank Italiane thinks so. That is why his company, Environ Corporation, has designed a computer-controlled chamber that offers its occupants a stress-free environment in which to modify behavior.

- - - - -
ODDS: 99%
ETA: 1999
PRICE: $30,000
- - - - -

101

The Environ chamber is designed to help manage pain, stress, and various behavioral problems through the use of sensory stimulation. Filtered, ionized air gives you a feeling of invigoration; mood-changing aromas waft in; multidimensional audio surrounds you, and the lighting continually changes colors, patterns, and intensity. Once you have achieved a relaxed state, says Italiane, "information is delivered to the multiple levels of a person's consciousness" using learning behavioral techniques for stress management, personal motivation, career development, weight reduction, or other topics. With your senses stimulated, the information you hear will be better acquired and retained.

The design of Environ incorporates NASA anthropometric technology. Anthropometry is the study of the size, shape, and motion characteristics of the human body and is fundamental to the design of clothing, equipment, and workplaces in NASA's flight vehicles. Environ also employs a NASA-designed pulse-monitoring electrode.

The chamber—which is 7½ feet tall, 6 feet long, and 4 feet wide—is currently being tested at Century City Hospital in Los Angeles and at the Headache and Pain Center in Beverly Hills. The first generation of Environ will be sold to hospitals, corporations, and other medical concerns, but less expensive models will be designed for home use by the year 2000.

MINI ROVER

Want to feel like an English country gentleman and tour your estate? Well, first you might want to have an estate to tour—or secure rights to trespass on someone else's—but if all that is in order, just hop on board the Mini Rover and inspect the fences in the far fields.

ODDS: 100%

ETA: 1991

PRICE: $8,900

Developed by the British and picked up by Hammacher Schlemmer, the Mini Rover travels at 5 miles per hour maximum speed (but only 2 mph in reverse). It's about half as wide as a golf cart and seats only one person. It's a little shorter, too. Actually, with the hood up, it looks like a high-tech baby pram with lights.

Good for "plein air" cruising, it has an open front end, but comes with a clear plastic hood for rainy afternoons. The hood can also be left half open. Rechargeable batteries, similar to ones used on boats, are stored neatly underneath. The tires are thick and puncture-resistant, with each back wheel independently motorized to ensure better traction in mud, snow, and gravel.

Start the engine and steer with the throttle. When you twist it, you're going to travel. When you let go, you'll stop. Tired of the back fields? Take yourself into town, but you better know the back roads or the uncrowded sidewalks. The Mini Rover is not street legal.

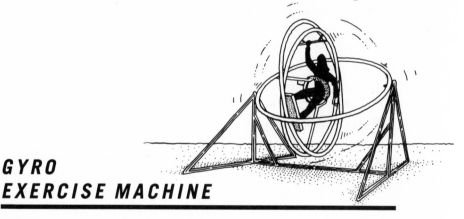

GYRO EXERCISE MACHINE

Picture three giant concentric hula hoops standing on end. Now imagine yourself strapped into the innermost hoop. Move a muscle and the three connected rings start to sway. Strain a little harder and you begin to spin. Nod your head and you somersault right over.

• • • • •
ODDS: 100%
ETA: 1990
PRICE: $4,000
• • • • •

103

This is an exercise machine for people bored by exercise machines. The design is based on the gyroscope, a compass device that's been around since the 1850s.

Gyro stands 9 feet high and wide. The three rings—one green, one red, one yellow—are made of tubular steel and rotate around one another, each on its own axis. The rider is fastened into the innermost ring with a foot-binding system and a padded waist device that allows for minimal movement. There are handle bars overhead for easy access and control that also help stretch and support the body.

Once you are in place, the slightest body movement will get the whole system turning. Through subtle shifts in weight and isometric muscle contracting, the rider can create and control the action, speed, and duration of the exercise. The rings move in every direction, the outer ones keeping the whole apparatus in balance. It's possible to do forward dives, back flips, lateral rotations, cartwheels, and more, all with the weightlessness of an astronaut in space.

"It's an exciting and exhilarating workout," says Julie Larsen, the public-relations director for Gyro North America. "Everybody who gets on this machine grins from ear to ear. They really enjoy every movement." It's also safe, she reports. And no one gets sick. You can slow it down or stop it and return to an upright position simply by bending your knees, which lowers your center of gravity. However, Larsen does suggest that a monitor be nearby for beginners.

The benefits? Stress on the joints is minimal. The three-ring ride is great for toning the body and provides a whopping aerobic workout, or a moderate one, as preferred. It's even beautiful to look at.

104

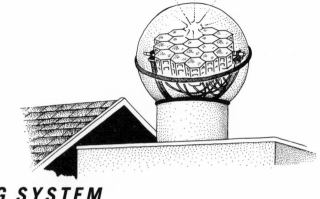

SOLAR LIGHTING SYSTEM

Imagine growing flowers and vegetables in a room with no windows but with plenty of real sunlight. This seemingly impossible scenario is already a reality in Japan, where Dr. Kei Mori, chairman of La Foret Engineering & Information Service Co., Ltd., has invented the Himawari (Japanese for sunflower) solar lighting system.

ODDS: 100%
ETA: 1992
PRICE: $7,700

The main feature is a clear acrylic bubble, installed on the roof. It's a 6½-foot-wide solar collector that weighs 1,320 pounds and contains nineteen hexagonal lenses. These lenses follow the path of the sun, much the way a sunflower does. A solar cell communicates the sun's position to a microcomputer, which controls motors that point the collector in the right direction. When the sun is obscured by clouds, the computer signals a timer to reposition the collector when the sun reappears. At the end of the day, the computer turns the collector east for the next morning's sunrise.

Below each lens in the collector is a cable of tiny optical fibers, which deliver the concentrated sunlight to the rooms below. Light collected by one lens and sent through 130 feet of cable is equal to that of a 100-watt quartz-halogen bulb.

An important feature of the system is that the acrylic bubble filters out most of the sun's harmful rays. Indeed, Dr. Mori claims that not only will the filtered sunlight grow plants, but it promotes the healing of various human ailments.

105

Though expensive to install—a home-size system sells for about $7,700 and a full-size commercial system for $200,000—it is inexpensive to operate.

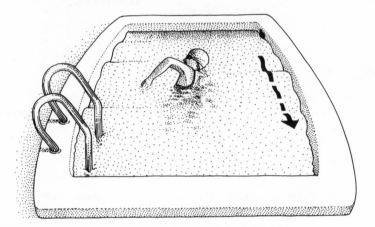

AQUATIC EXERCISE MACHINE

SwimEx Systems Inc. of Warren, Rhode Island, has created a swim-in-place mini-pool that will do for swimmers what the treadmill does for runners—and with less possibility of injury, because of the low-impact nature of exercising in water.

• • • • •

ODDS: 100%

ETA: 1990

PRICE: $19,950, WITHOUT INSTALLATION

• • • • •

A broad, even, adjustable current of water flows toward the swimmer, so that no matter how hard one swims, one goes nowhere.

The aquatic exercise machine is 17.6 feet long, 7.8 feet wide and 5 feet deep. The rear section of the machine has a paddlewheel—separated from the swimming area by a heavy grate—that propels water forward in a channel under the bottom of the swim area. The constant current of water then resurfaces when it enters the front of the swim area and flows back against the swimmer. The current can be adjusted to twenty-five different speed settings to meet the individual requirements of any swimmer.

In its first year, the company sold fewer than one hundred machines. But SwimEx executive director Alain Chardon is convinced that with the right marketing, SwimEx will soon be found in thousands of households and commercial institutions.

HOME BODY-CONDITIONING SPA

And now, for the man or woman who has everything, there's the Vibrosaun Body Conditioner, a space-age contraption that lets you shake, sweat, and sing along with Springsteen all at the same time.

ODDS: 100%

ETA: 1991

PRICE: $5,495

Invented in Australia, the Vibrosaun—a sauna/vibrator/sound system—can relax even the hardcore stressaholic. The user lies on a comfortable vinyl bed. An overhead fiberglass casing, hinged to the main fiberglass body at the toe end, comes down to cover the user, who's left with just neck and head sticking out. The user is now embraced in a vibrating, dry-heat sauna that can be jacked up to 175 degrees Fahrenheit.

A variable-speed fan cools the face, while the vinyl headrest emits ionized air to produce an exhilarating feeling. "It's the purest of air, like when you walk into a rain forest," says Ray Lang, from research and development at Vibrosaun International, the Thief River Falls, Minnesota, firm that manufactures and markets the product. "You feel completely rejuvenated."

The Vibrosaun Body Conditioner is 8 feet long by 3 feet wide and weighs 240 pounds. All of the features—the heat, music, vibration, and fan—can be operated from inside the sauna. Available in four colors, the unit sells for $5,495. Thus far, units are being used by chiropractic clinics, tanning/beauty salons, and the like. But Vibrosaun International is looking into distribution channels to make the product "a household name," says Lang. He adds that the price should

107

go down as "our volume increases and we become more efficient in the engineering and design of the machine."

SOLAR-POWERED BRIEFCASE

The briefcase of the future will not be carrying pens, pencils, books, and file folders. Rather, it will hold a wide variety of business tools, all powered by solar energy. A solar panel on the side of the briefcase produces electricity, which

• • • • •

ODDS: 100%

ETA: 1991

PRICE: $300–$8,000

• • • • •

charges a battery pack that will run the portable equipment within. Samsonite Corporation is already making the cases "on special order." But in the future, solar briefcases should be available to every business person.

You'll be able to buy the equipment separately or purchase a custom-designed briefcase complete with equipment for your special needs. A possible package might include a lap-top computer, a cellular phone, and a fax machine. A field engineer's case might include a Geiger counter, while a doctor who makes house calls could take along specialized medical equipment.

The price depends on the size and number of tools the briefcase can accommodate and how much equipment is included. Right now prices are high, according to Peter G. Dulka, a sales manager at Samsonite, because cases are specially ordered; but prices should drop dramatically when solar-powered briefcases are mass-produced.

• • • • •

SUPERCART

The supercart is a flatbed-style, electrically operated pushcart designed for handymen, gardeners, and serious putter-around-the-housers.

ODDS: 90%

ETA: 1991

PRICE: $1,000

It's quiet, small (36 inches high, 28 inches wide, 35 inches long), and light (100 pounds), yet it can handle loads of 400 pounds. It has a handle like a lawn mower, sphere-like pneumatic tires in the rear, and pivoting casters in the front. Supercart moves at a walking speed and maneuvers easily over carpet, tile, gravel, dirt, and concrete.

Although you can't really use it inside your home, it's great for bricks, garbage, heavy tools, small trees, or anything else that outdoor do-it-yourselfers need to move.

The Supercart should be available in stores like Sears by 1991, according to Donavan Harpool, vice president of marketing for Watkins Inc., the Wichita, Kansas, company that's marketing Supercart.

ROTATING HOME OBSERVATORY

Galileo and his friends would have had a field day with the Sirius Observatory, an outdoor observation dome from which you and three friends can enjoy maximum views of the stars.

· · · · ·
ODDS: 100%
ETA: 1990
PRICE: $5,900
· · · · ·

A standard-size telescope, which you provide, can be permanently installed and polar-aligned in the dome. Nylon rollers enable the observatory to rotate 360 degrees, for continuous tracking of the constellations. The unique construction of the dome keeps it from buffeting in the wind, and its interior absorbs light so that heavenly images aren't distorted. Made of white, weatherproof fiberglass, the observatory requires no maintenance and protects your telescope from condensation buildup.

If you're wondering how you're going to fit something like this in your backyard, never fear. The structure is only 8 feet, 8 inches in height and 4 feet, 8 inches in diameter, and can be attached to a concrete patio or deck. Assembly time is about one hour.

The Sirius Observatory, manufactured by Sabre Fibreglass, a division of Sabre Yachts of Australia, is available only at Hammacher Schlemmer in New York, Chicago, and Beverly Hills, or through the company's mail-order department, 1-800-543-3366. Wall lockers and shelves for books or extra equipment are optional.

110

· · · · ·

AUTOMATIC POOL COVER

This device will let you get the most out of your indoor-pool room. When the family is not frolicking in the water, you can lower the "ceiling"/floor and change the pool room into a recreation room with the covered pool serving as the floor.

ODDS: 100%

ETA: 1990

PRICE: $30,000

A wall-mounted control panel, which requires a key to operate, switches on the power. A warning buzzer sounds to alert people, and the floor/ceiling is raised or lowered in about two minutes. Custom-made to the dimensions of the room, the plywood floor can support 50 pounds per square foot. The 7-inch-thick covering is carpeted on the "top," while the "bottom" is a moisture-proof, heavy vinyl in pool blue. A ratchet safety catch secures the lift mechanism (hidden in the ceiling), preventing any sudden drop of the floor.

It is touted as a safety feature, since a covered pool is just plain less dangerous. Another advantage is that it results in less maintenance. "There is 40 percent less chemical treatment needed than for a pool without a cover," according to a spokesman for the manufacturer.

It's available from Auto Pool Floor, Inc., Hancock, Minnesota.

111

ROBOT DOG

I t's not very cuddly, it's bizarre-looking, and it may never be your best friend, but if you're allergic to animals or hate hair on the carpet, a robot dog may be the ideal pet.

ODDS: 50%

ETA: 1991

PRICE: $1,350

This "pet" can obey fifteen commands, turn in different directions, pick up objects, and detect a human presence. And it has an infrared sensing system so that it doesn't bump into furniture or walls. The dog doesn't bark, but can speak. It will issue a warning message to intruders, and its synthetic speaking voice also enables it to ask and answer questions.

William Holden, an Australian, came up with the idea at a robot show in the United States. "I tried to combine the idea of technology with the concept of a pet," he says. Once back in Australia, he watched how the koala bears moved around at the zoo. The Robot Dog was developed with those observations in mind.

Robot Dog has three 1.5-watt DC motors and is powered by six AA rechargeable batteries. A recharging unit plugs into household outlets.

Robot Dog does not have to be taken for walks, nor will it leave little batteries on your carpet.

9

at the supermarket

THE ELECTRONIC SUPERMARKET

S upermarkets are about to change radically, and for the better. Coming soon is a system of electronic price tagging that's going to make your store more efficient, at the same time as it makes you a smarter shopper.

• • • • •
ODDS: 100%
ETA: 1991
PRICE: N/A
• • • • •

When you pull your cart up to the tuna fish, instead of paper tags showing the shelf prices, you'll find an easy-to-read LCD screen displaying not only the price per can but the unit price, so that you can compare product value ounce for ounce.

The LCD display is a great little communicator. Along with price information, it can print messages such as ON SALE, BEST VALUE, LOW CALORIE, or DOUBLE COUPONS. Every one of the store's mini-screens is connected to the manager's main computer via low-power radio

113

signals. Prices can be changed on one product or on all products just by keying in some numbers. And the new prices are instantly transmitted to the cashier's checkout scanner. So the price you see in the aisle is the one you'll pay at the register.

The company at the forefront of this technology is Telepanel Inc. of Markham, Ontario, Canada. It has already installed the system in several test supermarkets. "Consumer response has been very, very positive," says Garth Aasen, the company's sales manager. "People like the large display, the easy comparison shopping, and the consistency."

Store owners love it, too. It reduces the workload and offers tremendous competitive flexibility. If, for example, it's discovered that prices in the drugstore section are being beaten because there's a sale down the street, the manager can instantly reduce the prices on all his drugstore stock. Managers will also be able to affect customer flow in their stores. If Saturdays are busiest, a big sale on Tuesday would probably attract some of those weekend shoppers.

SUPERMARKET SELF-CHECKOUT

What automatic teller machines did for banks, self-checkout machines will do for supermarkets.

• • • • •
ODDS: 100%
ETA: 1995
PRICE: N/A
• • • • •

The idea was developed by one David R. Humble while waiting in a supermarket checkout line. The person in front of him took the liberty of scanning a purchase by himself when the checkout person was distracted. The customer apparently was thrilled to run the bar codes over the scanning device and hence was born the idea—in Humble's mind—that shoppers might like to check out their own groceries.

Humble, who invented security tags for garments in clothing stores, has developed the first system for self-checkout in supermarkets, and founded a company, CheckRobot Inc. The system is now being used in four stores, and more will soon follow.

The Automated Checkout Machine (ACM) lets shoppers scan their own groceries, just as the checkout person does now. Once each purchase is scanned, the item goes down a conveyer belt with built-in security—lest a product sneak by unnoticed. At the same time, the price and description of each item is displayed on a touch-sensitive screen. The screen has a TOUCH button for a running total of purchases—a welcome addition to grocery shopping—as well as one for the final total. A human still bags the groceries and puts them in a cart. And if the shopper feels confused at any point, a HELP button on the screen will summon a store employee.

After all the purchases have been scanned, the shopper touches TOTAL on the screen to see what is owed and gets a printed receipt. The shopper then proceeds with the bagged groceries in a cart to a payment station manned by an employee. If all goes well, shoppers could be spending a lot less time waiting in checkout lines.

ELECTRONIC PROMOTIONS

Some people have systems for filing coupons; others don't. Some people can find the coupon they need when they want it; others can't. Some people cut coupons out of the paper; others won't. Soon, "To clip or not to clip" will no longer be a question. Just go shop!

• • • • •

ODDS: 100%

ETA: 1995

PRICE: N/A

• • • • •

A joint venture between CheckRobot, the company that is bringing self-checkout to the grocery store (see page 114), Procter & Gamble and Donnelley Marketing (a Dun & Bradstreet Company) is about to bring us electronic promotions at the checkout. The electronic system, called Vision 1000—and sure to be commonplace by the year 2000—can deliver instant refunds, generate coupons on other promotional

115

material, and administer frequent shopper programs (see Grocery Smart Card, below). The Vision System will work at conventional checkout counters or with CheckRobot's Automated Checkout Machine (ACM).

If your store has this system, the 20-cent refund you saw posted in the aisle for the purchase of two packages of cheese will be automatically credited to your bill when you buy two packages. The system will know electronically that you bought the two packages because the cashier scanned them both past the system's discerning eye.

There's more. If your grocery order contains baking items such as flour and sugar, the Vision 1000 system will print out a recipe for oatmeal raisin cookies, along with a coupon for a particular brand of raisins.

And more! "One type of promotion we offer is what we call a mystery product," says Kathy Robinson, a marketing and communications coordinator for Advanced Promotion Technologies, the company promoting Vision 1000. Consumers buying one of the "mystery" products chosen for that day could win a bottle of store-brand soda or some other item. "It makes grocery shopping fun," says Robinson.

GROCERY SMART CARD

Smart cards for the grocery store might be as popular in the future as automatic teller machines. They will debit and credit your account (see Smart Cards, page 201) and will be able to verify checks, if you want.

ODDS: 90%

ETA: 1994

PRICE: N/A

116

But most importantly, with a "frequent shopper" program—much like the frequent flyer one—customers will accumulate points for coming back to the same supermarket chain, just like they do when they fly often with a particular airline. Once a Smart Card shows a certain number of points, its owner will be entitled to a bonus, maybe some free items in the store, some money off on their purchases, or who knows? Would a trip to Disneyland be out of the question?

Store owners and manufacturers can automatically gear promotions to customers who are most likely to take advantage of them. A card inserted into the screen at the checkout line may reveal a long list of past baby-item purchases. The system might be programmed to respond with an automatic coupon for a new flavor of baby food, or money off on the shopper's next purchase of a favorite brand of diapers.

All information will be stored on the card as if it were a disk for a computer. No more need to store all those niggly coupons in your wallet. The system will know what promotions are being offered and will alert you to them on the screen.

The cards are being tested for customer satisfaction in a few stores around the country. The intention of Advanced Promotion Technologies, the company behind this concept, is to make grocery shopping easier for the customer. Time will tell.

SAFER TAMPER-PROOF PACKAGING

A safer, surer method of ensuring that a product has not been opened prior to its sale has been developed by a research scientist at Frito-Lay, Inc. It could give the term "tamper resistant" a whole new meaning and do away with safety overwraps and protective tabs.

• • • • •
ODDS: 50%
ETA: 1999
PRICE: N/A
• • • • •

117

Dr. Kim Krumhar came up with the idea while working as a post-doctoral fellow in the Massachusetts Institute of Technology's now-defunct Applied Biological Sciences Department. It was an off-the-wall idea, he recalls. The object was to find a common, non-toxic substance for food and drug use that would cause a seal to change color permanently when exposed to air, thereby indicating that someone had tampered with the product. Three years later, Dr. Krumhar, now with Frito-Lay, is perfecting his design. The sensor, at present, changes from blue to pumpkin orange when exposed to air. What he wants is a more dramatic and meaningful color change—such as from green to bright red.

He envisions his inventions being used on over-the-counter drugs, cosmetics, and some foods.

Dr. Krumhar's prediction that his invention has only a 50 percent chance of success by the turn of the century may be very conservative; it could be here a lot sooner.

THE SELF-COOLING CAN

For an extra dime, picnic lovers, warm-soda haters, and people with packed refrigerators will be able to buy drinks in self-cooling cans.

• • • • •
ODDS: 95%
ETA: 1991
PRICE: 10¢
• • • •

Dr. Israel Siegel, a biologist from Miami, Florida, has invented a container that works on the same principle as refrigerators and air conditioners. The difference is that those appliances use a chemical coolant called Freon, which is toxic and expensive. Dr. Siegel uses a coolant that is non-toxic and cheap: ordinary H_2O. When water is placed in a vacuum, it has the same cooling properties as Freon, and is ideal for use with ingestible products—in this case, soda. Dr. Siegel has simply surrounded a standard soda can with a vacuum chamber, filled the vacuum with water, and added a desiccant (a substance which absorbs water vapor from the vacuum chamber) on the outside. The cooling properties of the can last for as long as the container is unopened.

118

Self-cooling cans will be about 25 percent larger than regular cans and can be made from the same aluminum alloy.

Dr. Siegel has licensed his can to Zephyr, a Long Island, New York, manufacturer, which will make the containers and sell them to beverage companies.

RESEALABLE CAN

"It's back to the drawing board," says Lee Gunton, marketing director for Reynolds Can. Reynolds came up with a soda can that you can open and close again with a plastic plug over the top. But the soft-drink companies rejected it. They didn't like the fact that the cap became detached from the can.

ODDS: 50%

ETA: 1991

PRICE: N/A

No, it wasn't because it litters our national parks or our sidewalks. The reason given is that most soft-drink companies have been sued in cases where the caps on plastic bottles popped off like champagne corks. That happens only under extreme pressure or heat, but as it can hurt people, the soft-drink companies aren't taking any chances. So the Reynolds people are working on another version with a non-detachable cap. The soft-drink companies probably won't go head-to-head against plastic bottles with resealable cans. Instead, look for a specialized marketing, such as larger cans that fit into picnic coolers.

119

FRESH-FRUIT WRAP

I magine, non-bruised, firm, fresh apples, as well as other fruits and vegetables, available any time of year in any part of the world. That's the vision of food-science researchers at Cornell University.

· · · · ·
ODDS: 100%
ETA: 1991
PRICE: N/A
· · · · ·

The vision is well on its way to becoming reality. The researchers have developed a prototype of a retail-sized food package that extends the storage life of apples for more than six months. The package, made of a specially designed heavy-duty plastic tray, is wrapped and sealed with a plastic film which controls the amount of oxygen and carbon dioxide passed to and from the apples. Other plastic wraps totally seal the apples and don't allow any passage of the gases.

Currently, fruits like apples are stored in rooms with a mechanically controlled atmosphere. However, once these rooms are opened, the apples rapidly begin to lose their eating quality. And, as the saying goes, you can't mix apples and oranges in these rooms, as their storage requirements differ. With the new, high-tech packaging, different food products can be stored together because "each package simulates a miniature controlled atmosphere storage system all its own," says inventor Sayed S. H. Rizvi, an associate professor of food science at Cornell. The plastic tray allows for stacking without bruising.

The researchers estimate that buying a dozen apples in this new package will cost only slightly more than what twelve apples in a bag currently cost. And the benefits will reach far beyond the shelves of your corner grocery. NASA has expressed interest in the new packaging, as it would provide a way to serve astronauts fresh fruits and vegetables during space flights.

· · · · ·

COMPUTERIZED MEAL PLANNING

Traditionally, it's taken the average homemaker twenty minutes to make a shopping list for the week's groceries. Now it can take just two. A Kansas software company has created a meal-planning computer program that coughs up customized menus and accompanying shopping lists right at the supermarket.

• • • • •

ODDS: 100%

ETA: 1991

PRICE: FREE–$30 A YEAR FOR A FAMILY OF SIX

• • • • •

"This is a harried world we live in," says Roland Morreale, president of Computerized Meal Planning Systems, Inc. "People are dying for a service like this to eliminate the tedium of writing up shopping lists week after week."

Here's how the system works: The shopper inserts a personalized card, similar to automated bank teller cards, into a computer at a supermarket that has leased or purchased the system. In two minutes, the computer prints out a seven-day meal plan for the entire family. An accompanying shopping list details all the foods required for the week. The foods are categorized under "produce," "meat," etc., for headache-free shopping.

The kicker is that all the menus are designed for healthful living. Computer printouts detail individualized meal and nutritional data, as well as portion-control information, for every member of the family. The computer "knows" what each member needs because it has been fed information on age, sex, and activity level. According to Morreale, the nutritional standards are based on those established by the American Cancer Society, the American Heart Association, and other health-oriented organizations. The computer also goes by the height and weight limitation standards of Metropolitan Life Insurance.

The meals vary from week to week, and shoppers can delete from their program any foods they don't like. "Most people eliminate brussels sprouts right off the bat," says Morreale. Many high-sodium packaged foods are excluded, so if you're a TV-dinner freak, this

121

program may not be for you, he adds. "The shopper has to demonstrate a commitment to healthful living for this to work."

Computerized Meal Planning Systems hopes to have its meal-planning service available in a thousand supermarkets nationwide by the end of 1990. The cost to the consumer will vary at the discretion of the supermarkets, but will probably range from no charge to $20 a year for a family of two, $25 for a family of four, and $30 for a family of six.

10

potato ice cream & other nutritious treats

POTATO ICE CREAM

Al & Reed's Corporation is giving its frozen-dessert competitors a licking. Two years ago, the Idaho Falls company started making potato-based ice creams, fruit sorbets, and frozen yogurts. They've become a hit in the West and

ODDS: 100%

ETA: 1990

PRICE: $2.90 PER QUART

123

should reach the rest of the country in the early nineties.

Much of the milk solids are replaced with potato flakes that have gone through a special heating and cooling process that turns starch into fructose, nature's sweetener. The fructose is better for you than sugar, and the potato base slims the calories of Al & Reed's desserts by half.

According to Alan Reed, president of Reed's Dairy, he came up with the idea after his father, Leroy, made a tongue-in-cheek remark. He and his father, who was then president of the National Potato Board, were discussing the board's promotional budget. Alan commented that he wished the board would offer some funding to his then all-dairy ice cream business. His dad quipped that if his son put some potatoes in the ice cream, the board might consider it. Alan's no potato-head. He took his father's advice seriously and developed the Al & Reed's (a play on his name) line of frozen dairy products. He now distributes to over two hundred stores in the West, and is hoping to expand into the East soon.

The desserts, which have the taste and consistency of the more fattening goodies, come in traditional chocolate, vanilla, and strawberry, as well as raspberry and orange cream.

MAMEY

When Cubans cry for *mamey*, they want their fruit, not their mother. As one of the national passions of Cuba, mamey looks like a huge apricot, grows like an avocado, and tastes like, well, like mamey.

ODDS: 100%

ETA: 1991

PRICE: N/A

The tropical grenade-shaped fruit is a dull gray on the outside, with pinkish-orange flesh on the inside. Its flavor is sweet and nutty, and it has a texture similar to an avocado.

The Cubans are mad about the fruit, and judging from the acres of mamey trees that are starting to be cultivated in southern Florida, agriculturalists expect that Americans will love it, too. Meeting the anticipated demand may be difficult, particularly since the fruit grows slowly. "There's not enough tropical area in the United States to produce the amount the country will ultimately want," says Noel Vietmeyer, a specialist in exotic resources for the National Academy of Sciences in Washington, D.C. He predicts that the first mature fruit will be snapped up by Cubans living in southern Florida. He also thinks that, like the kiwi fruit, mamey will be introduced at a high price that will eventually come down. To capitalize on this anticipated hungry market, "farmers are planting trees in southern Florida as fast as they can," says Vietmeyer.

Again, like the kiwi, which was considered exotic for a time, mamey is almost certain to spark the interest of inventive gourmets. In restaurants and at dinner parties, mamey pies, tarts, and sorbets will almost certainly be the rage.

In the world of fruit, a star is about to be born.

ARRACACHA

I f you're planning to make a stew—say in 1993—you'll want to make sure you have plenty of meat, potatoes, onions, and arracacha to throw into the pot. Already a VIV (Very Important Vegetable) in South America, arracacha is expected to

• • • • •
ODDS: 75%
ETA: 1992
PRICE: N/A
• • • • •

catch the imagination of U.S. cooks looking for new flavors to add to old recipes.

A subtropical product of the Andes, arracacha tastes like a cross between a carrot and celery. The plant's edible portion is its turnip-like white root. And while it can't be eaten raw, arracacha has a very pleasant flavor when boiled.

Noel Vietmeyer, of the National Academy of Sciences, Washington,

125

D.C., predicts that arracacha will be grown in the United States soon, since shoppers are demanding a bigger selection and more unusual produce from their supermarkets. And considering that we rely on just twenty-two crops for much of our food—with more than 20,000 edible plants existing in the world—a little more variety might be good for us.

Although arracacha will never threaten the popularity of celery, the root will be found in a few years squeezed in alongside broccoli, which, incidentally, most Americans had never heard of before 1944 when the first commercial fields were planted.

OCA

O ca is one of a number of "new" vegetables that could become an American staple in years to come. It looks like a potato, only softer and thinner in shape. But the best thing about oca is the taste. It's like a baked spud with the sour cream already on it.

· · · · ·
ODDS: 75%
ETA: 1994
PRICE: N/A
· · · · ·

"Some are as sweet as candy or as sweet as the best sweet corn," says Noel Vietmeyer, of the National Academy of Sciences. "But it also has a sourish flavor that's not at all unpleasant."

An interesting phenomenon is spurring industry interest in unfamiliar fruits and vegetables. According to Vietmeyer, specialty produce is now a driving force in the supermarket business. (See Arracacha, page 125.) Surveys show that more and more customers shop where there is an interesting variety of produce, as opposed to the quality of the meat.

But there are problems to be solved before we become oca eaters. Grown primarily in South America, oca doesn't do well in America's long summer days. Northern California and Washington State seem like the best bets for oca growing, but the plant will need some treatment before it's transplanted here.

CARBONATED MILK

Anyone who's ever had an authentic New York egg cream is used to contemplating the profound mysteries of the drink. Like how come it's called an egg cream when there's no egg and no cream in it? And how can anything that tastes so wonderful and rich sound so awful and have such plain ingredients: milk, seltzer, and chocolate syrup?

ODDS: 90%

ETA: 1992

PRICE: $1.50

Even more baffling is why no company has ever bottled the stuff. Well, DRINC, the research arm of the United Dairy Industry Association, is now working to develop a broad-based consumer application for carbonated-milk drinks.

The reasons for their interest are actually sound. The UDIA represents dairy organizations who are understandably alarmed that milk consumption has gone down steadily in the past ten years, while soft-drink consumption has hit an all-time high every year.

The idea is to attract new, loyal milk drinkers by developing a milk-based soft drink, to be marketed not only in the dairy case but alongside nutritionally devoid Coke, Pepsi, and 7-Up. If it tastes good enough, they reason, no one need know that it's actually healthy for you.

DRINC's drink has a skim-milk base, to which fizz and flavor are added. Flavors under development include strawberry, peach, orange, banana, piña colada, chocolate, root beer, cola, and rum. Right now the experimental batches are packaged in 16-ounce bottles, like soda, and require refrigeration, although processing methods are being tested that either extend shelf life and/or make refrigeration unnecessary.

127

Food chemists insist that carbonated milk, strangely enough, doesn't taste anything like milk. If it's plain (unflavored), it tastes like seltzer; if it's fruit-flavored, it tastes like a fruit drink.

DRINC is hoping to sell their idea to the big soft-drink companies, who have the marketing and distribution clout to make a dent in the mega-billion-dollar beverage industry.

HIGH-FIBER CUPCAKES

Cupcake lovers are reading this and saying that cupcakes are perfect just the way they are. But we're telling you cupcakes will *stay* perfect *and* be good for you. Yes, your favorite high-calorie, low-nutrition hunk of heavenly junk will actually be just what the doctor ordered.

ODDS: 100%
ETA: 1992
PRICE: N/A

Years ago, we learned that certain forms of cancer may possibly be prevented with fiber. Americans averaged only 15 grams of fiber in their normal daily diet, while researchers told us we need 30. At about the time this research was reported in the press, Mike Gould and his team of USDA biochemists had come up with a way to soften the non-digestible (fiber) portion of cell walls in farm products. They were looking for something else, but as their mission was to find new uses for basic farm products such as oats, wheat, and corn, it occurred to them: "Hmmm. These grains also contain cellulose, and that's fiber!"

Indeed, it's 100 percent fiber. Experiments started immediately to replace some of the flour content in baked goods with their softened cellulose product. The researchers knew nobody was going to suddenly start eating twice the amount of fiber because it would prevent cancer. Most people eat what tastes good. So Gould *et al.* tried to put fiber in foods that people already liked. The trick was to do it undetected.

And success was theirs! The cellulose fiber can replace up to two-

128

thirds of the flour used in baked goods, depending on the product. "We made hundreds of cakes, brownies, doughnuts, pancakes, and breads," says Gould. A cake was developed that substituted cellulose for 40 percent of the flour normally used in the recipe. A professional taste panel couldn't differentiate the cake from another one made with the regular amount of flour. They compared taste, texture, mouth feel, and seven other criteria. "There was as much fiber in one slice of that cake as in a half a head of lettuce." That was 7½ grams, or one-fourth of the minimum amount suggested by the cancer researchers.

Cellulose fiber can go in gravy, sauces, ice cream, and any other products that require a bulking agent or a thickener, and it has no calories. Not one. It passes right through the body. Mind you, it has no nutritional value either. But if you like cupcakes, you won't care.

PICKLE QUICK

If you've ever tasted a pickle straight from the barrel, you've experienced a rare treat. That flavor comes from a mix of fermenting cultures used only on pickles made in barrels. Most bottled pickles sold in supermarkets are simply soaked in vinegar and some spices. Charlie Rosen is a man with at least ten careers behind him—one of them dealing with artificial intelligence. But Rosen is now having "fun with food," he says, marketing for home use a dry mixture of those special fermenting cultures used in those exotic ethnic pickles.

• • • • •
ODDS: 100%
ETA: 1993
PRICE: 90 CENTS PER PACKAGE. MAKES 1 QUART
• • • • •

The cultures are similar to the ones used in yogurt and sour cream. They are combined with a bit of sugar (to encourage the cultures to grow), some acids (to discourage any bacteria from growing), and spices to make up Pickle Quick dry mix. When it is added to water and a bunch of washed cucumbers, you will have half-sours within

129

three days; in ten days to two weeks you will have fully sour pickles. When the pickles are at the taste you desire, just put them in the refrigerator and they will stop fermenting.

A special blend (that includes caraway seeds) is also available for fermented sauerkraut. The sauerkraut version is called Crispy Kraut.

"The big thing we did is to eliminate the guesswork and make it very easy to make high-quality fermented pickles and sauerkraut," says Rosen. However, distribution has proved more difficult than making pickles. "It's quite difficult to penetrate these large food chains. And they represent 80 percent of the market." Still, Rosen and his colleagues at Cultured Foods Corporation, 973 Linda Vista, Mountain View, CA 94043, are determined to bite into the market. They have started with a little piece, mostly in California.

SUPER CARROTS

Put a super carrot next to an ordinary, run-of-the-mill, supermarket-variety carrot and you won't notice much difference. Only that the super carrot is a bit thinner and slightly darker in color. Still, it really is a super carrot. It contains twice as much all-important carotene, a rich source of vitamin A.

ODDS: 100%

ETA: 1990

PRICE: SAME AS REGULAR CARROTS

The official name of this special carrot is Beta III. The United States Department of Agriculture spent four years developing it for distribution to areas such as India and East Africa, where populations suffer from vitamin A deficiencies.

130

Beta III will not make an appearance at your fruit and vegetable stand for some time. However, it will be available to American carrot lovers by 1990 through seed catalogues. Beta III should appeal to the health-conscious. There is research indicating that the orange pigments can protect against various forms of cancer. Also, vitamin A tablet takers risk the problem of toxicity, a danger that does not arise if one consumes an excess of carrots.

SUPER SPUD

D r. Jesse Jaynes, a professor of bio-chemistry at Louisiana State Univer-sity, has spent four years working on the perfect potato. So far, he has developed a "nearly" perfect spud that contains a more complex protein than the ordinary variety.

ODDS: 90%

ETA: 1994

PRICE: COMPETITIVE

Dr. Jaynes, working with Dr. John Dodds of Peru's International Potato Center, is using recombinant DNA technology to beef up this important staple. Considering that in some Third World countries the potato may comprise 80 percent of the daily diet, a better spud could go a long way in the fight against malnutrition. And for vegetarians and health-conscious Americans who are cutting back on red meat, these high-protein potatoes will surely spark an interest.

Dr. Jaynes and Dr. Dodds have supplemented the proteins already present in potatoes with man-made ones that are higher in essential amino acids—the building blocks that make up protein. But they are continuing to work on developing even better protein genes in hopes of creating a truly perfect spud.

Taste and texture won't change. Nor will the price. Super spuds will just make people stronger.

131

BUFFALO MEAT

Ralph Lauren, look what you've done. Your nouveau prairie togs have turned us back to when buffalo roamed the range. Buffalo meat, higher in protein and fiber than beef and lower in cholesterol, has even less saturated fat than chicken. It's easier to eat than lobster and

· · · · ·

ODDS: 85%

ETA: 1997

PRICE: DOUBLE THE PRICE OF BEEF

· · · · ·

is supposed to taste great. But even with our current penchant for down-home American cuisine, the annual Fourth of July Buffalo Bar-B-Que is still in the distant future.

Americans are basically squeamish eaters, slow to take to new foods, which is good, for now, since there's not nearly enough buffalo to go around. "Only 80,000 head," says Paul Butler, manager of Livestock Research and Innovation, "or about enough to last the population of New York for two days." But hold on to your hat. Butler's organization of scientists and ranchers is convinced that in cholesterol-conscious America, the demand for buffalo will someday far outstrip the supply.

To prepare for that day, the Cheyenne, Wyoming, group is planning to breed the American bison, using cattle as surrogate mothers. Using cows, production could increase fivefold. The technique involves artificially inseminating the female buffalo and transferring the embryo to a cow. Cows have rejected the embryos so far, but scientists are not deterred.

Buffalo ranchers—and health-conscious eaters—are optimistic that if scientists can find a way to dramatically increase the number of animals, buffalo meat could be an American staple by the year 2000.

132

11

less is
better

NO-CALORIE SUGAR

This could be the breakthrough for which every chocoholic, desserta-holic, and junk-food junkie has been waiting—sugars with near-zero calories.

They exist all right, and always have. They're called left-handed sugars because they are the molecular mirror image of right-handed sugars, the ones we know and love. The two sugars are chemically identical, except that they face in opposite directions. Reportedly, their taste quality is the same. The key difference is that the body's digestive enzymes know how to break down only the right-handed kind. The lefties get passed through the digestive tract completely unnoticed.

Left-handed sugars are found in tiny quantities in mountain ash-

• • • • •

ODDS: 85%

ETA: 1995

PRICE: COMPETITIVE WITH OTHER NON–CALORIC SWEETENERS

• • • • •

133

berries, seaweed, flaxseed gum, red algae, and snails' eggs. Not the stuff we normally eat. And not in sufficient quantities to be farmed.

Which brings us to Dr. Gilbert Levin, the founder of Biospherics Inc. of Beltsville, Maryland. He and his company have managed to synthesize left-handed sugar, which he calls Lev-O-Cal. The name Dr. Levin coined has nothing to do with his own. *Lev* is a Greek word meaning to rotate to the left. The *O* stands for zero and *Cal* for calories.

Although Biospherics has managed to produce left-handed sugar, the process has been far too expensive to actually market Lev-O-Cal. From 1982 to 1987, Biospherics, a relatively small company, invested $700,000 to produce a few ounces of left-handed sugar. Big-time help was needed. That assistance has come in the form of two Italian companies—Montedison and Eridania; the latter is Europe's largest sugar company. FDA approval is expected sometime before 1995, providing that no negative side effects are discovered.

The price objective is to be competitive with other non-caloric sweeteners, according to a spokesman for Biospherics.

Besides the pure sugar taste, Lev-O-Cal has another advantage. It provides texture in baked goods. Other sweeteners need additives to serve as bulking agents.

Optimistically, Lev-O-Cal could be on supermarket shelves before 1995, good news for the average American, who consumes 130 pounds of sugar a year.

NON-FATTENING FAT

For the millions of health-conscious Americans who love to eat, the idea of non-fattening fat is almost too good to be true. But it is on the horizon.

ODDS: 70%

ETA: 1993

PRICE: N/A

Procter & Gamble has conducted over a hundred tests on a substance called oles-tra, which looks, tastes, and smells like real fat but contains only a small fraction of the calories and none of the risks to your heart. Ironically, olestra was discovered when Procter & Gamble researchers were looking for a way to improve the digestibility of fats and oils for people who need to gain weight. What they found was that olestra molecules are too large to be absorbed by the body and thus pass right through. In other words, you will be able to eat french fries, potato chips, and pie with lower fat content and reduce health risks and weight gain.

Procter & Gamble is presently awaiting FDA approval on olestra. The company hopes that it will be okayed for use as a replacement for 75 percent of the fat in commercial preparations of deep-frying oils and salted snacks and 35 percent of the fat in home-cooking shortenings and oils.

Industry observers say the chances are good that long before the turn of the century gastronomes will be able to take care of their hearts and waistlines with a lot less sacrifice.

135

CHOLESTEROL-REDUCING POWDER

"Ten years from now we'll have shakers on the table for salt and pepper—and one for the cholesterol slasher." So says researcher Donald Beitz, head of the Iowa State University team developing a way to remove cholesterol from animal products.

· · · · ·

ODDS: 80%

ETA: 1992

PRICE: SAME AS MEAT TENDERIZER

· · · · ·

They've already established that eubacteria, which is naturally found in the body, contains an enzyme that alters cholesterol so that it is absorbed poorly. Once the cholesterol is converted into the poorly absorbed state, it would pass right through the body without stopping at the hips for a few months. The enzyme could eliminate as much as 80 percent of the cholesterol we absorb from our foods.

The trick is to isolate the enzyme and reproduce it in quantity, probably through genetic engineering. Beitz says it may not require FDA approval, because the enzyme occurs naturally in the body. It could be sold as a nutritional condiment for use at your table, or it could be used in packaged foods, such as luncheon meats, that are available on supermarket shelves. Sausage and eggs, anyone?

· · · · ·

LOW-PROOF LIQUOR

A mericans just don't drink the way they used to. It's not that they don't imbibe at all, but for health reasons and concerns about weight and driving, many Americans opt for a light beer, a glass of wine, or even a glass of juice instead of hard liquor.

.....
ODDS: 90%
ETA: 1991
PRICE: N/A
.....

Which is fine if you're not heir to a distillery or you actually like the softer stuff. But what about those who, as concerned as the next person about health and safety, still prize the flavor of a fine single-malt Scotch? Don't you think there should be a product for them? A small company called Sepracor in Marlborough, Massachusetts, sure thinks so. They've developed a means of removing the alcohol—and nothing more—from spirits.

Alcohol can be removed from spirits by using extracting solvents that unfortunately mess up the flavor of the liquid. Sepracor, however, inserts a very thin polymer film (made from an organic substance) between the beverage and the extracting solvent. The solvent can still absorb the alcohol out of the liquor, but the liquor is not touched by the solvent. The system can actually drain away as much as 95 percent of the alcohol while "the flavor and aroma components are left behind," according to Steve Brandt, director of marketing for the company. Brandt, whose company plans to manufacture the equipment to make the membrane and license the technology to use it, already is working with a "major distiller." He says he does not expect the system to be used to produce alcohol-free drinks, but rather to produce flavor concentrates and reduced-alcohol spirits only.

And, it shouldn't surprise you, the less-potent versions will be less caloric than their unadulterated relatives.

137

.....

LOW-CALORIE BEEF

At last. It's once again possible to be a red-blooded American carnivore; a skinny, red-meat American feeding on low-calorie, low-guilt beef.

This answer to a twentieth-century prayer comes to us from the friendly (really) folks at Dakota Lean Meats, a South Dakota outfit with nine stockholders, most of them stockbreeders.

• • • • •
ODDS: 100%
ETA: 1990
PRICE: $39.75 FOR A PACKAGE OF 24 OUNCES OF STEAK AND 3 POUNDS OF GROUND BEEF
• • • • •

Plugged in the best-seller *The 8-Week Cholesterol Cure* by Robert E. Kowalski, this beef is a popular entree on the menus at the celebrated La Costa Resort Hotel & Spa. It comes in 3-ounce rib-eye steaks that contain only 1 percent more fat than a comparable fish fillet. In fact, the vital statistics on each steak are: 102 calories, 1.08 grams of fat, and about 30 milligrams of cholesterol. A regular 3-ounce steak has about 378 calories, 33 grams of fat, and 75 to 85 milligrams of cholesterol.

According to Sheryl Krog, Dakota Lean's general manager, part of the secret is early slaughtering. Mostly, however, the beef is the product of genetic selection which involved thirty years of cross-breeding three types of cattle. The cattle were raised without hormones or antibiotics, and a computer tracked their intake of mixed grains.

Dakota Lean plans to market the beef, which comes as ground meat as well as steak, to some restaurants, and to distribute it through specialty meat markets. "We find that the supermarkets are more interested in price than quality," Krog says. "We're more expensive than other beef, but we're not the same kind of beef either."

Right now, you can have low-cal beef delivered to your door by calling 1-800-727-5326.

138

• • • • •

CHOLESTEROL-FREE EGGS

Eggs that are 95 percent cholesterol-free could be on your supermarket shelf by late 1991 or early 1992, according to technologists at the Phasex Corporation of Massachusetts.

ODDS: 90%

ETA: 1992

PRICE: N/A

The key to this health breakthrough is an extraction process called supercritical fluid extraction. Basically, what scientists have found is that pure carbon dioxide dissolves cholesterol from eggs. Supercritical fluid extraction is already being used by a German company owned by General Foods to remove caffeine from coffee. According to Val Krukonis, a Phasex technologist, the coffee tastes excellent.

Cholesterol-free eggs may actually appear as an ingredient in breads and cakes as early as 1990. But the eggs, as a separate product in powder or liquid form, are still being tested to ensure that taste is retained, that they maintain their functionality, and that the product will be cost-effective. Cholesterol-free eggs should taste better than the artificial kind on the market now, which remove the yolks and add food coloring.

50% LEANER PORK

I f you're a meat lover who's cut back on chops and steaks because of the dietary dangers of fat, cholesterol, and calories, here's some good news. Terry Etherton, a professor of animal nutrition at Penn State University, has found a way to produce pork with only half the usual amount of fat.

ODDS: 100%

ETA: 1992

PRICE: N/A

Etherton injected pigs daily with a natural pig growth hormone that he produced in quantity with recombinant DNA techniques. After eleven weeks, he found that the pigs' body fat fell by as much as 80 percent, while muscle increased as much as 50 percent. Growth hormones are natural proteins that occur in the muscle tissue of all animals and are therefore harmless to ingest. Etherton says the hormone stimulates protein buildup in muscle tissue while it inhibits the synthesis of fat—although he's not certain exactly how it does this.

But the next step, he knows, is to find a more economical and commercially viable way to deliver the hormone to the animals. Several companies are already working on development of a slow-release, long-term delivery system, possibly putting the hormone inside tiny biodegradable beads that can release it slowly. Farmers would then need to inject the animals only two or three times in the sixty-day growth period, instead of every day.

Etherton guesses that this leaner meat will be available to consumers within a few years, depending on when the technology receives FDA approval. "We're not in this for the economic incentive to the producer," says Etherton, "but rather, to make a leaner product for the consumer and to help fight the battle against coronary heart disease and saturated fat."

for

parents

FEVER CHECK

· · · · ·

ODDS: 95%

ETA: 1992

PRICE: N/A

· · · · ·

Anyone who has ever pulled an all-night fever watch next to the bed of a sick child knows the fearful feelings caused by such a vigil.

Harry Bloch, the father of three children, experienced that fear on several occasions, the first time when he woke to find his daughter's temperature had spiked to a startling 105 degrees as she slept. "My wife and I were uncomfortable all night. We didn't want to have to keep waking her every hour to take her temperature, but we knew we had to track the situation. Later, we faced a similar dilemma with our son," said Bloch.

The solution for Bloch, a Pennsylvania mortgage banker, was to invent a temperature monitoring system that constantly tracks a fever by sewing temperature sensors inside the armpits of a garment top. The temperature can then be displayed in several ways. First, there's the illuminated display located on each sleeve of the garment—so that it's visible in the dark. Second, there's the wireless transmission—using the same principle as currently available with wireless intercoms—which sends a beep to a unit in the caretaker's bedroom or activates an alarm if the temperature rises above a preset degree.

Officially patented as the Infant Temperature Measuring Apparatus and Methods, Bloch feels the device has uses beyond childcare. He envisions people in need of constant monitoring—such as geriatric patients—also benefiting from his device, which is "more sanitary and less intrusive than an oral thermometer."

VELCRO CLOTH DIAPERS

Of the many decisions facing young parents, one of the most perplexing is the diaper dilemma: cloth or disposable? Cloth diapers are cheaper and pose no burden to the ecology, while pin-free disposables, besides being infinitely more convenient to use, fit better!

• • • • •
ODDS: 100%
ETA: 1991
PRICE: SAME AS REGULAR CLOTH DIAPERS
• • • • •

A product called Didee-Snugs may end the debate once and for all. They are the only form-fitting and reusable cloth diapers patented in the United States that are shaped like an hourglass with elastic around the legs. Didee-Snugs incorporate the pin-free convenience of disposable diapers with the durability and financial savings of cloth. Instead of pins or plastic tags, the diapers use Velcro closures. They are designed to last for years and are available in three sizes.

Culley Davis, the president and founder of Vencor International, notes that the diapers have widespread appeal. "Fathers who are afraid of pins like the Velcro, as do children in potty training who can

142

participate themselves in the transition out of diapers," he said.

Besides being an ecological improvement over disposables, Velcro cloth diapers don't take up as much shelf space, which should please the supermarkets. And with plastic diapers costing about $45 a month, consumers will be pleased to return to the old-fashioned price of cloth diapers—a mere $13 a month.

PREGAPHONE

The Pregaphone is one of those wonderful ideas that started out as a joke and turned into a business. The device— an oversized stethoscope in bright yellow with a mouthpiece at one end and a funnel at the other—is used to communicate with unborn children.

ODDS: 100%

ETA: 1990

PRICE: $14

Dawn Hodson, a California business consultant, gave it to a friend as a shower gift. She now runs Pregaphone Inc. "Research has shown that at six months children hear and learn in the womb," Ms. Hodson explained. And according to a study conducted by California prenatal specialist Dr. Rene Van De Carr, they not only hear, but children who were spoken to in the womb scored significantly higher than other children in tests dealing with early speech and use of compound words. "There is also evidence that the bonding between child and parent is stronger when there is prenatal communication," says Ms. Hodson.

The Pregaphone is available at a number of maternity shops or directly from Pregaphone, in Ventura, California.

143

KIDS' TV MONITOR

Platinium Communications Systems Inc., a Vancouver, Canada, company, is in the business of making monitors that watch your kids watch TV. They have one product, the Eye Guardian, on the market and two more on the way.

ODDS: 100%
ETA: 1990
PRICE: $70

The Eye Guardian is an electronic device that sits on top of your TV and, using a "presence detector," disrupts viewing when a child sits too close to the screen. "Too close," according to the American Optometric Association, is a "non-viewing zone" that can be measured by multiplying the width of your screen by five. So if you have a 15-inch screen, no one should be closer to the TV than 75 inches. A child sitting too close can develop eye strain and have problems focusing.

"Kids respect technology, and this effectively conditions them to sit back, away from the set without their parents having to nag constantly," says Mike Stevens, president of Platinium Communications Systems. If a child penetrates the zone, the Eye Guardian will interrupt the program and produce "snow" on the screen. When the child returns to a safe distance, the picture is restored.

The Eye Guardian is being sold now through the Hammacher Schlemmer catalogue. Soon a model that lets parents control the times their children are allowed to watch TV will be available. Also under development is a device which will give parents the ability to select which channels the kids watch.

So, no more tantrums and no more hazardous spinning of the dial.

144

INFANT SAFE SEAT

Anyone who has ever tried to restrain an antsy toddler while heeding nature's call or sought a safe, clean, and quiet spot in a public place to change a diaper will welcome The Sitter.

ODDS: 70%

ETA: 1991

PRICE: N/A

It was Jacqueline Siani, now three years old, who inspired her parents—Vincent and Marie—and her grandfather—Stephen Rinaldi—to invent this changing table/safety seat. "It came down to a matter of safety," said Mrs. Siani. "When we went somewhere and I had to use the bathroom, or even a dressing room, it was impossible to hold on to her and take care of my own needs. Likewise with finding a place to change her. I just got disgusted by the lack of facilities for children."

The solution was The Sitter. Bolted to a wall in restrooms or dressing-room stalls, the compact unit has safety doors that fold out to make a full-length changing table—complete with a safety strap for holding baby in place; or they can be pulled up and snapped into place to form a seat equipped with safety bars.

A prototype has been shown to people at a Health Department clinic in New York, an airport in Connecticut, and a famous hotel/casino in Atlantic City. Interest seems high and the Siani clan is optimistic. They will soon begin to manufacture their patented product and make it available around the world.

One question remains unanswered, however. For every Sitter sold for a public ladies' lounge, will the inventors be able to sell one for a men's room too?

145

MEALS FOR KIDS

Mary Anne Jackson came up with this idea while juggling motherhood with her career in the food business. As a manager in a major food corporation in Illinois, she devoted Sunday nights to preparing healthy meals that would be easy

ODDS: 100%

ETA: 1991

PRICE: UNDER $3

for a babysitter to serve to her infant. When Ms. Jackson lost her job, she turned her Sunday nights into a business.

My Own Meals is her trademark. These nutritious meals are the first to be packaged for mass-market distribution with the two- to eight-year-old in mind. The meals are made without artificial ingredients, MSG, or preservatives. The food is vacuum-sealed in a special air- and moisture-proof pouch and cooked under pressure. Sterilization is reached faster with the thin pouch than with jars or cans. Therefore, the process seals in more of the natural flavor, color, and nutritional value of the food, as well as a firmer texture. The "retort" packaging, as it is called, renders the product "shelf stable" for as long as a year. That means no refrigeration is necessary. They'll be displayed next to the dry pasta in your supermarket.

Ms. Jackson experimented with twenty-five different meals before she whittled her menu down to five. After much consultation with her prospective market—kids—the winners include My Favorite Pasta, My Meatballs & Shells, My Turkey Meatballs, My Kind of Chicken, and Chicken, Please.

The meals should take away some of the guilt from parents who don't have time to cook. "Because mothers have to remove the food from the pouch and arrange it and put it on a plate, they feel as if they are serving a meal," says Jackson.

BIODEGRADABLE DIAPERS

Roughly 26 billion disposable diapers a year are thrown away in this country. And it takes 200 to 400 years for those diapers to break down in landfills. That's a lot of diapers and a lot of years. But now a new biodegradable product is headed for the baby market that will take two to seven years to return to nature. The diapers are from Tendercare and will be marketed by the Rocky Mountain Medical Corporation in Montrose, Colorado.

• • • • •
ODDS: 100%
ETA: 1990
PRICE: $59 PER CASE
• • • • •

According to Suzanne Shelton-Foley of Rocky Mountain, the new diapers contain a recently developed FDA-approved plastic with a starch-based additive to speed enzyme and bacterial processes that disintegrate the diapers. "We are convinced," says Shelton-Foley, "that all plastic consumer products will eventually be biodegradable. They'll have to be."

A case of the diapers—264 for newborns, 192 medium, 132 large, and 112 in toddler size—will sell for $59.

HOME SHOPPING FOR KIDS

The trend has gone from Tupperware to sexy underwear and now to kids' clothing. What we're talking about here, of course, are those at-home shopping parties.

• • • • •
ODDS: 90%
ETA: 1991
PRICE: FREE SERVICE
• • • • •

Two New York working mothers figured it made good sense to extend the concept to children's apparel. Says Margot Ravon, one of the entrepreneurs, "I hated shopping with my

147

kids, particularly in small Manhattan boutiques, because it was a nightmare and the kids hated going." So Ravon and her partner, Cindy Brown, founded Clothes to Home. You invite a few friends over and buy your kids' stuff in the comfort of your own living room. A salesperson makes a short presentation and takes orders.

So far, so good, for Ravon and Brown. Other mothers apparently shared their unpleasant feelings about shopping with tots on the town. Business has expanded to the New York City suburbs, and Ravon and Brown are now talking to investors about rolling out to other parts of the country.

Clothes to Home's merchandise is supplied by a number of designers and is quite up-market. Prices are reasonable and wrong sizes can be returned. "Our clothes are very much what I would call hip adult wear shrunk down," says Ravon. Their idea seems pretty hip as well.

TODDLER HAIR-WASHING BOARD

Anyone who has ever tried to wash a toddler's hair in the bathroom sink knows that it's no easy task. How does someone with only two hands keep a struggling child from rolling off the counter, or banging his head on the sink, while getting the job done?

ODDS: 75%
ETA: 1991
PRICE: $15

Arlene Boyhan of Bridgeport, Connecticut, thinks she has the answer: a device that will safely keep a child still on a countertop, leaving the parent free to use both hands in the effort. It's a plastic surface with safety straps that hold the child in place, suction cups to secure the board to the countertop, and neck and headrests like those in a beauty parlor.

Boyhan's personal experience led her to believe there was a need for such a product. "I would lay my daughter out on the counter and fight to hold her still as I washed her hair with my free hand. She'd be crying and complaining, and I was wishing someone would invent something to make it easier." Well, Boyhan waited too long to make it easier for herself—her children are past the "head in the sink" stage—but other parents may soon be able to buy the Boyhan board. She estimates that the board would be useful in bathing children between two and five years old. For parents with squirming kids, the Boyhan device might be the most welcome addition to bathtime since the rubber ducky.

13

get
smart

CD ROM

R esearch can be a drag. You end up spending more time "locating" than actually "learning" anything. But if looking things up is a big part of your life, here's some happy news—CD ROM! It's a five-inch silvery circle that stands to revolutionize our libraries.

· · · · ·

ODDS: 100%

ETA: 1990

PRICE: $125–$1,000 PER DISC
$600–$800 FOR DRIVE UNIT

· · · · ·

CD ROM stands for Compact Disc Read-Only Memory. These discs are similar to those used by audio enthusiasts except that instead of music, they contain text and graphics just like in a book. If you like how

151

long the audio versions play, you might be impressed that one CD ROM holds as much information as 1,500 floppy disks now used in computers. You'll need a special CD drive unit that plugs into your current computer ($600–$800).

Some software companies have packed whole stacks of dictionary-size reference books onto one disc. Whole encyclopedias and the twelve-volume Oxford English Dictionary with 252,000 main entries are also available on CD ROM already. A few discs with combinations of various volumes could put a library at your fingertips. For computer pioneers who once dreamed of volumes of information pouring across small screens around the world, welcome to your dream.

ELECTRONIC BOOK

D o you love cozying up with a good book? Well, try cozying up with five hundred at a time!

This is the electronic book. The huge storage capacity is brought to you by CD ROM (see page 151), the floppy disk with room to spare. A specially designed small computer unit with a detachable display panel makes up the hardware. The software is just plastic, indestructible CDs, with a capacity for five hundred manuscripts on each one. The display panel weighs only 5 pounds, and is roughly the size of a legal notepad (7 inches by 14 inches by 2 inches). A 15-foot cord attaches it to the similarly small base unit, and a touch-sensitive screen makes it work. The viewing area is 10 by 6 inches.

There's no fussing with computer lingo, or even a keyboard. This perfect product for the literary computerphobe responds to your touch. When you want to turn the page, just touch the button displayed on the screen in the corner. Judy Bolger of the Massachusetts company marketing the first model, called DynaBook, confidently reports, "A

• • • • •
ODDS: 100%
ETA: 1991
PRICE: $12 FOR 500 TEXTS
$15,000 FOR VIEWER UNIT
• • • • •

152

six-year-old who knows how to read can use it without ever having used a computer before."

Now that you're convinced it could be comfortable, you're wondering who in the world wants to read from a computer screen? It's bad enough using computers in the office, but the added eyestrain of using one at home sounds ludicrous, right? Wrong! With a visual image identical to the high quality associated with the printed word, the electronic book doesn't cause eyestrain. Even the graphics don't look like computer graphics. Photographs look like real photographs. The technology is so refined that art books look great on DynaBook. Take an electronic tour of the Louvre. You won't be disappointed.

If you're thinking of putting your whole library onto disk and using the wall space for a Rembrandt, you're out of luck. The cost of making your own disk could be as much as $1,500 (but to produce a duplicate of it will run only $2.50). You also could have some problems with publishing rights. Think of this more in terms of buying records. They come permanently engraved, are non-erasable, and they'll probably have your favorite author's "greatest hits" by the time you're ready to buy the unit.

LARGE-CAPACITY SMART CARDS

Large-capacity Smart Cards are the real future in information storage.

They will eventually replace floppy disks, because they are two hundred times faster at retrieving information, yet small enough to fit into a wallet. They're more versatile than CD ROM (you'll remember ROM stands for Read Only Memory), be-

ODDS: 100%

ETA: 1993

PRICE: $300 FOR READER; $200 PER BLANK CARD

cause you can erase and input information. The only downside is the $200 for a blank card compared to a few bucks for a floppy disk. But, oh, the storage capacity. On a space the size of a MasterCard

153

you can store 4 million bytes (2,000 pages), as opposed to a mere
1¼ million, tops, on current floppy disks. And all this information
can be retrieved on a reader ($300) as fast as you can flip from ABC
to CBS on your TV.

Jerome Svigals, a thirty-year IBM veteran and author of the book
Smart Cards (see page 201), says the floppy disk will compete nobly
with large-capacity Smart Cards as engineers improve the disks' storage capacity. But you'll still need a personal computer at a cost of
several thousand dollars. Laser optical cards will also compete, but
they'll be used primarily in industry because of the high cost of their
readers. And again, CD ROM will be for reading only.

Smart Cards—small, fast, with high capacity and low-cost readers—could be the first choice of consumers in the nineties.

THE WRITE-TOP COMPUTER

I t looks like an Etch A Sketch and acts
like an Etch A Sketch, but kids beware. The Write Top's no toy.

ODDS: 100%

ETA: 1990

PRICE: $3,000

A portable PC, the Write Top actually
lets the user input just by writing. There
is no keyboard, though one can be con-
nected as an option. Instead, a unique clear-glass screen acts as an
electronic notepad: the writer "writes" with a stylus (a mechanical
pen) that produces "electronic ink."

"The great thing about the Write Top is that you don't have to know
how to use a PC. You only have to know how to write," says Brooks
Puckett, dealer manager at Linus Technologies, Inc., in Reston,
Virginia, which markets the product. The user makes notes, then

pushes a button to transform his handwriting into print. The user has a chance to edit for mistakes—the computer may have misread something—before saving it on disk. Mistakes are eliminated simply by writing over notes or by drawing a line through an entire sentence.

The Write Top saves the user the laborious step of inputting his notes into a computer. And it minimizes the chance for error. "The inputter may miskey," says Puckett. "Or, if you're using a secretary, *they* may misread your handwriting. Then you've got the added chore of going back and proofreading everything that's been keyed in."

The Write Top, which in all other respects can serve as a standard IBM-compatible PC, has some added features. A glossary option allows the user to call up frequently used information—phone numbers, client contacts, etc.—at the push of a button. And the computer can be used for filling out forms, which are drawn onto the screen and saved for repeated use. Finally, the 2.5-pound Write Top screen can be dislodged to serve as a clipboard. A three-foot cable links the screen to the rest of the computer, which, at 6 pounds, can hang in a shoulder bag.

The first Write Tops are out now. By the early 1990s, they should be widespread.

ELECTRONIC NEWSPAPER

I magine reading all the newspapers in the world and not getting a smidgen of ink on your fingers.

Cleanliness and vast volume are not the only features of the electronic newspaper, however. The main advantage is customized access. If you don't care about Sylvester Stallone and *Rambo*, Part XII, you won't even have to know that he or the movie exists. Interested in only OPEC oil prices and

• • • • •

ODDS: 100%

ETA: 1991

PRICE: $125
ONE-TIME FEE

• • • • •

155

Chinese volleyball scores? Just enter key words into the system and receive only articles on subjects that interest you.

Based on NewsPeek, originally developed in an undergraduate thesis at M.I.T. by Fen Labalm, the electronic newspaper offers a large "peek" from any angle at a wide variety of information sources. A company in Denver called X*Press has already started marketing the service. Among its sources are The Associated Press and nine other international wire services, including the Soviet Union's Tass. Pro-sports scores, worldwide weather reports, editorials, life-style and entertainment news, shopping bargains, computer information, and even letters to the editor are included. Personalized stock quotes are updated three times a day, and a special business version of the news is available for an extra $20 a month.

The X*Press mainframe computer collects all the communiqués and sends them out in a unified form to cable systems around the country. Your cable-TV line picks it up, and with the help of a "splitter"—made available when you buy the service—it goes straight into your home computer without affecting your television hookup. Your computer can store your customized "NewsPeek" in its memory or you can print it out. It's a twenty-four-hour delivery of information as reliable as cable TV.

X*Press offers everything from worldwide instant news coverage to soap-opera updates and horoscopes. Everything . . . but the comics!

THE IDEA SALON

156

Psst! A little short on inspiration? Are your creative juices ebbing? Need a good idea? Call TIM. TIM, aka The Idea Machine, makes its home in the Idea Salon on the campus of Virginia Polytechnic Institute and State University in Blacksburg.

. . . . .
ODDS: 80%
ETA: 1998
PRICE: ABOUT $500 PER IDEA
. . . . .

TIM is designed to help generate ideas and solutions by drawing on a wealth of data in an electronic library. TIM utilizes printed, visual, audio, and aromatic (would you believe an odor compact disc!) information in the fields of science, art, music, religion, physics, engineering, sociology, and business. All are intended to trigger your creativity. TIM's creator is Dr. John Dickey, a professor at Virginia Tech and president of IdeaPlex, Inc. He explains that right now any person or company that needs problem-solving help can call the Salon or come to Blacksburg and sit down at TIM's keyboard.

There are six steps in TIM's creative process. First, the problem is identified. Second, a number of key words are chosen from TIM's data bank to describe it. Number three: ideas are generated by using encyclopedic information, listening, smelling, seeing pictures, and a review of previous ideas. In step four, the ideas are screened to see what worked and didn't work in the past, and to decide which ones merit more consideration. In step five, TIM helps package similar ideas and evaluates each one. Finally, in step six, a report is produced on a desktop publishing system.

Dr. Dickey believes that industry, government, business, and schools, as well as artists and authors, can benefit from TIM. (Even TIM can be improved by TIM, he says.) The suggestions TIM has helped come up with range from practical to strange. For example, when asked "If you ran a railroad, what would you do with all the used railroad ties?" TIM triggered ideas that ranged from building insect-proof structures to having a Railroad Tie Festival.

Dr. Dickey envisions a world where Idea Salons are located on city corners, available to anyone seeking inspiration. In the meantime, he's talking with hotel and conference center executives about setting up Salons on the premises. Sort of "mental workout rooms."

• • • • •

THE "SMARTS" CHAIR

Do you want to know what the future's answer is to the La-Z-Boy lounge chair? Are you ready for the "smarts" chair? Well, your colleague is, and your boss surely will be, so you'd better sit yourself down real quick.

. . . . .

ODDS: 90%

ETA: 1992

PRICE: $280
PER MONTH
FOR HOME USE

. . . . .

Cerebrex is the brainchild of Dr. Yoshiro NakaMats, a sixty-one-year-old Japanese inventor who holds the most patents ever—over 2,300. He himself starts each day by sitting in his invention for twenty to thirty minutes. Special short frequency waves are transmitted through his feet, causing blood to rush to his head, which in turn brings more oxygen to the brain, giving a relaxed, euphoric feeling. After being caressed at the same time with alpha waves and the gentle trickling sound of a stream, his brain feels as refreshed as if he had just awakened from eight hours of sleep.

All of this is supposed to erase fatigue, help you think better, prevent senility, and increase memory, sexual potency, and creativity. Already available in Japan, Cerebrex is found in offices or in "brain-tuning" centers, where several of the chairs are lined up as in a beauty parlor. The chairs are scheduled to be leased in the United States to companies interested in increasing staff productivity. Other U.S. applications will follow.

Dr. NakaMats started inventing when he was five years old and eventually became famous for the invention of the floppy disk, among other items. He vows he would discard all his other inventions before ridding himself of his futuristic chair and the Brain Revolution Program he has designed to go along with it. In addition to sitting in the "smarts" chair for twenty to thirty minutes a day, the regimen includes exercise, his patented "Brain Snacks," and meditation.

158

CHAPTER

14

future
games

UPHILL SKIING

How many times have you skied down a challenging slope, only to realize the bigger challenge of getting back up to the top for another run? John Stanford and Phil Huff decided to use their parachuting and skiing experience to design a product that would solve that dilemma. The result is a lightweight parachute powerful enough to propel skiers up steep slopes, yet small enough to be easily packed away for the trip back down.

· · · · ·
ODDS: 100%
ETA: 1991
PRICE: $1,300
· · · · ·

Coming up with a prototype was fairly simple—since Stanford's company manufactures parachutes—but testing it was downright thrilling. "We realized that uphill skiing was more fun than skiing

159

downhill," says Stanford. So once they received a patent, the sport of "upskiing" was born.

The parachute can be used on snow-covered lakes or steep mountain slopes, in winds as low as 7 or 8 mph. Stanford and Huff have upskied in 50 mph winds, but describe the experience as "terrifying" and "dangerous" and strongly advise against it.

Like sailing, upskiing is a wind sport. After putting on your skis and strapping yourself into the harness, lift part of the canopy (with the help of control lines) so that it fills with wind. Then just lean back and go. On a modest slope with firm snow and average winds of about 10 to 15 mph, you can move at twice the speed of the wind. To get yourself up a very steep slope, however, you'll need stronger winds of about 18 to 20 mph.

A control center attached to the harness allows you to increase or decrease your speed and, in the case of an emergency, release yourself from the equipment. The parachute itself is 28 feet in diameter, and the whole system weighs a mere 13 pounds and folds up to the size of a backpack.

The product can be purchased from UpSki, Inc., P.O. Box 1269, Frisco, CO 80443. Customers are required to participate in a short demonstration of how the system and its emergency features work.

OVERSIZED GOLF

ODDS: 100%

ETA: 1991

PRICE: $4 PER GAME

Some 16 million Americans now crowd the nation's golf courses, but apparently many other prospective players shy away because of long delays on the public links and high fees on the private ones. In addition, novices are often intimidated by the sand traps, dog legs, and other course obstacles that can get in the way of a good time.

Well, here's a game for the disenfranchised. It's easier to play, it's faster to play, and the courses are tiny by golf standards. Golfun Equities in Washington State has come up with a pressurized plastic ball the size of a grapefruit. The game requires oversized tees, but players use standard clubs. The air-filled ball (available in hot pink and other colors) travels one-third as far as regular golf balls, and, better yet, only 6½ acres is required for a nine-hole course, compared to the customary 180 acres. It takes only about an hour to complete a game of Golfun.

"It is intended both as family recreation and as a training ground for regular golfers," says Jim Contini, co-owner of the firm. Contini adds that he and his partner intend to establish Golfun franchises around the world through contacts with real-estate developers, amusement parks, city and county officials, and anyone else with enough land on hand.

WIND WEAPON

This is a toy that is definitely not for everyone. But if you're a surfer or a hang glider, or preferably both, then this contraption is a dream come true.

· · · · ·
ODDS: 100%
ETA: 1990
PRICE: $1,275
· · · · ·

It's called the Wind Weapon and it's the brainchild of Windsurfer Tom Magruder and hang-gliding expert Robert Crowell. The Wind Weapon is a sailboard rig with a sophisticated aluminum-and-mylar pivoting wing that enables the board and rider to leap as high as 40 feet above the water's surface.

This is not a sport for novices. First, says Magruder, you should have Windsurfing experience. Then, expect to experiment for a good week before you get the hang of it. These modern-day Wright Brothers say that once you get good, you can stay in flight for up to ten seconds.

The Wind Weapon is available at a few Windsurfing shops or from Wind Weapon International, Inc., in Hood River, Oregon.

FIVE-BLADED BOOMERANG

The Aborigines wouldn't recognize it, but a boomerang it is. Designed in a star shape with five blades and a hole in the center, the Bee-Bak is a space-age version of the old boomerang.

· · · · ·
ODDS: 100%
ETA: 1990
PRICE: $5–$7
· · · · ·

162

Unlike a conventional L-shaped boomerang, which travels on a horizontal plane in a wide arc, the Bee-Bak soars vertically, traveling some 20 to 40 yards in distance and three stories in height before making the return trip. When it reaches its farthest point, the boomerang stalls, flips over, and flies straight back on the same course.

The toy was designed by J. Turner Hunt, an aerospace engineer who does conceptual work on fighter planes and space vehicles for the McDonnell Douglas Corporation. Allied Toy Company, a Kansas City, Missouri, manufacturer, is mass-producing them.

Tossing the boomerang requires more practice than strength, says Steven Pack, president of Allied Toy. "It's a lot easier to master than a standard boomerang, and it's lighter and softer, so it won't hurt anyone. And, unlike a Frisbee, you don't have to have someone to toss it with you—or a dog to fetch it."

Instructions come with the product, but the principle is to throw the Bee-Bak up and out, either sidearm or overhand. Although the toy seems simple in design, the manufacturer insists that it has very tight tolerances, with precise specifications on the blade size, thickness, and angle. It's made of a special plastic compound that gives it a great deal of flexibility and has a high resistance to impact.

The Aborigines, of course, used their boomerangs to hunt animals, but the Bee-Bak should serve as a "good, healthy outdoor toy," says Pack.

NIGHT GOLF

Golf nuts, say thank you to a group of New Hampshire entrepreneurs. They've come up with illuminated equipment, so you can now play your favorite sport at night. Right now only luminous tees and balls are for sale, but look for a $50 Nitelite putter to be available soon as well.

• • • • •
ODDS: 100%
ETA: 1990
PRICE: $6 FOR TEE AND BALL
• • • • •

163

The golf balls are translucent and made of polyurethane, with a hole for a one-and-a-half-inch chemi-luminescent light stick that is inserted into the ball by the golfer before playing. The sticks emit a green glow that lasts for about six hours.

Pick Point Enterprises of Mirror Lake, New Hampshire, is the company making the Nitelite line of balls, tees, and putters. According to Corky Newcomb, vice president of Pick Point, these strange balls drive, chip, and putt just like the daylight white ones. Up in New Hampshire, Newcomb is already running nocturnal tournaments with fairways, flag pins, and cups all lit by chemi-luminescent sticks. Players use flashlights and lighted carts to get around.

Nitelite is great news for golfers; bad news for golf widows.

SIMULATED GOLF

A small company on the windblown prairies of Canada has developed an indoor simulated golf game that is so real, so scientific, and so entertaining that it could revolutionize the sport.

• • • • •
ODDS: 90%
ETA: 1990
PRICE: $18,000
• • • • •

Its first markets will be Japan, where course space is at a premium, and Canada, where cold weather minimizes the season. But there are two test units in the United States already set up in Atlanta and San Francisco.

The game, called GS 2020 Interactive Golf Simulator, has four components: an interactive video with a large screen, a tethered ball, a scale that measures the weight or power stroke that goes into the golfer's swing, and a set of optical sensors that measure the swing of the club. An actual course is played: the famed Banff Springs Golf

Club course in Alberta, Canada. New courses will be available at the rate of two per year.

The golfer begins with a view from the first tee seen on a 19-inch monitor. He chooses his club and feeds that information into the computer. He swings, and on the screen actually sees the flight of the ball and the spot where it lands. He picks his next club after he sees the view for the second shot. The computer takes into account the club used, how much power went into the swing, how cleanly the ball was hit, and the wind factor, in determining how far, how high, and how straight the ball will travel.

According to a spokesman for Joytec Ltd., of Saskatoon, Saskatchewan, "The computer operates a 12-inch laser disc with 54,000 frames." That means there is enough video for hundreds of possible shots. You can end up in the woods, water, or sand traps, and even see wildlife scurrying across the fairway. And, of course, the game includes putting.

Hotels, golf centers, and clubs are the first places likely to offer the GS 2020. But the entire operation needs only a 12-by-12-foot playing area with a 10-foot ceiling, so Joytec expects to be selling a version of the Golf Simulator for home use. Joytec has already made a deal with a major Japanese corporation for marketing in that country. In 1990, it's expected the game will be on sale in the United States.

165

• • • • •

ROBOT
HORSE RACING

A West German magazine described the sport this way: "Remote-control robot riders race small hackney ponies around an indoor track. A new spectator spectacle from the land of unlimited possibilities."

ODDS: 80%

ETA: 1991

PRICE: N/A

The land, of course, is the United States. The robots are made of metal and fiberglass, weigh 22 pounds, and are shaped and brightly painted like little legless jockeys. The ponies are live and about half the size of thoroughbreds, stand 45 to 52 inches high, weigh about 500 pounds, and apparently don't know the difference between a human rider and a robot which is fortunate for Charles McVean, a commodity trader and the president of Super Jock and Mid-South Indoor Racing in Memphis, Tennessee, who expects this new sport to sweep America.

The Super Jock (that's what he calls the intense-looking, legless rider) is operated by a "trainer" in the infield using a hand-held remote-control box. A joystick moves the arms, which hold the reins, while the push of a button brings down the riding crop, which is attached to the robot's derriere. The trainer can urge his pony on with shouts of "Giddyap," or whatever, which a microphone relays to a speaker implanted in Super Jock's head.

166

McVean came up with the idea for robot horse racing in 1984, when cattle were missing on his ranch in Missouri. He called a friend, David Kime, now his partner in Super Jock, who devised a system for monitoring fence lines with a small remote-controlled helicopter equipped with a camera. Then Kime saw his first hackney pony and thought, Why not use the remote technology to create a robot cowboy? "When David called me to come and look at it, I saw this squeaky box thing sitting on a little pony," McVean recalled. "I immediately thought, indoor horse racing." He describes the hackney pony as hot-blooded, with great stamina and strength, and, because of its diminutive size, able to make the tight turns on a 240-foot-long indoor track.

The advantages to indoor racing, he claims, are increased visibility, enhanced perception of speed, and all-weather operation. Plus, "excitement is much more contagious indoors than out."

With 300 ponies and 100 robots in training at his Memphis track, McVean is only a racing license away from establishing his first Super Jock Indoor Racing meet. "People love horses," McVean says, though he personally is allergic to them, "and this invention makes horses more adaptable to man's modern urban environment."

WATER WALKERS

To "walk on water" has long been synonymous with doing the impossible. Which may have been the motivation for Ben Watson's fifteen-year quest to do just that—develop an apparatus so that man can stride across lakes and rivers.

. . . . .
ODDS: 85%
ETA: 1991
PRICE: $850
. . . . .

Well, Mr. Watson of Renton, Washington, has created water walkers, tested them, obtained a patent, and is now seeking a manufacturer. In the meantime, he's still taking test walks on a local lake at about 5 miles per hour.

His invention looks a bit like a pair of bulky skis (6 feet long and

167

9 inches wide), except that each walker is 9 inches deep and the foot is inserted inside a foot well instead of a boot. Each of the walkers, or floats—to be more accurate—is equipped with eight flaps on the underside to propel motion forward. The walkers are made of foam and fiberglass, and a pair weighs 30 pounds. They can support up to 300 pounds. The actual motion one uses to make headway is more like skating or cross-country skiing than walking, as the floats never leave the water.

Now, the big question is, Who wants or needs to "walk" on water enough to spend $850? Mr. Watson claims his water walkers are stable enough for fishing or hunting and provide a challenging aerobic off-season workout for skiers and other athletes. And one has to admit there would be head-turning excitement about walking across the lake on a bright summer day.

And, "for more fun and excitement," Mr. Watson has also devised sails to convert your walkers into a little catamaran.

15

sports stuff

SWINGSPEED BAT

When his son was a college baseball hopeful in 1985, Robert Cobb, a dean at the University of Maine, wanted to help him be better prepared. "Bat speed and strength are critical variables," says Cobb, who looked for something that would indicate how hard and how well a bat was swung.

- - - - -
ODDS: 100%
ETA: 1991
PRICE: UNDER $100
- - - - -

Finding no such product on the market, Cobb enlisted physicist and fellow dean at the university, Charles Tarr, "who is very adept at working with microprocessors," to help develop a device for measuring and recording swing speed. "It took us three years, working down in the basement," says Cobb, who was an undergraduate physical-education major. His contribution to the project was his knowledge of "the parameters and measurements of athletic performance."

169

The Swingspeed Bat, which weighs as much as a regular bat, has a weight implanted in the wide end. This is attached to a slide potentiometer, a device which registers the centrifugal force of a swing in electronic impulses. These impulses are monitored by a microprocessor, which converts them into a digital readout on the top of the bat. A later model computes the average of all swings, indicates the fastest one, and automatically converts the information to miles per hour.

Cobb, who believes the bat will appeal to both the toy and the sporting goods/athletic markets, would like to keep the price below $100 to make it more available to kids as a developmental tool.

By the way, Cobb's son made the Harvard University varsity baseball team.

SWIMMING PROPULSION DEVICE

They look like two torpedoes; you strap them on, stretch your arms, flick a switch, and the next thing you know, you're jetting through the water *à la* James Bond.

ODDS: 50%
ETA: 1992
PRICE: $300 PER PAIR

The device doesn't have a catchy name yet or, for that matter, a manufacturer, but with the popularity of scuba diving, snorkeling, and plain old swimming, it will probably have both soon.

The propulsion device can do 4 miles per hour for forty-five minutes in a lake, ocean, or pond. Each of the units includes a battery, a motor, and a propeller in a watertight housing. Within easy reach of your fingers is a control panel with an on/off switch. One model will also have a light switch for night swimming. The contoured units strap snugly under the arms and extend from the hand to the elbow.

The device was invented and patented by California diver Michael

Borges. Kessler Sales Corporation of Ohio is assisting Borges in his search for a company to produce and market the product.

SWEET-SPOT TENNIS RACQUET

I f you've ever played a game of tennis, you probably know the "sweet" sensation of hitting the ball with the center of the racquet. The center, responsible for the sound and feel of that *whomp*, is understandably referred to as "the sweet spot." You've probably also felt the momentary twinge that shoots up your arm when you don't hit the ball so well. The strain to your tendons causes painful tennis elbow.

• • • • •
ODDS: 100%
ETA: 1990
PRICE: $149–$196
• • • • •

A company called Dynaspot is making a totally "sweet" racquet that puts a "sweet spot" in every shot and reduces the forces that cause tennis elbow by about 40 percent. Marvin Sassler, president, is an electrical engineer and tennis player who had experienced a bout of tennis elbow. While recuperating, he came up with the idea of a racquet with a sweet spot that moves. Gerald Geraldi, Sassler's chief engineer, designed a racquet frame of lightweight graphite with partially filled tubes of liquid on either face that absorb the torque when the ball is hit. The fluid acts as a "dynamic" balancing system, meaning that the weights move, thereby cushioning the impact of the ball and reducing the stress on the player's muscles. The energy in your swing is delivered to the ball, and not absorbed by your arm.

Sassler's revolutionary racquet has been spotted at both the French and Geneva Opens, but not yet in the United States. Look for it soon.

171

• • • • •

"UMPIRE" TENNIS BALLS

Cheaters beware! In the future, you won't be able to win that desperately needed point by calling a close ball out.

Engineer John A. Van Auken has developed special tennis balls, called Accu-Call balls, that contain electricity-conducting metallic fibers. On standard tennis courts, these balls perform the same as any others. But when used in conjunction with special sensor-embedded courts, these balls can make line calls themselves. Every time the ball makes contact with the court, a signal is emitted to a lap-top console held by someone at courtside. This signal indicates to within one one-hundredth of an inch whether the ball landed inside, on, or outside the line.

So far the balls have been successfully tested by John McEnroe and Jimmy Connors. Their only problem is a slightly gray color caused by the metallic fibers. But a spokesman for Penn Athletics, manufacturer of the balls, says this problem can be corrected.

Initially the balls will be available on a rental basis at private clubs equipped with the special courts. While current agreements do not call for sale of the balls to the public, at some point in the future, consumers will likely be able to purchase them at athletic stores for use on private or public electronic courts.

• • • • •

ODDS: 75%

ETA: 1999

PRICE: N/A

• • • • •

• • • • •

NO-SLIP RACQUETBALL GLOVE

P art-time inventor Noel Hames of De-
catur, Alabama, has invented a
racquetball glove that will eliminate at
least one excuse for why your game isn't
better.

· · · · ·
ODDS: 95%
ETA: 1991
PRICE: $20
· · · · ·

An avid racquetball and tennis player,
Hames observed that the racquet is always in and out of the hand,
so the grip and consequently the angle of the swing are constantly
changing. "I was always twisting my racquet, so my game was not
consistent," he says. In racquetball, because the racquet is so short,
there is tremendous percussion when the ball is hit. This is what
causes the racquet to slip in the hand.

Hames now has a glove that will keep the racquet in place. The
part of Hames's glove that grips the racquet is made of suede per-
forated with tiny holes, while the back of the glove is spandex. Straps
over the fingers (except the thumb) merge into one lead strap that
fastens with Velcro around the racquet to the glove back. In this way,
the racquet is locked into the hand, preventing slippage. "Most racquetball gloves being developed now are aimed at increasing grip
capacity, with different leathers or even sticky lubricants. But with
suede, the wetter it gets, the better it grips," says Hames.

The glove, which took Hames a year and a half to develop, has
been tested by racquetball pros at colleges in Alabama. "When that
racquet is strapped into your hand, it becomes an extension of your
arm," says Hames. "It really increases the power of your swing. We're
just flabbergasted."

With slight modifications, the glove could be applied to any racquet
sport. Hames plans to sell the gloves at racquetball centers and
eventually in sporting-goods stores.

173

· · · · ·

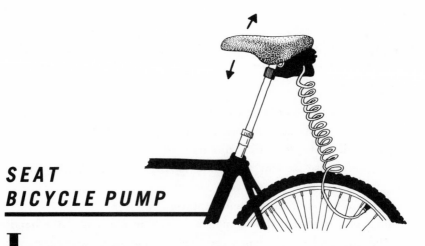

SEAT BICYCLE PUMP

If out of sight really is out of mind, there's less chance this innovative bicycle pump will ever get stolen . . . or, for that matter, lost. The Seat Post Tire Pump from Bike-O-Matic actually becomes part of your bicycle.

ODDS: 100%

ETA: 1990

PRICE: N/A

What you do is replace the seat post (the bar that holds the seat and connects to the body of the bike) with the Seat Post Tire Pump. Attached to the pump and nestled under the seat is a storage bag containing a coiled hose. When a tire needs filling, you simply pull out the hose and connect it to the tire's air valve.

Pumping it up is the neat part. Your seat serves as the handle. Move it up and down to fill the tire with air. When you're finished, the seat snaps back into place. The 12-ounce Seat Post Tire Pump was invented by Gilmore Chappell, a mechanical engineer from Philadelphia who also created the bike automatic transmission.

AUTOMATIC TABLE TENNIS SERVER

For those who take their table tennis seriously, the Taiwanese (and we know *they* do) have come up with a mind-boggling gadget called the Challenger 108.

ODDS: 100%
ETA: 1992
PRICE: N/A

Not unlike tennis servers or baseball pitching machines, the Challenger 108 sprays balls at its human opponent 108 different ways. You can control the speed, the direction, the interval, the slice, the left-right motion, and anything else you can think of that can be done to a table tennis ball.

From Holy Industry Company of Taipei, Taiwan.

ARCHER'S LASER RANGE FINDER

From Robin Hood to Robin Hines, archers have had a problem gauging the distance to their prey. Now finally, after centuries of guesswork, the latter Robin has invented a way to calculate the space exactly.

ODDS: 100%
ETA: 1990
PRICE: $300

Distance is crucial when you hunt with a bow and arrow. For unlike a bullet, an arrow drops off sharply in flight. The hunter has to determine how high to aim and how hard to pull on the bow string based on the distance to the prey.

Hines, a native of Tullahoma, Tennessee, has come up with the Laser Range Finder, a hand-held device that focuses a laser beam of light on the target. A photo sensor then picks up the deflected light

175

wave and the device determines the distance the light has traveled. This measurement is displayed in yards on a small LCD display.

The Range Finder weighs 1.5 pounds, measures 4 inches by 4 feet by 2 feet and uses rechargeable batteries. The invisible beam is 1 inch in diameter, with a range of 50 yards.

Hines's company, Quantine Inc., is producing and marketing the Range Finder in a joint venture with Cubic Precision, a division of the Cubic Corporation of San Diego, California.

THE SKI VALET

As many skiers know, negotiating a double black-diamond mogul run through trees can be easier than lugging your equipment through a crowded airport or an icy parking lot.

ODDS: 100%

ETA: 1990

PRICE: $70

Enter the Husski Ski Valet, designed by the Bresslergroup of Philadelphia, to alleviate the problem of getting your skis, poles, and boots to the slope. This is a folding device on wheels that's about 2 feet long. You unfold it, latch on your equipment, and secure everything with a padlock or cable lock. There are three bags that attach to the Husski—a saddle bag for the boots, an airline bag–type cover for the skis and poles, and a snap-on duffel for your parka, sweater, and other gear.

The valet is weight-stabilized so that it can be pushed or pulled easily over ice, snow, gravel, and mud and up and down stairs.

The Husski can be mounted on a car ski rack and meets all airline baggage requirements.

SPORTS SHOCK METER

John Carlin, a Denver entrepreneur and sports fan, has patented a device that he believes could make all contact sports safer. Called the Measureguard, it gauges the accumulated shock sustained by an athlete during the course of a game.

ODDS: 95%
ETA: 1992
PRICE: $20

In effect, this meter will tell coaches and officials how "used" a player has become and the likelihood that he is susceptible to certain kinds of injuries. The Measureguard, attached to the back of a football helmet or other athletic gear, monitors the accumulated shock with a vibration sensor. Each jolt produces electrical signals that are converted to numbers and displayed on the tiny screen attached to the helmet. The signals fade as time passes but increase with each new blow.

"An official can see who is overused—and thus prone to injury—just by looking at the back of the helmets," says Carlin. In his view, the Measureguard could prevent many tragic high school, college, and professional injuries. In fact, Carlin came up with the idea after his sixteen-year-old nephew was hurt playing football.

PUNCH METER

John Carlin, inventor of the Measureguard (see above), has also patented the Measureband, a device that measures the effectiveness of punches thrown by a boxer.

Vibration sensors worn around each

ODDS: 95%
ETA: 1992
PRICE: $20

177

wrist gauge the shock when fists meet target. This information is transmitted by radio signal to a processor that records the number of blows, the time of each blow, the frequency, force, and accumulation of force. The information is digitally displayed on a TV screen. Using this feedback, trainers and fighters can determine which combinations, punches, and techniques produce the most devastating results. Also, spectators could appreciate boxing more by knowing instantly the effectiveness of each punch.

To determine both give and take, the boxer can also wear the Measureguard which gauges how much shock is absorbed by the body during competition.

PERFECT LINE GOLF BALL

To the duffer, every golf ball may look like every other golf ball. They're white and have dimples. But the Acushnet Company, which manufactures 40 percent of the golf balls in the United States, has developed a super golf ball for precision putting.

ODDS: 75%

ETA: 1991

PRICE: N/A

The experts line up their putts along the ball's parting line, an axis that divides the ball in half. Presumably, when the putter hits the ball along its "equator," the ball should run true.

Most designs are based on dimples arranged in equilateral triangles, giving the ball bilateral symmetry (where one half is the mirror image of the other). William Gobush, manager of aerodynamic research and testing, has patented a design for Acushnet in which the ball's dimples are arranged in twenty-four isosceles triangles (two sides are of equal length). This, in effect, gives the ball six planes of bilateral symmetry. So golfers have a much better chance of stroking true putts. "When driving, a pro will usually hit the ball's 'pole' region as opposed to its parting line. But in putting, the force on the putter is more con-

178

trolled and he'll get a symmetrical hit if he can find that parting line axis."

Gobush admits, however, that this design may not be for the Saturday-afternoon golfer with an 18 handicap. But for Ben Crenshaw, or a low-handicap club player who cares that a millimeter to the right or left can make a difference . . . this ball's for you!

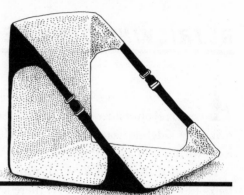

THE DRY SPORTS CHAIR

Communing with nature is one thing. Doing it with a wet tush is quite another. That's why Louise Chandler and Rob Hart, two former Outward Bound instructors, decided to get to the bottom of the problem with their product, the "Crazy Creek Chair."

ODDS: 100%

ETA: 1990

PRICE: $35–$43.50

"When you spend a lot of time outdoors, you're always trying to find ways to be more comfortable. After all, our society is comfort-driven," says Ms. Chandler. The end result of these two Montanans' brainstorming was a portable, lightweight, waterproof chair made with a tightly woven packcloth seat designed to withstand everything from the rigors of the wild to sports stadiums. The seat, which can be folded into a backpack or duffel bag and strapped onto a bicycle or raft, has even been used by a few innovative golfers to hold ice and beer while on the course. "We've also heard the chair can act as a flotation device," noted Ms. Chandler.

Weighing in at about 20 ounces, the chair comes in three models— regular, large, and the power lounger. All fold out into a sleeping pad—and come in a choice of twelve colors, including camouflage.

179

Currently marketed in a few catalogues and retail shops, the chair can be purchased directly from Chandler and Hart's Crazy Creek Products, Inc., in Red Lodge, Montana.

RETRIEVING DUCK DECOY

A new kind of duck-hunting decoy could revolutionize the sport and permanently sideline your faithful Labrador retriever.

ODDS: 100%

ETA: 1992

PRICE: $1,250

It's called Robo-Duck, and while it looks like any other duck decoy, there are some chilling differences. This battery-powered, propeller-driven decoy is operated by remote control from behind a blind. A joystick controls its movements, including the opening and closing of 20-inch steel talons, with which it can retrieve two mallards or one large goose.

"They remind me of the jaws of an alligator," says Jean Bogner, owner of Outdoorsmen's Herter's in Beaver Dam, Wisconsin, Robo-Duck's exclusive mail-order distributor. Bogner feels that while the "aesthetics" of what he calls the Benedict Arnold duck may take a little getting used to, the decoy should be fairly widespread within five to ten years. "We've gotten a lot of calls about it," he comments, including one from a customer in Saudi Arabia who wanted a Robo-Duck for his private duck pond.

Future-minded duck hunters can call Outdoorsmen's Herter's at 800-654-3825.

180

ELECTRONIC FISHING LURE

Chemical engineer Michael Garr was surf-casting in Maine in 1983 when the inspiration for his electronic fishing lure was born. "I wasn't having much luck, but the guy next to me kept reeling them in," he recalls. "He was using the 3-inch-long end of a broomstick, painted red, with a bolt for an eye and a hook on the end." Garr resolved then and there to develop the ultimate fishing lure.

ODDS: 100%
ETA: 1991
PRICE: $3–$10

Over the next few years, Garr's lure evolved from painted broomstick ends and rolling-pin handles with glass eyes and small electric Christmas lights to today's clear plastic, battery-operated models complete with tiny microprocessor chips inside. The lures flash colorful lights, attracting innocent fish that don't yet know about these high-tech fisherman schemes.

The idea behind it all, says Garr, is that different species of fish are attracted to different angles and colors of light. Sounds fishy, but heck, if a broomstick works . . .

that's entertainment!

INTERACTIVE SATELLITE THEATER

Beckett is on Broadway, there's a Seurat auction at Sotheby's, and the Dior fashion show is in Dallas. Meanwhile, you're stuck in Sausalito. Don't despair. Someday soon, all these events—plus a gourmet meal—will be as close as your country club or resort hotel, through the Club Theatre Network.

· · · · ·
ODDS: 95%
ETA: 1993
PRICE: $25–$100
· · · · ·

"We've combined 35mm film, live theater, satellite transmission, computers, and gourmet dining in one experience," says Club Theatre Network president, Ron Ratner. Events such as first-run movies, live auctions, and fashion shows will be presented in small theaters located in private country clubs, resort hotels, or high-rise condominium complexes. Each event, whether a matinee or an evening performance, will begin with a four- to six-course gourmet meal. Guests will then move to a small theater, where the performance takes place. But you are not there simply to watch. Club Theatre Network allows the audience to participate, whether to place a bid on a work of art, order a designer dress, or discuss a movie premiere with the director.

"The key to Club Theatre Network is audience interaction," says Ratner. The theater's seats are computerized so that you can press a button in the armrest and access a hookup to ask a question, place a bid, or enter a credit-card number. Handsets at the seat will let you talk directly to those on screen during post-performance question-and-answer sessions, or while bidding. And the events will all be transmitted by satellite to high-definition, CinemaScope-size screens.

Other programs will include concerts, and even shareholders' meetings, with prices varying according to the event. Club Theatre Network has just begun operating in Florida. The plan is to expand nationwide and to Europe during the nineties.

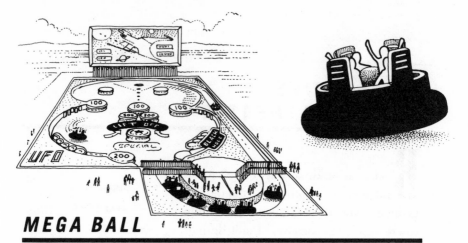

MEGA BALL

I magine yourself hurtling off the walls of a giant pinball machine, actually sitting inside the ball as you spin and bounce off bumper posts, and you start to get the picture of what Mega Ball is all about.

ODDS: 75%

ETA: 1996

PRICE: $2 PER RIDE

An amusement park ride for the next generation of pinball wizards, Mega Ball is the brainchild of the Swiss Intamin Inc., a company

184

responsible for such adventures in gravity loss as the Free Fall, Rapid River, and Tidal Wave, all currently found in amusement parks across the country. "If it's over 50 feet high, it's probably ours," boasts Intamin vice president Kurt Lukas, who says the twenty-year-old company also specializes in manufacturing monorails and aerial tramways.

But this is more than your ordinary thrill ride. With Mega Ball, you're actually *in* the ride—providing vicarious thrills for hordes of spectators while you hurtle around the insides of a giant pinball machine.

The Mega Ball experience starts with you and three friends sitting in one of approximately twenty round bumper cars on a 183 by 76-foot-wide inclined plane. After traveling up to the top of the ride, the four-passenger "ball" is released to roll down the colorfully painted platform, bouncing off walls and posts to the accompaniment of flashing lights and electronic buzzers. You can control the giant flippers from within the ball, through a radio-frequency hookup—but even more dastardly, a coin-operated pushbutton outside the ride will allow sadistic spectators to "bump" Mega Ball's hapless riders back up the platform for another shot!

With an average ride time of two minutes, Intamin expects that once it's on the market, Mega Ball will have a capacity of 1,200 to 1,500 passengers per hour.

INTERACTIVE GAME PAVILION

Computers have allowed us to work at home, to talk without speaking, and to interface without ever coming face-to-face. Edwin Schlossberg, creator of innovative museum exhibits, wants to put the fun back into people being together. "Technical advancements created situations that isolated people. Now it's time we create situations where people can learn to interact with one another," he says.

•••••
ODDS: 90%
ETA: 1991
PRICE: $20 ADMISSION
•••••

His creation is the interactive game pavilion—a place where people can play with each other through technology. Each pavilion will house up to twenty-two different games. Bruce Falstein, director of business development for Edwin Schlossberg Inc., calls the games "theatrical events where players are both the actors and the audience." Here are a few examples:

Beat the System: A stock-market game in which players, individually or by forming cartels, trade fictitious stocks to increase their portfolios.

The Robot Cocktail Party: Set in a bar, each person in a separate booth operates a 3-foot mobile robot equipped with a microphone. Each player has a part of a phrase, such as "birds of a feather." The object is to move your robot around and have it converse with other robots until it finds one with the other half of the phrase.

Big Picture: Fifty players are seated in a movie theater. Each one has a touch screen computer capable of creating images. Each player's creation is displayed on one-fiftieth of the big movie screen in front. The idea is to work together to create one large picture.

On your mark, get set, communicate!

186

•••••

IN-FLIGHT ENTERTAINMENT SYSTEM

More entertainment in the sky will be a high priority for the airlines in the 1990s. Boeing and Sony have teamed up to create an in-flight information and entertainment system that rivals anything you might now have in your home.

• • • • •
ODDS: 75%
ETA: 1995
PRICE: N/A
• • • • •

It was set to be installed in Boeing's new 7J7 mid-range jet, but full-scale development of the plane has been postponed because of lack of orders.

Here's what Boeing and Sony have in mind: a 4-inch flat-panel display screen located on each seatback, allowing passengers to choose their own entertainment. The choices are movies, TV shows, video games, or live viewing of the landing and takeoff of your plane. Passengers will also be able to order food and drink and even duty-free goods through the system.

Other available information will include gate directories, the status of connecting flights, and a moving route map. Service on board should improve as well. The individual consoles will be linked to a central cabin management system that will give flight attendants instant information on passenger needs and keep a food and beverage inventory and a cabin maintenance report.

187

• • • • •

SUPER MOVIES

As television races to look as good as film, the movie industry is moving to introduce its own improvements. At the top of the list is Showscan, a process that involves projecting 70mm film at 60 frames per second. Traditional movies are shot on 35mm film and rolled past the projector's light source at 24 frames per second. The increased image area of the 70mm film plus the more rapid frame speed creates a larger, more detailed, more lifelike picture.

ODDS: 90%

ETA: 1995

PRICE: SLIGHTLY HIGHER THAN TODAY'S MOVIE ADMISSION

Showscan was first developed by Douglas Trumbull, the special-effects master behind *2001: A Space Odyssey* and *Close Encounters of the Third Kind*. Trumbull has been trying to convince the studios and the theaters to convert, but some would rather fight than switch. The larger film requires a modified projector, a better sound system, and a larger screen. The projector can be changed back to accommodate the slower speed film in half a day, if needed. The Catch-22, however, is that theater owners are waiting for films shot in Showscan before they finance any conversion. Meanwhile, the film producers are waiting for the theater owners to convert their projectors before they start making Showscan films.

But there are those willing to push this along. Aaron Russo, producer of the movie *The Rose*, is acquiring the rights to produce three films in the new process. Columbia Pictures has bought 6.6 percent of the stock in Showscan Film, and Paramount Pictures has expressed interest.

As for the film critics, Roger Ebert says that Showscan is "incomparably more realistic than anything I've ever seen on a movie screen."

188

MOTION SIMULATOR

W ant to go on a roller-coaster ride but it's a rainy day? Want to go on the Ferris wheel but you're afraid of heights? A Swiss company based in Maryland has a solution. Just sit yourself down in one of its Dynamic Motion Simulator Theaters.

• • • • •
ODDS: 100%
ETA: 1995
PRICE: $10 PER MOVIE
• • • • •

In one of these specially designed theaters, you will find yourself in what appears to be a relatively normal-looking seat. But when the movie begins, hold on to your cowboy hat! The seat will rise and fall, and shimmy and shake, in perfect synchronization with the action before you. The roller coaster on screen will have a whole new authenticity. When it dips at 60 miles per hour, you will dip with it enough for your stomach to feel as if it's in your mouth.

The system employs hydraulically activated seats that move in conjunction with a super-high-resolution film technique called Showscan (see page 188) to yield a total viewing experience. Kurt Lukas, vice president of Intamin, stresses that the system works best with this new film projection because "Showscan's really the only one that's good enough for the Dynamic Motion Simulator."

The motion theaters already exist in France and San Francisco. Others are in the works for Japan and Korea. Intamin has plans to install more in U.S. shopping centers, entertainment malls, and amusement parks.

189

17

look!
no hands!

VOICE-ACTIVATED TYPEWRITER

For bosses, secretaries, students, writers—anyone who strains over a typewriter or word processor—it seems too good to be true. Will we really be able to sit back, put our feet up, and let our vocal cords do the typing? Chances are we will.

• • • • •
ODDS: 90%
ETA: 1995
PRICE: $5,000
• • • • •

Raymond Kurzweil of Kurzweil Applied Intelligence, Inc., in Waltham, Massachusetts, is a master of artificial intelligence machines. He is already selling a working system that, in a limited way, operates like a voice-activated typewriter.

It's called KVR (Kurzweil VoiceReport) and works like this: The operator speaks into a microphone, inserting brief pauses—at least one-tenth of a second—between words. This is called "discrete speech." The words are then displayed on a computer screen for verification or editing. If something is wrong, you say "Scratch that" and the incorrect words are erased. When the dictated text is ready to be put on paper, you simply command "Print report."

First, however, each person who will use KVR must "train" it to recognize his or her voice. That's because KVR is "speaker dependent": It will only recognize the speech of users who first pronounce each word of KVR's vocabulary into the system's microphone. The system's computer creates a digital record of the way the user pronounces each word, and stores that record in its memory for comparison purposes during the actual speech recognition process.

Right now, KVR has a vocabulary of 5,000 words, so its applications are limited. But Kurzweil has developed a number of specialized programs that make the most of this relatively small vocabulary. For example, VoiceRAD for radiologists and VoiceEM for emergency medical physicians both eliminate the need for human transcribers by making it possible for doctors to dictate, edit, and print accurate patient records in minutes.

These programs include a feature called "trigger phrases." A spoken word or phrase will trigger frequently used sentences or paragraphs to be printed in their entirety. The KVR is even able to distinguish and use homonyms correctly, such as *to, too,* and *two.* This is how close technology is right now to a fully voice-activated typewriter or word processor.

Robert Joseph, marketing vice president for Kurzweil Applied Intelligence, feels it won't be long before a generation of easy-to-use, reasonably priced, voice-controlled word processors are in homes and offices. These machines will have an unlimited vocabulary and will be able to recognize continuous speech (with no pauses between words). Then we'll all be able to put up our feet, relax, and dictate.

BUTLER-IN-A-BOX

It's a magic lantern of sorts, but there's no rubbing and there's no genie. It just sits in the corner, but if you talk to it, it talks back and anything can happen.

• • • • •
ODDS: 100%
ETA: 1990
PRICE: $1,575
• • • • •

Butler-in-a-Box is a wonderfully eccentric enhancement to automated home technology. A mini–smart house (see page 4), this voice-activated box will not only turn on the heat in the upstairs bedroom, or turn off the light in the bathroom, it will perform any of thirty-two commands you tell it to do. All told—using voice, timed control, and keypad—the Butler can control 256 household devices.

But first, the 3-by-9-by-11-inch box needs to be given a name—maybe Godfrey—because it thinks it is a real butler, and it needs to be trained. A few entries are made on its built-in keypad and then you must recite ten phrases so that Godfrey knows what you sound like. Finally you must enter each desired command that you will want Godfrey to perform. Godfrey can be programmed to be charming or cantankerous, as you wish, and can respond in a foreign accent or a foreign language.

Ask him to order a pizza, and Godfrey can locate the correct number in his files and dial for you. He'll also activate the phone if a call comes in; you can talk over the speaker phone to the caller. And like his human counterparts, if Godfrey makes a mistake he apologizes by saying "I'm sorry" or "Please forgive me, master."

Godfrey can pick out his master's voice in a packed room and won't be confused by the television. He is trained to respond to only the four voices entered into his system. If a burglar enters your abode, Godfrey will ask, "Hello, may I help you?" Without the correct response of a secret password, Godfrey will throw a veritable tantrum, and all the lights in the house will start flashing, the stereo will blare, and the alarm will go off.

Gus Searcy, a professional magician and computer buff, got tired of people asking "Can you make the lights go on?" whenever he pulled

193

rabbits out of hats. So he designed the voice-activated box out of which anyone can pull a butler!

Available from Mastervoice Inc., 10523 Humbolt St., Los Alamitos, CA 90720.

VOICEKEY

N o more searching purse or pockets for your keys to the house. The mere dulcet sound of your own voice will open doors of the future. That's the idea behind Ecco Industries' new security system— VoiceKey.

ODDS: 100%
ETA: 1991
PRICE: $1,200

Whether you're from the North, South, East, or West; whether you stutter, lisp, drawl, twang, or carefully modulate your words—it matters not to VoiceKey, a device that uses the individual patterns of each human voice as its combination for unlocking doors.

In this latest innovation in voice-verification technology, a user is "enrolled" in VoiceKey during a one-time 20-second procedure. A voice sample is spoken into a built-in microphone and then stored in the compact unit that mounts on the wall next to your door. The user also chooses a personal identification number and the password, which is spoken. To gain entry past the area VoiceKey guards, a user punches in his ID number and utters the password. In a half second, a decision will be made by VoiceKey to grant or deny access. Each time access is granted, the system updates the acoustic voice pattern of the user to reflect daily fluctuations.

Michael T. Dougherty, national sales manager for the company in Danvers, Massachusetts, explains that what makes a system such as this more effective than keys or cards is that, like fingerprints, no two voices are exactly alike. And while the voice reader allows for natural changes in the human voice—groggy, hung-over, a cold—it will not respond to recordings.

SMART SHADES

When it's hot outside, the window shades come down. And when it cools off, the shades go up.

The technology behind Smart Shades is really rather simple. A thermometer in a glass tube is positioned outside the window to monitor changing temperatures. "The system operates very much like a thermostat on an air-conditioning system," explains John Schnebly, chairman and technical director of Comfortex Corporation, the Cohoes, New York, manufacturer. You set the temperature at, say, 80 degrees, and when the thermometer hits 80, the shades lower. If the temperature drops, the shades go back up. Smart Shades are solar-powered, and one sunny day provides enough energy to run the shades for thirty cloudy days.

If privacy or life-style determine when your shades are up or down, the timer can be set to raise or lower them as many times as desired. Smart Shades are made of Duette fabric, an insulating polyester material, and they run along a geared track.

When computer-controlled "smart houses" come on the market, says Schnebly, his company will provide Smart Shades that are compatible, and in twenty colors, too!

WEED KICKER

John J. Terhune lives in Arizona's high desert near the Mexican border. He's a retired electronic engineer who still spends much of his time tinkering with labor-saving devices. His wife, Toshiko, comes from a long line of Japanese gardeners. It was her suggestion that inspired Terhune to develop a line of back-saving "foot" tools.

• • • • •
ODDS: 90%
ETA: 1992
PRICE: $20 PER SET
• • • • •

Where they live, the biggest problem is weeds. His wife was tired of bending over to pull out dandelions, so Terhune developed a little V-tip foot tool that attaches to a metal frame strapped to the toe of your shoe and extracts the unwanted weeds. A semicircular tool attachment complements the weed kicker. It will till the soil, dig trenches for drainage, and edge the lawn.

With the foot tools, both hands are free to push the lawn mower, or use the hose or rake. "It's particularly good for senior citizens," says Terhune, but the main advantage is saving your back and getting a little exercise while performing a useful task. "Oh yes, another advantage is that we're erect while gardening so we can wave hello to our neighbors as they drive by," adds the inventor.

What do the neighbors think? They use them all the time, just like Toshiko. Terhune now has a patent and is selling his device by mail order from 4852 Apache Ave., Sierra Vista, AZ 85635.

• • • • •

TOUCHLESS FAUCET

If you're concerned about hygiene or just like to conserve water, the touchless turn-on faucet from Mile High Precision Instrument Company is something you should know about.

• • • • •
ODDS: 100%
ETA: 1990
PRICE: $120–$170
• • • • •

The device, called Lampson's Automatic Mixing Faucet, runs on infrared technology: When hands or any other object are brought to within 4 to 6 inches of the tap, an infrared beam activates an electric valve that opens to unleash water. The flow automatically stops when the object is moved away.

The touchless faucet—completely dripless—is designed for water conservation. Says Gordon Lewis, general manager of Mile High Precision Instrument in Aurora, Colorado, "One hundred and fifty families of four can save a million gallons of water each year using this faucet just to brush their teeth." That's more than 6,000 gallons per family. The average brusher sends 3.5 gallons of water down the drain; with the touchless faucet, only a half gallon or less is expended.

The faucet also speaks to current life-style concerns about personal health and hygiene. "You're not going to be as exposed to as many colds or transmittable diseases if you're not coming into physical contact with the faucet," says Lewis. The faucets run on electricity. A 12-volt transformer plugs into a regular wall socket via a 12-foot cord.

Mile High Precision Instrument, exclusive distributor of Lampson's Automatic Mixing Faucet, has manufacturers working on a soap dispenser that would also operate via infrared beam. The company hopes to market its faucet, soap dispenser, and an infrared-activated hand dryer together as a package in 1990.

197

• • • • •

ROBOT LAWN MOWER

Hi ho, etc. Introducing the Lawn Ranger, a computer-guided robotic mower that behaves as though it has eyes and a brain. It's riding to the rescue of those summer afternoons when you'd rather be on a golf course than your own front lawn.

• • • • •
ODDS: 95%
ETA: 1992
PRICE: $900
• • • • •

Developed by Technical Solutions Incorporated of Sterling, Virginia, the Lawn Ranger has sensors that let it "see" where there's grass to be cut and the "know how" to get there. But first you have to guide the Lawn Ranger around the perimeter of your yard by using a joystick on the hand-held control panel. The Lawn Ranger takes over after that.

"What we have here is a computer that guides the mower, using sonar and sensors," explained Ray Rafaels, the mower's designer. "The sonar helps the mower detect obstacles in its path, and the sensors detect the height of the grass."

The Lawn Ranger will steer itself around the yard, mowing any area where the grass exceeds the height you have preset for the sensors. When the job is done, the Lawn Ranger automatically turns itself off.

Safety features include (1) a bumper switch that automatically shuts off the mower if contact is made with another object; (2) a remote cutoff switch that allows the operator to stop the motor from a distance; and (3) a sonar detector that steers the mower around trees and shrubs. The unit weighs 120 pounds, stands about 2 feet off the ground, and is rectangular in shape (about 3 feet by 2 feet).

Right now Rafaels and his partner, Jim Hammond, have a patent and a prototype and a lot of interest from large companies who want to put the Lawn Ranger into production. Hi ho . . . and away!

18

rent-a-cat
& other
essential
services

RENT-A-CAT

The Anderson Hotel in Wabasha, Minnesota, provides feline companionship on request to any guest. It's an idea that in pet-mad America (just think, pet cemeteries, schools, and gourmet foods) is liable to catch on. Hotel owner John Hall had the idea when a guest complained that he was

• • • • •
ODDS: 50%
ETA: 1993
PRICE: N/A
• • • • •

199

so lonely, even his wife's cat would be good company. Hall loaned him his housecat and a new hotel service was born.

Hall now has fifteen cats for loan. Each comes with its own litter box, food, and water bowl. Guests are lapping it up. Hall estimates that one in five who stay at the fifty-one-room hotel take the feline option. "The biggest problem we have with the cats is that we don't have enough! Every weekend, they're all out. They are as common as a bucket of ice would be in other hotels," says Hall.

Which makes one think that it won't be long until Holiday Inn and Ramada enter the business. There's no charge for cats at the Anderson Hotel. That may not be the case if the chains get in on the action.

CUSTOMIZED MUSIC CASSETTES

W hat we have here is a development that promises to revolutionize the way you buy recorded music. For just a little more than you now spend on an album, you will come home with one cassette tape bearing up to twenty-five songs that you, personally, have selected from

• • • • •

ODDS: 95%

ETA: 1990

PRICE: 50 CENTS–$1.25
PER SONG

• • • • •

the entire spectrum of recorded sounds. Only your favorites, professionally produced using Dolby technology, in just the order you'd like to hear them. And this can be done in under five minutes.

"It's an idea that has occurred to many people in their showers," says Charles Garvin, president of Personics Corporation and the man who turned the idea into a reality.

So, how do you make this reality yours? Just go to the record store and fill out an order form. Checking the catalogue section of Personic's monthly magazine, *Music Makers*, you fill in the names of your selections and their ID numbers in the order you want them. Then you hand the form to the clerk behind the counter. He punches in your selections on a high-speed-recording jukebox and, in less than five minutes, you get an album-length cassette tape complete with printed song titles, copyright info, your personal album title, and a matching cassette jacket. Furthermore, you can listen to a short segment of every song in the catalogue before you make your picks. Every store featuring the Personics system is equipped with both the jukebox recorder and a listening post. You just put on the headphones and punch in the ID numbers. Listening is free.

A boon to the consumer, the system also protects the rights of the artists. "As long as the system is being used, royalties are being generated," says Garvin.

Instituted with some 2,000 titles in fourteen categories, the current system is designed to offer up to 15,000. That's certainly enough for starters.

SMART CARDS

S mart Cards will replace most of the magnetic stripe cards you now carry in your wallet. You'll be able to use your Smart Card in any automatic teller machine to get cash or conduct any banking transaction. It will also be able to replace the variety of store and bank credit cards you now carry—up to sixteen of them.

ODDS: 95%

ETA: 1996

PRICE: FREE

"It's like a shopping center with sixteen different stores," explains Jerome Svigals, editor of the newsletter *Smart Cards and Comments*. "Once you enter a shop, the card will know just how to conduct itself." The card will know if you have enough money in your account to buy what you want. Hardware units in stores will read your smart card and not only approve your purchase; the transaction will be immediately registered in your account and onto your card. The card comes with safety precautions like any other credit card—the card won't open for transactions unless your personal code is entered, and

201

it can be cancelled or replaced if it is lost or stolen. You may want to purchase your own reader unit for home use ($50), so that you can check the status of your account at any time.

Credit-card companies are enthusiastic about Smart Cards because they will prevent you from exceeding your credit limit. Merchants will like them because they'll eliminate those time-wasting and annoying phone calls to check on your credit.

And you'll like them, too. With up-to-the-minute knowledge of your balance, you can avoid those embarrassing scenes when the salesclerk or waiter says, "Sorry, your card has been rejected!"

VISUAL SMART CARDS

These Smart Cards come with a built-in pocket calculator. They are "visual" because you can look at the mini-display screen and actually see your transaction take place.

ODDS: 95%

ETA: 1999

PRICE: $10–$20

There is a keyboard and a display unit just like a calculator. The cards still can be used in machines set up for magnetic stripe, but they don't need to be read by a hardware unit in stores when you buy something. Visual Smart Cards allow you to review your spending history and to authorize your own transactions without plugging into a machine or having a salesperson make a phone call. To authorize a purchase, all you do is punch in CREDIT-CARD MODE on your mini-keyboard. On the display screen the card will print HOW MUCH IS THIS TRANSACTION FOR? You input the value and hit the OK button. If there is enough money in your credit-card account to cover the purchase, then a six-digit authorization code will appear on the screen. If you don't have enough funds, you can then have the machine check to see if you can get credit beyond your limit. To complete the purchase, the salesperson simply copies the authorization number from your card onto a conventional credit-card slip and makes an imprint with your card.

Jerome Svigals, who developed the first magnetic stripe cards, says he's certain we'll all be using visual cards in the future. "They're already being tested by five different companies, and VISA has registered a name for them."

And what is the name? Super Smart Cards, of course.

COMPUTER SHOP-AT-HOME

By now you've heard about computer shopping. A couple of services tried it but failed in the early eighties. Still, one way or another, the opportunity to shop for goods and services from your home will be with us in the nineties. And a system called Prodigy is the one most likely to succeed.

· · · · ·
ODDS: 100%
ETA: 1992
PRICE: $10 PER MONTH
· · · · ·

Prodigy, already in eight markets and soon to be in more, is accessed through your home computer. You need a modem—the unit that transmits information over the phone wires—and a graphics card, both of which are available at your local computer store. A floppy disk that comes with the start-up kit automatically dials into the network of merchants. Once the modem is connected to your phone and the graphics card is adapted to your computer, just insert the software and you are on-line and ready to start spending money.

When you see the coat of your dreams come up on your screen, just hit the ACTION key. The store will process your order and deliver the coat to your door. You can even charge it to your account or to a credit card. And all this for the price of a phone call. You'll be charged for a local call on your phone bill, plus the monthly fee of $10. Information goes "from your computer, through our computer, and on to the retailer you're buying from," says Mike Darcy from Prodigy's headquarters in White Plains, New York.

203

Darcy tells us that, besides shopping from department stores, you can buy groceries, trade stocks, get stock quotes, make travel reservations, do your banking, and get news and sports information. You can even get expert advice on anything from household hints to what movies to see. The "experts" include Jane Fonda, Sylvia Porter, *American Health* magazine, and many others.

The bottom 20 percent of the Prodigy screen is all advertising. If you see an ad for something that interests you, just hit the LOOK button to get more information about the product. There will be ads for sales, too, so you won't miss out if you didn't have time to go through the Sunday papers.

DRIVE-BUY ADVERTISEMENTS

Does the world really need more advertising? Well, need or not, more is on the way. It's called Drive-Buy Radio, and it does have its advantages.

ODDS: 90%
ETA: 1990
PRICE: N/A

For example, if you're cruising for real estate—looking at houses or apartment buildings sporting FOR SALE or FOR RENT signs—you won't have to get out of your car to get the details. Instead, you'll tune your car radio to the setting indicated on the FOR SALE sign. On that station, you'll hear a description of the home, price, amenities, etc.

Drive-Buy Radio will, of course, work just as well for other kinds of products. An appliance store can promote a sale or your supermarket can announce specials. Passing motorists can tune in to find out the particulars.

Drive-Buy is the brainchild of INR Technologies of Canoga Park, California. A short-range radio transmitter the size of a clock radio broadcasts the prerecorded messages on an open FM radio channel

204

over a 400-foot radius. "So far, it has been most successful in the real-estate business," says Steven Rand, INR president.

SPY-SATELLITE PHOTOS

Did you know that anyone—you, your neighbor, your boss, the company you work for, the competition, an environmental group—yes, anyone can order spy satellite photographs?

ODDS: 100%

ETA: 1990

PRICE: $3,000 PER PHOTO

Christer Larsson and his colleagues at Space Media Network in Stockholm, Sweden, make satellite photos available to the public. Several countries had thought of the idea but got nowhere. Larsson *et al.* have done it privately with the help of a Swedish billionaire and philanthropist who agreed to absorb the $140,000 current losses each year until the spy-photo business gets off the ground. Their goal is a safer environment and world peace.

The first big wave-maker occurred when Space Media Network sold pictures of the 1986 Chernobyl disaster, thus forcing the Soviet Union to publicly acknowledge the catastrophe. But along with nuclear-disaster reporting, the pictures have been used to spot Chinese missile sites in Saudi Arabia, giant forest fires in China, and several military installations and nuclear test sites around the world.

The photos are immediately analyzed by international scientists, but often nothing is released for as much as a year until Space Media Network is sure of its findings.

Most of Space Media Network's customers are members of the press, but with its ability to photograph something as small as 30 feet across, businesses might want a peek at their competitors' factory behind the Iron Curtain or in Asia. The cost is a bit steep, but as more satellites go up, the cost of doing business in the spy-photo mart should start to descend.

205

DIAGRAMMATIC KNITTING INSTRUCTIONS

How many of you learned how to "knit one, purl two," create a popcorn stitch, even make fancy cables on a practice swatch, but never quite mastered the intricacies of following directions on knitting patterns? Well, with a little boost in the home-craft market, diagrammatic knitting instructions may help you save face.

ODDS: 70%

ETA: 1994

PRICE: SLIGHTLY MORE THAN OTHER INSTRUCTIONS

Six years ago, Estelle Leighton of New Paltz, New York, discovered she had a talent for crocheting. But although she crocheted up a storm, she never could follow any crocheting instructions. "They're very confusing," she says of conventional instructions. "I can't understand them. I thought if I could see it, I could understand it." Hence her patented instructions for both knitting and crocheting.

The diagrams show line by line what stitches are required for any item you might want to make. If a row of knit is required, the instructions will show KKKKKKK. A row of purl: PPPPPPP. Each stitch can be color-coded for patterns. To indicate increasing a stitch, there would be two letters where there would usually be one. Decreases are marked in lower case, and so on.

Leighton says the diagrams work for beginners. Even Charles Blaich, a first-time knitter who is helping to market her invention, knitted a piece just by following Leighton's instructions. Yarn companies have been very encouraging, as have editors at knitting magazines, but this knit-by-letter technique has not yet received the backing it needs. "The industry is at an all-time low with so many women out working. They don't have the time for crafts," Leighton surmises.

206

But with so many economists forecasting a slowdown in the economy, Mrs. Leighton's helpful instructions may soon take off as people start to spend more time at home.

VENDING MACHINE FRENCH FRIES

Seven years ago, while recovering from open-heart surgery, William Bartfield, a Palm Springs accountant and inventor, found himself reading the classifieds out of boredom. A two-line ad offering a french-fried-potato vending machine at a "sacrifice price" of $200 caught his eye. Recognizing the potential for automated Americana, he bought the machine.

• • • • •
ODDS: 100%
ETA: 1991
PRICE: 75 CENTS–$1.00
• • • • •

Five million dollars and countless hours of research and testing later, Bartfield is ready to offer the world Prize Frize. Others had tried and failed with the coin-operated french-fry concept because they hadn't figured out a way to eliminate potato storage and spoilage problems. Bartfield's quest for a solution took him to Twin Falls, Idaho, where a casual conversation with a fellow hotel guest gave him the answer he needed: submarine powder. Submarine powder, explains Bartfield, is a concentrated potato product manufactured by San Francisco Basic American Foods for use on U.S. Navy submarines and other small vessels, where galley space is limited and spoilage is a key concern.

Armed with the exclusive rights for the use of Basic American's potato product in vending machines, Bartfield and his partners then designed a computerized vending system. When a customer drops 75 cents into the slot, the dehydrated potato is sent into the mixing chamber, where it is showered with hot water, extruded into french-fry shapes, cooked, allowed to drain, and then put into a serving cup, which holds in its recessed bottom ketchup and salt. All this is controlled by microprocessors which can simultaneously track two orders, ensure that fresh oil is constantly added to the fryer, and perform self-diagnoses if the machine malfunctions.

Bartfield envisions a world in which Prize Frize machines go where other vending dispensers are—and aren't: cafeterias, bars, even car washes.

207

MUSIC THERAPY

I t's taken the world nearly three hundred years to catch up with the advice of William Congreve, who eloquently pointed out that "Music hath charms to soothe a savage breast."

What Congreve obviously meant was that the right tune could alleviate tension, stress, anger, anxiety, or depression. Perhaps the most modern application of music therapy is the Biosonics System, the creation of Indiana educator Jerry Hampton.

. . . . .
ODDS: 100%
ETA: 1990
PRICE: $900 PER 4-WEEK TREATMENT; $16,900 FOR THE SYSTEM
. . . . .

"Science," states Hampton, "has proven that frequencies found pleasurable automatically induce relaxation. Likewise, unpleasant frequencies involuntarily increase tension." Putting the advice of poetry and science into practice, Hampton devised a type of musical massage.

Soothing frequencies are heard and felt as one lies in a darkened room on a therapeutic table suspended within a geometrical, aluminum, resonating frame called a Vector. Through wireless sensors, the Biosonics System monitors the patient's electromagnetic field—or aura—to determine which music relaxes the patient. The volume of this music is then increased, encouraging the patient to "think pleasant thoughts."

A series of seminars or experiential workshops is conducted in conjunction with the therapy so that individuals can learn to reduce their stress levels away from the clinic. Called the Discovery Program, the whole package of music massage and "stress mastering" takes four weeks to complete and costs $900.

208

"This is not a panacea or a quick fix for what may have taken years for an individual to develop psychologically or physiologically," notes Hampton, who is president of Innovation of Indiana, the marketing company for the Biosonics System. "It is intended to create a pleasant environment for self-learning and stress-reduction through the magic of music."

Currently Biosonics "personal-growth centers" can be found only in Indiana and New Orleans. But Hampton's concept seems to be catching on. By 1990, there should be other centers in Florida, Nevada, and Colorado.

19

looking good, feeling good

KISS MOISTURIZER

A t last, relief from the turnoff of a dry kiss!

Actually, the process is pretty scientific and has applications far beyond lipstick and a good kiss. The key is a "micro-sponge," a microscopic, synthetic sphere that can be programmed to release cosmetic or pharmaceutical agents

• • • • •
ODDS: 95%
ETA: 1991
PRICE: $4.50
• • • • •

211

in response to pressure, time, or temperature. In other words, when you pucker, your lips get moist.

Microsponges are the brainchild of Advanced Polymer Systems of Redwood City, California, and the process, called "Command Release," has been licensed to a cosmetic firm, Pavion Ltd. of Nyack, New York. The collaboration will result in the first remoisturizing lipstick.

Soon to be available at your drugstore, the lipstick not only will remoisturize but will renew its color all day long when you press your lips together.

ELECTRONIC DEODORANT

Drionic, an electronic sweat-control device, will relieve perspiration problems for the 26 percent of our population that suffers from profuse sweating. It may someday also relieve us of endless, nauseating deodorant commercials.

ODDS: 100%
ETA: 1990
PRICE: $125

Users administer a series of approximately twelve half-hour treatments to obtain about six weeks of sweat-free protection. From then on, it's two to three treatments for six weeks of protection. The process employed is called iontophoresis, which has been university-tested and FDA-released. Iontophoresis stops emotion-related heavy perspiration by causing hyperkeratotic (thickening of a particular layer of the skin) plugs to form in sweat ducts. Studies have shown that when excess sweating of the hands, feet, and underarms is stopped, there is no effect on the body's thermoregulation.

Drionic is here now. It is available with a prescription at a limited number of pharmacies or from the manufacturer, General Medical Company in Los Angeles, California. It should be widely available within a couple of years. The Drionic battery-operated devices come in shapes that fit under your arms, hands, or feet. Each pair costs $125.

SUPER PORE CLEANER

From the dermatologist who brought you Retin-A comes a new cosmetic skin treatment that cleans pores more completely than any treatments currently on the market. It's like having a professional come in and clean the rugs, or having the exterior of a building cleaned: The difference between the before and the after is amazing.

ODDS: 90%
ETA: 1990
PRICE: N/A

Retin-A, you will recall, is that wonder acne medicine that millions believe reduces facial wrinkles. Well, Dr. Albert M. Kligman's new discovery may not cause quite the same sensation, but for those who suffer the indignity of blackheads and the accompanying enlarged pores, a ten-minute treatment should bring relief.

What makes it so super? A substance similar to what is found in glue! (Now don't rush to the utility drawer and put glue on your face. That not only won't work, but it will hurt.) A liquid containing the key ingredient is applied to the skin—only by a trained professional for the time being. When it dries, it is peeled off, taking with it dirt, oil, and bacteria from the pores.

According to Kligman, it works best on blackheads, removing the debris that makes them look enlarged. It is effective before or after a blemish flare-up (okay, pimple) but not during. In other words, it is not for whiteheads, though it will help acne sufferers since it removes from open pores any excess oil and bacteria buildup. Compared to masques currently available, Kligman says his product is 100 percent better—or close to that. "Masques are not in the business of cleaning pores in the way that this product does."

According to the patent, "a little discomfort" and temporary red-dening is sometimes experienced, but the skin then becomes "healthy, clean and smooth."

WRINKLE-REDUCING PILLOW

Everyone knows that too much sun, too much worrying, and too much smiling can cause wrinkles, but now experts claim that even sleeping can damage the skin.

- - - - -

ODDS: 100%

ETA: 1990

PRICE: $80

- - - - -

Ordinary pillows—whether soft and fluffy or hard as a rock—put pressure on the face, thus stretching the tissue and eventually causing wrinkles. The Goodbye Sleeplines pillow is designed to alleviate that pressure, while providing proper support for the head. Billed as an alternative to collagen treatments, the pillow helps the skin maintain its tone and elasticity.

The 16-by-23-inch rectangular pillow has a hollow center cut out in a shape that improves the circulation of blood to the face. Since most people sleep on their sides, they put pressure on their faces, says Carol Bianco, executive vice president of the Sleeplines Division of La Jeunesse, a Kirkland, Washington, company. "You're pressing in creases every night, and they become increasingly more pro-nounced. It's almost like ironing in the same wrinkles every time you lie down."

The product was invented by Kerry Lake, an interior designer, who noticed that she never looked her best for breakfast meetings. So, Ms. Lake designed a foam support that didn't press against her skin. In a short time, she was looking a lot better in the early A.M.

The pillow is also ideal for anyone recovering from facial or dental surgery, Bianco says. "There's no pressure on the face, so healing is accelerated." One early user of the special pillow was face-lift veteran Phyllis Diller. Made of polymeric urethane foam, the pillow is also recommended for people who need optimal back and neck support, since it puts the spine in correct alignment for all sleeping positions.

Goodbye Sleeplines, which comes with an acetate satin pillowcase, is presently distributed through the Hammacher Schlemmer catalogue (1-800-543-3366) and a few retail stores.

LIVING SKIN EQUIVALENT

N o guarantees exist yet, but the chances are good that in the future we will be able to patch up our skin just like an old pair of jeans!

ODDS: 80%

ETA: 1996

PRICE: N/A

A former MIT biology professor, Dr. Eugene Bell, is producing living skin. Organogenesis, the company founded by Dr. Bell in Cambridge, Massachusetts, is not just growing skin cells; it is keeping the cells together in a total skinlike structure. According to Doug Billings, manager of corporate development for the publicly owned company, growing live skin cells is not the tricky part. "What makes us unique," claims Billings, "is that we have a patented process that allows us to create skin 'structure' from those cells, thereby making full-thickness skin." The patent involves collagen extracted from cows.

Reconstructive Tissue Filler (RCTF), one kind of skin the company grows, is a deep fatty tissue sometimes called "deep tissue." It is this tissue that could be used in plastic surgery to make certain parts of the body fleshier. However, animal trials have not yet been started for this purpose, leaving human application several years away.

The immediate focus of the company is on their Living Skin Equivalent (LSE) product, which uses the same cell culture technology as

215

RCTF. It is grown from cells in the outer layer of the skin, the epidermis, and from cells in the inner layer, the dermis. After successful animal trials, LSE is just now being tested for safety on humans.

So far LSE and RCTF have no color or odor and are unable to grow hair. The company is working on pigmentation of LSE so it can be used to replace scar tissue with a natural look.

Animal-rights activists will be glad to hear that except for skin grafting, the first applications of LSE will test the effects of certain chemicals on human tissue, dismissing the animals usually used for this purpose.

SUNTAN IN A BOTTLE

Worried about getting skin cancer? Your concern may soon fade away like last year's tan. With Melano-Tan, people may get a perfectly natural tan without exposing themselves to the sun or other harmful rays.

• • • • •
ODDS: 85%
ETA: 1995
PRICE: N/A
• • • • •

Scientists at the University of Arizona have now synthesized and patented a hormone that triggers the body to create a tan. Taken orally or applied to the skin as a cream, the hormone enters the bloodstream and stimulates melanocytes to produce melanin, the ingredient that makes your skin brown. It could take two weeks to produce a dark, uniform tan, and preliminary studies show that a Melano-Tan has no side effects—like aging the skin and cancer. It is expected to last at least as long as a regular tan.

With the depletion of the ozone layer and estimates of skin cancer attacking over 500,000 people a year, Dr. Mac E. Hadley, the endocrinologist who discovered the hormone, says a product like this could someday be necessary for survival.

Melano-Tan, which will need FDA approval, should be on sale by 1995. For those who believe you can't be too rich, too thin, or too tan—it can't get here too soon.

SUNBURN PROTECTION METER

A $20 device the size of a pocket cal-culator will be able to protect you from painful sunburn, ruined vacations, and severe skin damage.

ODDS: 95%

ETA: 1991

PRICE: $20

It's called the Sunsor UV Meter. Point it to the sun and it will measure the strength of the sun's ultraviolet rays. You may think you know how long you can lie in the sun without burning, but because on some days ultraviolet rays are stronger than on others, you're really only guessing.

The Sunsor UV Meter will electronically measure ultraviolet-ray strength on a scale from 1 to 120 and display its finding on an LCD screen. Generally speaking, a reading of 100 will reflect the sun's strength in mid-summer on a clear day at high noon in southern Florida. Now, if you get a reading of, say, 80, you turn the meter over and check the chart on the back. It will tell you in minutes how long until you will begin to burn. The chart is designed to indicate the effect of the sun's exposure on average, unprotected, untanned skin.

217

health

20

SONIC PAINKILLER

Throughout time some of the most intriguing discoveries have actually been accidents—look at penicillin and LSD. Now a Sicilian-born physical chemist with two hundred inventions to his credit may have serendipitously hit on

· · · · ·
ODDS: 95%
ETA: 1993
PRICE: N/A
· · · · ·

something that can relieve the intense, crippling pain of arthritis.

Dr. Alphonse Di Mino was investigating ways to reduce ohmic levels in electronic resistors. To test one of his theories, he built a device called a Sonotron, which combined low-frequency radio and audio waves. When the Sonotron is on, it throws off a neon-purple spark about the size and shape of a Tootsie Pop. It also generates a good deal of heat. On a lark, Dr. Di Mino decided to treat the arthritic pain in his hand using the spark as a sort of electronic heating pad.

219

To his amazement, the pain stopped instantly. Other informal trials with different arthritics yielded similar results. After several years of clinical testing in universities, researchers still aren't sure how or why it works, but their results indicate that the mysterious purple spark can ease lameness in horses and reduce the pain from arthritis in people.

Similar in size and shape to a stereo speaker, with the addition of an 8-inch, silo-shaped appurtenance, the Sonotron is being manufactured for use in doctors' offices, hospitals, and clinics. According to Dr. Di Mino, a smaller, less expensive model is under development for home use. He hopes to have it on the market by 1993.

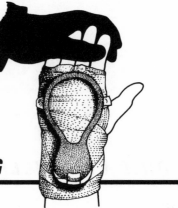

THE ELECTRONIC
BANDAGE DRESSING

Dr. Richard Bentall, a British surgeon, has created a disposable Electronic Bandage that will lend Mother Nature a hand by accelerating the body's natural healing process.

• • • • •

ODDS: 100%

ETA: 1995

PRICE: $10

• • • • •

Actually a mini electric system, the heart of which is about the size of a wristwatch, it speeds the body's natural healing process by pulsing electromagnetic radio waves into the cells of a wound. The Electronic Bandage can heal up to 30 percent faster, reduces swelling, and leaves less scar tissue.

As Dr. Bentall explains it, an injured cell is like a rechargeable battery that has gone flat. The device, manufactured by Bioelectronics Corporation of Washington, D.C., recharges the battery, so to speak, by introducing an electronic charge. It can help heal internal wounds as well as external ones, and is normally left on for ten to fourteen days after surgery.

The system, which Dr. Bentall expects will win FDA approval by 1990, will be available at first on a prescription basis and in hospitals for about $100. He is optimistic that the system will eventually be sold over the counter for a much lower price as production increases and costs go down.

X-RAY-LESS MAMMOGRAM

U p to now, the best way to detect breast cancer was to have an X-ray. But X-rays can cause the tissue to become cancerous. Result? Only 11 percent of the women who should be monitoring their breast tissue for cancer actually do.

ODDS: 100%

ETA: 1995

PRICE: $35 PER EXAM

Soon the detection method of choice will be an X-ray-less mammogram developed by Somanetics, a company in Troy, Michigan. Using harmless light rays, the INVOS 2100 System measures the chemical makeup of the breast tissue. The "likeliness" of an abnormal growth developing is indicated by a risk factor called the INVOS Value, which is available immediately. The system doesn't actually diagnose the situation; it determines the risk. "It measures the biochemistry of the breast to determine the likelihood of breast cancer developing or already existing," states David Weaver, vice president of the company. As for accuracy, when the system was originally tested, it detected 13 percent of cancers missed by conventional X-ray tests.

The new procedure is painless, harmless, low cost, and takes only five minutes. It can be performed as often as needed without causing any harm to your body. Although the system will be available mostly

221

in doctors' offices, look for breast clinics to provide this sort of testing as well. Please note: One woman in ten develops breast cancer in her life; early detection is the best cure.

NON-INVASIVE HOME GLUCOSE TEST

Millions of American adults and children suffer from diabetes. And while the disease can be controlled, it takes constant monitoring, insulin shots, and a special diet. To make life easier for diabetics, a new device is being developed that can measure glucose levels simply by being held against a person's skin.

ODDS: 90%
ETA: 1992
PRICE: N/A

And this may be just the beginning. Using the same technology, similar devices should be able to measure other chemicals in the blood, such as cholesterol and drugs.

The glucose tester has been developed by Biocontrol Technology Inc. in Indiana, Pennsylvania, with the assistance of Toronto's Hospital for Sick Children in Canada and the Battelle Memorial Institute in Columbus, Ohio. The device works by emitting a flow of energy directly into the patient's body tissue. The testing device registers numerically how the energy flow interacts with the tissue, indicating the glucose level in the body.

A large and expensive research instrument already exists. By 1991 there should be a smaller unit about the size of a briefcase. Researchers hope to reduce the size to a hand-held model by 1992.

HOME STREP TEST

Strep throat is more than a sore throat. It is most prevalent among children and if not treated can lead to rheumatic fever and eventually rheumatic heart disease. But kids come down with all sorts of colds and flus, so the doctor bills can

ODDS: 85%

ETA: 1990

PRICE: $30

get out of hand if you seek medical attention every time.

A number of drug companies are looking into home diagnostic tests—especially one for strep. Tambrands, a company known for consumer pharmaceuticals, has a test already set to go. "Everybody believes in the value of the test," says Paul Konney, a vice president. "The thing that takes time is satisfying the FDA that it can be used properly."

How does it work? Just like at the doctor's. You take a swab of the child's throat with a big Q-Tip. Put the swabbed Q-Tip into one solution, which prepares the antigen (toxin) to be detected, if present, and then into a color solution to which the strep antigen will adhere. Next, the color solution itself goes into a test cup with a filter that will reveal a blue spot if the antigen is present. A control spot of blue will also be present, provided all systems are go and the kit isn't faulty in any way. In other words, if two spots show up, take the kid to the doctor. If one spot appears, send the kid to bed with a cup of chicken soup. If no spot appears, take the kit back to the drugstore and exchange it for another one.

Konney goes on to say, "If this is approved, it will be the first home diagnostic for an infectious disease, leading to the possibility of home diagnostics for sexually transmitted diseases and AIDS."

223

HOME CHOLESTEROL TEST

No more going to the doctor to check your cholesterol level. Just prick your finger and a hand-held analyzer will give you a digital readout at home.

ODDS: 100%
ETA: 1991
PRICE: $10

There's just one problem with the cholesterol device—the price. People with diabetes need the constant monitoring provided by the glucose test; but there's not the same urgency to monitor cholesterol, so people aren't willing to pay the same price. Several companies are working to develop a home cholesterol test that's highly accurate and lower-priced. Tambrands, a pharmaceutical company in Lake Success, New York, is one of them. Paul Konney, Tambrands vice president, put it succinctly: "The cholesterol test has got to be cheaper—a few generations beyond the glucose test."

Tambrands is working on a number of approaches, according to Konney. When they find the right one, the home diagnostic cholesterol kit will sell in drugstores alongside a related device that monitors blood pressure at home.

VITAL SYSTEMS HOME MONITOR

Health diagnostics are bound to hit big in the nineties. But this home unit gives you more—a personal history of vital body functions.

ODDS: 25%
ETA: 1999
PRICE: N/A

224

Med Module monitors your weight, your blood pressure, and your pulse. With frequent use, it will work up a personal history so you can be made aware of gradual but significant changes in your body functions. "It's the collectivity or pattern of readings that's significant," says Bill Griffiths of General Computer Corporation. The patterns can indicate high blood pressure, hypertension, and weight loss or gain that might have gone unnoticed.

Each person who uses Med Module must have a personal magnetic stripe card. The card instructs the machine (about the size of a small desk) to open the user's health file. Current readings are displayed along with a history of those readings.

General Computer will soon be introducing Med Modules in health clubs and pharmacies. They're expensive—$9,000. "But with the cost of the technology going down, it may well be an in-home device in the future," says Griffiths.

POISON IVY VACCINE

Remember those wonderful camping trips that were ruined by a casual stroll into a patch of poison ivy? Well, by the summer of '94, a vaccine should, once and for all, put an end to the scourge of poison ivy.

• • • • •
ODDS: 50%
ETA: 1994
PRICE: N/A
• • • • •

Dr. Vera Byers, a medical researcher at the University of California in San Francisco, has isolated the oil that causes poison ivy. The oil is called urushiol and is also prevalent in poison sumac, poison oak, and in the Japanese lacquer plant. It is well known among dermatologists and allergists—though not among the rest of us, according to Byers—that if you feed a person the oil for three months in gradually increased doses, the person will lose sensitivity to the poisonous plants. The problem is that the "cure" lasts for only one year. And the taste? "It's nasty," says Byers. "It comes in a green concentrate and tastes like motor oil."

Three months of increasing amounts of a vile taste is a high price

225

to pay for one year of immunity to poison ivy. So Byers took her medical know-how and invented a vaccine that is injected into the arm—one time only. It could be good for one year, and for the 80 percent of the American population that is sensitive to poison ivy and its relatives, this will bring relief.

Byers, in collaboration with Dr. William Epstein, has also developed a poison-ivy block that is applied like sun block to parts of the skin that might be exposed. A chemical in the poison-ivy block absorbs the urushiol oil, preventing it from contacting the skin.

The Food and Drug Administration will demand some fancy testing and long clinical trials before these products are allowed on the market because, says Byers, "they want to be sure you can't get any other viruses from them."

THE STING BUSTER

Every year, some two hundred people in the United States die from insect bites. Millions more suffer stings. Now a company in Oregon, Tec Laboratories, Inc., has come up with a small solution to this big problem.

· · · · ·
ODDS: 100%
ETA: 1991
PRICE: $5
· · · · ·

The Sting-X-tractor is a 3-inch-long, hand-held vacuum pump that eliminates the poison from insect bites or stings by suctioning out the venom that bees, wasps, hornets, fleas, mosquitoes, spiders, and scorpions leave behind. Steve Smith, Tec Laboratories' vice president, explains that the Sting-X-tractor works along the same lines as a syringe—minus the needle. Placed over the bite, a powerful but painless sucking motion made by drawing up on the mini-pump will bring the venom—often not much more than would fit on the head of a pin—to the surface of the skin. You then wash it off with soap and water. The Sting-X-tractor also removes stingers, such as those left behind by honeybees.

226

Removing the venom before it has the chance to spread to the rest of the body reduces and, in most cases, eliminates the itching of untreated insect stings, states Smith. However, he adds, if a sting victim has a known allergic reaction to stings or show signs of anaphylaxis, he should not rely solely on the Sting-X-tractor but seek medical attention immediately.

The Sting-X-tractor will be made available first in selected locations on the West Coast, in the Southeast and the Southwest.

SMOKE-CHECK BADGE

The Smoke Check badge should settle a few arguments. If you don't smoke and your spouse does, you'll be able to tell just how polluted your home is. At work, if you're in a nonsmoking cubicle but a colleague in the next space is puffing away, you'll be able to determine how much smoke is wafting over to your area.

ODDS: 100%

ETA: 1990

PRICE: $9.95 PER 3-PACK

The badge is a disposable device that turns from pale yellow to deeper shades of brown as it registers accumulated exposure to tobacco smoke in the air. It was developed by Assay Technology of Palo Alto, California, a company that manufactures industrial products to measure toxic chemical levels in the workplace.

What Smoke Check can't do is give you a reading in minutes or even hours, so it won't settle that argument in a restaurant between a smoker and a nonsmoker. It takes three to five days for an accurate reading on low-level exposure.

The product is presently available through the manufacturer in quantities of thirty or more.

227

FOUR NEW WAYS TO QUIT SMOKING

A s society grows increasingly intoler-
ant of cigarette smoking, it is also
finding out just how serious the addiction
can be. According to Dr. Jed Rose of the
Nicotine Research Laboratory run by
U.C.L.A. and the Veterans Administra-
tion Medical Center in Los Angeles, researchers are hard at work on
four innovative techniques for helping smokers to kick the habit.

· · · · ·
ODDS: 80%
ETA: 1992
PRICE: N/A
· · · · ·

Two of these are called habit/sensory replacement techniques, in
that they let you maintain the habit of smoking while reducing your
nicotine addiction. The first is a fine mist made from smoke dissolved
in water, which, when inhaled either through an imitation cigarette
or a device resembling an asthma inhaler, feels and tastes like smoke.
Very little of the mist reaches the lungs, settling mostly in the mouth
and throat. Administered as often as one would smoke, the mist
contains only one-twentieth of the tar and nicotine of a cigarette and
none of the carbon monoxide.

A citric-acid spray is the second of these. It would be administered
like the smoke-flavored mist and would create the same feeling as
smoke at the back of the throat.

A small adhesive patch that slowly and steadily delivers nicotine
to the blood vessels through the skin is also in development. The
patch, replaced daily, would eliminate nicotine-withdrawal symp-
toms, especially irritability.

Another innovation involves delivering nicotine through a nose
spray or an inhaler. Because it can irritate the nose and throat,
however, the nicotine is microencapsulated in liposomes—natural
substances found in the human lungs—in the form of tiny bubbles
that are suspended in solution. This way the nicotine slips by irritation
receptors in the throat and windpipe and is absorbed in the lungs.

Dr. Rose feels that some patients would benefit, in the beginning,
from a combination of a nicotine-replacement and a habit/sensory

228

replacement method, eventually quitting first one and then the other for good.

These four methods of weaning smokers from their habit are in various stages of development and will gradually become available to the public over the next five years. The nicotine-replacement devices will probably require FDA approval and a doctor's prescription, as nicotine is considered a drug. The other two could most likely be sold over the counter.

STRESS GUM

Stress gum is used by the Japanese as a quick and easy way of determining the state of their health and nerves. The gum reacts with the body's pH level to indicate the level of stress. After a few minutes of chewing, the user checks the color of the gum. Pink is a sign of health; green a signal that the user is suffering from unhealthy stress.

• • • • •
ODDS: 50%
ETA: 1995
PRICE: 65 CENTS
FOR 6 PIECES
• • • • •

In Japan, six pieces of gum sell for 65 cents. Right now, the manufacturer, S. B. Shokauhin Inc. of Tokyo, has no plans to market the product in the United States. However, with Americans increasingly interested in monitoring their own health, stress gum is a natural for these shores.

229

• • • • •

LE FUNELLE

In her own way, Lore Harp has done more for the women's liberation movement than others have in years. By inventing Le Funelle, a paper funnel with a scoop-like mouth and an easy-to-hold handle, women can now approach the toilet like a man—upright.

• • • • •
ODDS: 100%
ETA. 1991
PRICE: $4.99 FOR A
PACKET OF 10
• • • • •

Ms. Harp, who used to travel several hundred thousand miles a year for her microcomputer company, had had her fill of dirty public restrooms and worry about contracting a disease. "I was fed up with hovering over filthy toilet seats to avoid contact with them. I thought there has to be a better way," she explained.

There was. Le Funelle, which is based on your average kitchen funnel, is treated with a special coating and packaged with a sheet of toilet paper. It dissolves when flushed and is also biodegradable for hikers and campers who'd need to bury or burn it. But it's not just for business travelers or outdoorswomen. The elderly and handicapped, who have difficulty sitting and then standing, can also benefit from the device.

Ms. Harp, whose product is currently sold in drug stores and travel stores primarily on the West Coast, says consumer education is now her foremost concern. "People laugh when you talk about the product because what you're really speaking about is something personal and private. This product is going to involve some complex marketing. We have to overcome the resistance to talking about normal bodily functions and needs."

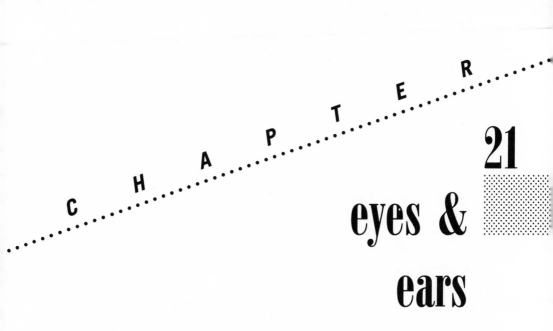

CHAPTER 21

eyes &
ears

TV EYEGLASSES

Farsighted researchers are taking the high-tech track to better vision with televisions so tiny they fit into eyeglasses.

ODDS: 75%
ETA: 1993
PRICE: N/A

Johns Hopkins's Wilmer Eye Institute and NASA are collaborating on an ingenious technology that will help people with uncorrectable or inoperable eye problems, such as tunnel vision, blind spots, peripheral field blindness, and night blindness.

Fiber optics, set in the bridge of the glasses, convey the image in front of the wearer to TV cameras and pump it through a battery-operated power pack worn at the hip or the shoulder. The images are computerized through the power pack and sent back to the glasses, to be displayed on little solid-state TV screens set into both the right and left lenses. "There will be one TV for each lens, to allow for

231

binocular, as opposed to monocular, viewing," says Marie Leinhaas, research associate with the Wilmer Eye Institute. "Most viewing aids today have the patient use whichever eye is better."

Because eyes move but glasses don't, the researchers are developing infrared eye trackers to stabilize the images. The images will appear in real time, and will be custom-tailored to meet the needs of the viewer by programming the computerized power pack for light/dark contrast and magnification. "Instead of looking at the world the way you and I do, the patient will see reality readjusted on the screen to compensate for his or her vision deficiencies," says Leinhaas.

Researchers still have to work out a few kinks, not the least of which is making the glasses "lightweight and cosmetically acceptable," says Leinhaas. A prototype of the first low-vision eyeglass device should be ready within a couple of years, and the Wilmer Eye Institute hopes to have the glasses available to the public on a limited basis by 1993. The price will be affordable to "the average aging person on a fixed income," says Leinhaas.

EYE BRACES

They're called intracorneal rings, they work much the same way on eyes as braces do on teeth, and they could eliminate eyeglasses and contact lenses.

Quite simply, a thin corneal ring will flatten the cornea to correct nearsightedness. A tighter ring will steepen the cornea to correct farsightedness. And any ring at all will round out the shape of the eye to correct astigmatism, caused by an oval eye shape.

According to Thomas M. Loarie, of KeraVision, Inc., the company

· · · · ·
ODDS: 75%

ETA: 1994

PRICE: $2,000
· · · · ·

developing the intracorneal rings, the device is placed in the cornea much like braces are placed on teeth. The rings can be removed at any time, they will cause no interference with normal eye functioning, and they could stay in indefinitely. This would mean no lost lenses, no cleansers, no discomfort. The rings will be surgically implanted by a physician on an outpatient basis. The procedure will cost $2,000, a steep price, but, compared to a lifetime of buying contact lenses or glasses, probably a bargain.

The rings are being tested successfully on animals, and with approval from the FDA, human testing could begin by late 1989. "Everybody is optimistic," says Loarie.

FISH-EYE LENS

The copilia, a very rare copepod— that's crustacean to you—found in the Bay of Naples and the Caribbean, is the inspiration for a new fish-eye lens that could give millions of legally blind people the chance to see. The lens will gather light like no other lens ever devised by man.

ODDS: 100%

ETA: 1991

PRICE: N/A

According to its developer, Professor Jerome J. Wolken of Carnegie-Mellon University, the lens is designed to take advantage of the way undersea creatures see while living in depths of 500 to 1,500 feet in almost total darkness. Over millions of years the lenses in their eyes have evolved to gather short flashes of light emitted by their neighbors as they move. "Using this type of lens held in an eyeglass frame," Professor Wolken says, "a visually impaired person can begin to see the world."

233

The lens, ten times more sensitive to light than a normal camera lens, is actually two lenses in one. The primary lens provides magnification, while the secondary "fish-eye" lens built behind it, as close to the eye as possible, collects the light. The lens, manufactured in glass or plastic, is being tested with encouraging results at low-vision clinics and schools for the visually-impaired in Pittsburgh and Philadelphia. As long as the optic nerve and even just part of the retina are functional, the lens works.

TIME-RELEASE EYE DROPS

Anyone who's had the misfortune of eye problems knows that administering the cure—usually in the form of eye drops—can be pure torture. Half the time you miss, and when you finally do get a drop in, it stings so much your eyes

ODDS: 100%
ETA: 1990
PRICE: N/A

well up with tears. When they overflow, up to 80 percent of the solution runs down your face or, worse, the back of your throat. Besides being nasty for the patient, this catch-as-catch-can administration is a serious problem when it comes to determining proper dosage. To the rescue: the soluble ophthalmic drug insert, SODI.

The inserts are made of a biodegradable polymer matrix permeated with various drugs used to treat an assortment of disorders, from simple infections to glaucoma. SODIs are roughly the size and shape of a Tic Tac mint, and are easier to insert than contact lenses. (Once they're in position under the lower eyelid, they're virtually impossible to feel.) The plastic is designed to dissolve over a period of twenty-four hours, steadily and predictably releasing medication. Because SODIs are time-released, patients don't have to apply drops ten or twelve times a day. And because the drug is reliably delivered, drugs can be used in much smaller concentrations and thus less likely to cause further irritation.

The implants were invented by Soviet scientists in the late 1970s to treat a disorder common among cosmonauts—conjunctivitis, caused by intense glare in space. In zero gravity, drops are useless, but inserts were found to work beautifully. The U.S. distributor,

234

Diversified Tech Inc. of Salt Lake City, Utah, plans to manufacture SODIs in the United States by 1990.

TELESCOPIC EYEGLASSES

A n accident at birth left Brandon Edwards with optic nerve damage so severe it rendered him, while not blind, incapable of fully operating in a sighted world. But it was no accident—just years of hard work—that led this Virginian to invent a vision-improvement device called a bi-level telemicroscopic apparatus, or BITA.

• • • • •
ODDS: 100%
ETA: 1991
PRICE: $2,200–$3,000
• • • • •

"I don't compete in a blind man's world; I compete in a sighted man's world," says Edwards, who, while in college fifteen years ago, began work on glasses that would help him pass his driver's license test. At age thirty, using the BITA eyeglasses, he received the license.

Today Edwards, a former teacher, devotes all his time to his Virginia Beach company, Edwards Optical Corporation, and improving and expanding upon the BITA vision system. The glasses have tiny telescopes built into the lenses, which are shaded to camouflage the 'scopes. Unlike other corrective optical devices, the BITA glasses do not force the wearer to give up depth perception, spacial orientation, or peripheral vision. Each of the 'scopes, which come in different magnifications, weighs less than a paper clip. In an effect akin to that of bifocals called Simul-vision, the BITA wearer will see two images: a regular field of view below the telescope and a magnified image of the field's center portion above.

235

Insurance will generally help cover the cost of the BITA glasses, which can only be fitted by a trained optometrist. "I'm not saying these glasses are a panacea," says Edwards. "There are some vision problems the BITA system just can't help. But when they work, they work extremely well."

HOLOGRAPH BIFOCAL CONTACT LENSES

A bifocal contact lens that uses holo-graphic technology should arrive on these shores from Britain early in the new decade. For people who need one lens for ordinary vision and another for reading, these new lenses are going to make life a lot easier.

ODDS: 95%
ETA: 1991
PRICE: $410

You've no doubt seen holographs. Most credit cards now have holograph double images that change as you move the card. Well, these hard contacts, called Diffrax, are etched with concentric rings that split incoming light and also make two images that have equal intensity but different focal points. Your brain will instinctively pick the proper image on which to focus, depending on where you're looking. There are currently other bifocal contact lenses on the market, but they work by dividing their surface into two separate lenses. They don't allow for a full range of vision and create a blurry image under certain conditions.

Pilkington Contact Lenses Ltd., the Surrey, England, manufacturer, has successfully tested the new lenses for two years. Diffrax lenses are easily fitted and take about a week to get used to.

DIGITAL HEARING AID

I f you've never had a hearing problem, you won't know what an advance this is. People who say they can't hear usually have difficulty deciphering sounds within certain frequency ranges. Conventional hearing aids use tiny microphones that, when turned up, cause every sound around to sound louder as well.

ODDS: 100%

ETA: 1990

PRICE: $1,500

Enter 3M—the purveyors of adhesive tapes—with something called a digital-analog hybrid hearing aid that allows you to select which sounds will be amplified. The MemoryMate hearing aid is worn behind one or both ears and can be custom-programmed for use in up to eight different "listening situations."

Bill Schnier, marketing manager for 3M Hearing Health, suggests a listener might want to eliminate city street noises, background music at parties, or background voices in a crowded room. "If you're at a concert," he says, "you could eliminate some nearby distractions and concentrate on just hearing the music." Should your hearing requirements change, you can quickly have your MemoryMate hearing aid reprogrammed to change all or some of your eight "listening situations." These different environmental settings are programmed by a computer that is controlled by your audiologist (or whoever sells you your hearing aid) according to your individual life-style. By pressing a button on your hearing aid, you can switch from one "listening situation" to another as it suits your need.

The next step to aid the hearing impaired will be a device similar to the MemoryMate aid, but one that adjusts automatically.

237

THE NOISE CANCELER

The drone of a vacuum cleaner. The buzz of a power saw. The grind of a lawn mower. Noise. Who needs it? A quieter world will soon be ours with a new technology that cancels out noise by counteracting it with electronically produced anti-noise waves. The principle has been known to scientists for years but was impossible to apply to the workaday world until recent advances in microprocessor technology opened the door.

ODDS: 100%
ETA: 1993
PRICE: N/A

"We now have the technology to effectively eliminate low-frequency repetitive noise and vibration," says Frank Siciliano, sales representative at Noise Cancellation Technologies in New York. The company has developed the NCT 2000, an industrial noise and vibration control system that electronically analyzes noise, then matches it precisely with an anti-noise wave to produce silence. An anti-noise wave is one which is exactly 180 degrees out of phase with the original noise wave and thus cancels it out.

Consumer applications of the noise control system will be developed on the prototype of an electronic muffler system for cars and trucks. Not only will the muffler serve to quiet the car, but it will relieve the vibration pressure on the engine, thereby prolonging the life of the motor, says Siciliano, adding that the muffler should be available in 1991 models of some cars.

Noise Cancellation Technologies will also be applying the technology to home products such as vacuum cleaners, lawn mowers, and snowblowers possibly within the next three years.

The one application which will have to wait is nullifying irregular noises—radio, television, children, etc.—in the home. The current technology can only gauge and match the consistent level of noise from machinery. It is not advanced enough yet to predict what Siciliano calls "random, or background" noises. However, "eventually, way way down the road, we hope we can use those applications," he says.

THE NOISE METER

More and more attention is being paid to noise pollution. But it's hard to know when you've been exposed to too much. Instruments exist that measure general noise levels in an area, but a person's ear receives 60 percent more

. . . . .
ODDS: 100%
ETA: 1998
PRICE: $500
. . . . .

screeching, drilling, hammering, and rock 'n' roll than whatever level is measured in an open environment. To accurately represent the decibels heard by the naked ear, a company in England has made an instrument called a Personal Noise Dosemeter. It is portable, small, and lightweight. The main unit fits in your pocket or clips onto a belt. A small microphone permanently attached to the dosemeter is mounted also with a small clip near the wearer's ear.

Dose percentage is displayed on a bright digital readout screen that can register from zero to 99.99 percent. At 100 percent, you have the maximum allowable exposure—set by the user according to a chart. If you switch it off, the instrument will store the dose last registered for up to several hours.

The Noise Dosemeter will mostly be used on the job at building and road sites and in factories, but parents, take heart, this item will provide long-needed evidence in the case against loud rock 'n' roll.

239

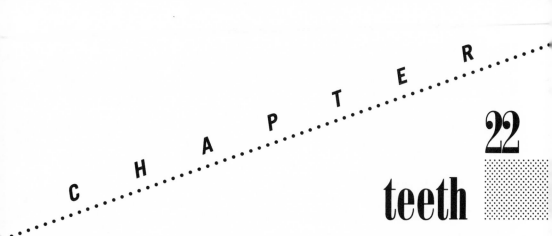

teeth

ANTICAVITY PILL

Medical researchers are saying that the anticavity pill will wipe out tooth decay with the same thoroughness that the polio vaccine eliminated that crippling disease.

ODDS: 70%
ETA: 1999
PRICE: N/A

But according to Dr. Richard Gregory, assistant professor of oral biology at Atlanta's Emory University, there is still considerable research to be done before the pills are on the market. The basic premise, he explained, is that the streptococcus mutans—the name of the whole bacteria that causes tooth decay—has a variety of antigens that collect on the outer wall of the bacteria cell. The research is isolating which antigen or which sets of antigens would be most effective in the vaccine.

Successful tests were first conducted on rats and monkeys, who

241

develop cavities at a faster pace than the eighteen months it takes for humans. A second set of successful tests has now been completed on sixteen humans. The Food and Drug Administration will require at least three more studies. They will "take their time," according to Dr. Gregory, to be sure there are no side effects, meaning that it will probably be around the turn of the century before the pills are approved.

For those who don't like taking pills, the same research will make plaque-fighting milk possible. Cows immunized with the vaccine produce a milk rich in antibodies that work against the bacteria, Dr. Gregory explained. When the milk was fed to rats, they were protected against cavities. "We envision this milk freeze-dried and used in food products."

TIME-RELEASE FLUORIDE PELLETS

C avity-prone? Concerned about better oral hygiene? Tired of the same old rinse-and-spit routine? Take one fluoride pellet and see your dentist in six months.

ODDS: 95%
ETA: 1993
PRICE: $5–$10

For years it has been accepted knowledge that frequent exposure to fluoride helps to eliminate tooth decay. If the United States National Institute of Dental Research has its way, by the mid-1990s these pellets, called Intraoral Fluoride Releasing Devices, should be part of life for millions of people.

The pellet is one-half the size of an aspirin tablet and filled with fluoride. According to Dale Mirth, a research chemist at the institute who worked on the device, a simple, painless, twenty-minute procedure in your dentist's office will be all it takes to attach the pellets comfortably to the side of a molar or bicuspid on both sides of the mouth.

Once inconspicuously in place, saliva triggers a reaction releasing measured amounts of the fluoride into the mouth. Each pellet lasts six months and is easily replaced.

Mirth and his colleagues envision the device initially being used by high-risk groups such as brace wearers or others with handicaps who find it difficult to keep teeth clean. But it is highly conceivable that someday everyone will be using these revolutionary anticavity pellets.

COMPUTER-DESIGNED DENTAL CROWNS

A ny invention that will save a trip to the dentist is okay in our book. So the University of Minnesota's new computer-designed dental crown, which eases pain and eliminates an appointment, is certainly good news.

ODDS: 99%

ETA: 1990

PRICE: $400

In the future, photographs—rather than impressions—will be taken of the injured tooth. These will be digitized to create a three-dimensional model of the crown on a computer screen. Software will then instruct a milling machine how to make the crown.

The process is less expensive, because stainless-steel and precast ceramics are used instead of gold and unformed ceramics. And perhaps best of all, the whole process takes about an hour, eliminating the need for a temporary crown and a second dental appointment.

Your dentist will need to spring for the whole system ($150,000) so he can manufacture the crown right in his office. Otherwise, he'll send it to a central laboratory and you'll have to come back for another visit.

PAINLESS DENTIST DRILL

S ince there are no "good" vibrations when it comes to the dentist's drill, *no* vibrations at all will be a major improvement. That's right, no high-power buzzing, no pain, no squirming; in short—no drilling!

ODDS: 90%

ETA: 1997

PRICE: N/A

Pfizer Laser Systems is working on the last details of a laser instrument that would replace the drill. The company already has been successful with a laser tool used for gum surgery. The trick to using the same technology on hard tooth enamel is getting the right amount of power—too much power can crack the tooth.

Pfizer's Barbara Pringle says the laser drill will "remove decay, seal fissures in an effort to prevent decay, and even seal any open ends after a root canal to prevent infection and/or the need for any repeat root canal." Great—but will it hurt? "Patients will feel maybe a slight heat sensation, but nothing else. Psychologically, the patient will love this."

The laser drill weighs only half a pound and is connected to a power console that weighs less than 10 pounds. A dentist in Paris, France, is already using a similar instrument. Pfizer plans to get FDA approval for use here as soon as possible.

safety

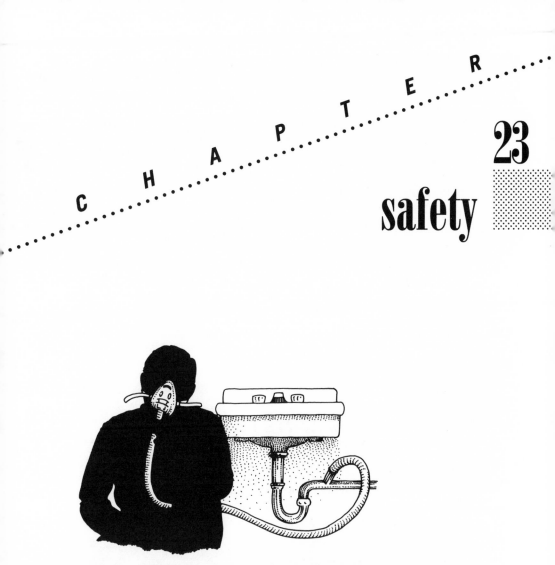

FIRE EMERGENCY LIFELINE

The vast majority of fire-related deaths are not caused by contact with fire but by smoke inhalation.

When fire fighter and licensed plumber Ray Tannatta of Schenectady, New York, found one such victim collapsed in the bathroom of a burning apartment building, he realized that an unlimited supply of air was just inches away in the drainpipe of the sink. "There's breathable air in the pipes under every sink in every bath-

ODDS: 100%

ETA: 1990

PRICE: $40

room," says Tannatta, who has invented the Llifeline, a breathing device that consists of two plastic air masks connected to a seven-foot hose. In a fire emergency, this hose can be hooked up to a sink drainpipe, allowing two people to acquire air through the pipe while awaiting rescue.

"The air in drainage lines is safe to breathe," says James Lunny, vice president of Llifeline Services Ltd. in Schenectady, the exclusive manufacturer and distributor of the product. Each is equipped with an activated carbon filter to prevent inhalation of any noxious fumes.

Llifeline is available in two models, one for home installation in high-rise buildings and the Travel-Safe model for the frequent traveler. The latter, which will be sold in hotel and airport shops, packs easily into a suitcase.

PANIC-ALARM WRISTWATCH

C onsidering the crime rate and the fact that watches today can do just about anything, it's surprising that this kind of alarm watch didn't arrive years ago.

The watch is really simple. A battery-powered siren is set off when the wearer opens the wristband or an attacker knocks it loose. The watch comes off easily, as the band has a Velcro fastener.

. . . . .
ODDS: 90%
ETA: 1991
PRICE: $30
. . . . .

The inventor is Nathan Feigenblatt, a retired safety engineer who lives in Tucson, Arizona. Feigenblatt patented the watch back in 1986 but as yet has no manufacturer to produce it.

246

. . . . .

BOLA-SNARE

It makes more sense than Mace and it's safer than a gun. It's called Bola-Snare, and it should give would-be muggers and robbers fits.

ODDS: 60%

ETA: 1994

PRICE: $60

This gas-operated device looks like a flashlight with a trigger. When you fire, four Teflon balls, each at the end of ten feet of flax/nylon string, are launched in a V formation. On contact, the twine wraps around the target like a spiderweb.

Bola-Snare's inventor, R. J. "George" Washington, a retired U.S. Navy bomb-disposal diver, is now seeking a distributor for his non-deadly weapon. "The best thing about the Bola-Snare," says Washington, "is that you protect yourself without seriously harming your target. Think of the wife who's home at night and mistakes her husband for a burglar. She hears strange noises coming from the kitchen, rushes in, and bashes him on the head with a baseball bat." That kind of domestic catastrophe can't happen with Bola-Snare. Nor can children spray it in each other's eyes like Mace. And no one can be accidentally killed cleaning the thing.

ELECTRICAL SHOCK HAZARD PROTECTOR

This invention won a National Safety Council award in 1987 for achievement in product safety. By the early nineties, it should actually arrive in your home. A little device with a big name—Immersion Detection Circuit Interrupter

ODDS: 100%

ETA: 1990

PRICE: N/A

247

(IDCI)—disconnects power when water is present in the current. In other words, if your hair dryer or radio falls into the bath, you should be protected from electric shock or electrocution.

About time, isn't it? Created by engineers at the Leviton Manufacturing Company in Little Neck, New York, it has already been licensed to some manufacturers of hair dryers and home health spas. It will not be sold directly to the public. You will have to buy a product already equipped with an IDCI.

According to Bernard Gershen, a member of the Leviton team that developed the IDCI, manufacturers have been slow to pick up on the product because of the additional $5 cost. But times are changing and lawsuits against manufacturers have been increasing, so it looks as if IDCIs are about to catch on.

If all electrical outlets were protected by Ground Fault Circuit Interrupters (GFCIs), there'd be no need for IDCIs. But GFCIs are required only in some outlets in new and reconditioned homes.

SAFE, NO-IRON COTTON

C an you remember ever walking into a clothing store and thinking that the store smelled odd? Chances are the odor came from Permapress cotton shirts that were treated with formaldehyde to make them wrinkle resistant. Now we have

• • • • •
ODDS: 90%
ETA: 1992
PRICE: N/A
• • • • •

learned that formaldehyde is a skin and eye irritant and can cause cancer in animals, and probably does some damage in humans, too.

The federal agency that controls health and safety, OSHA, is proposing that workers who are exposed to formaldehyde vapor be tested and that fabrics that are processed with it carry a warning label. However, the USDA is not waiting around to see if OSHA's proposals get approved, they are working on a new wrinkle-proofing agent that will not be hazardous to your health. They've come up with a family of chemicals called polycarboxylic acids that seem to be able to do the trick, each with varying complications. Clark Welch, a research chemist with the USDA in Louisiana, says that one of the acids, butanetetracarboxylic acid, seems to work the best. "It has surprisingly effective, smooth-drying properties."

But don't throw out your iron just yet. Welch says that the cost of producing this polycarboxylic acid has to come down before it can be commercially feasible. It now costs about $6.50 to manufacture one pound. Several companies are trying to cut the price by about three-fourths to get it ready for market.

RADON EXTRACTOR

Government studies estimate that 20 percent of American homes may have unacceptably high levels of radon. The colorless and odorless gas is dangerous—possibly causing up to 20,000 lung cancer deaths a year—only when it is trapped

. . . . .
ODDS: 100%
ETA: 1991
PRICE: $2,000
. . . . .

(much like gas from an oven). It comes from decaying uranium in the soil and seeps up from the ground into basements.

RAdsorb-222, a self-contained radon-removal unit, was developed by RAd Systems in Massachusetts. Richard Abrams, the company founder, explains that his system adsorbs radon-contaminated air into charcoal filters, where the air is purified and the radon is trapped. The radioactive gas is then vented to the outdoors, where it is rendered harmless. The unit removes 98 percent of the radon in the air and requires only a small amount of electricity to operate. The use of two charcoal filters allows one to detox while the other is adsorbing, leaving your home under constant protection.

Install RAdsorb-222 in your basement. It's a 4-foot-high box that weighs 200 pounds. The charcoal is good for five to ten years, depending on concentration levels of the gas.

249

THE VILEST TASTE

U.S. Patent #4,661,504 at first taste is an unlikely candidate for a marketable product. It is described as "the bitterest substance in the world" by its manufacturer, Atomergic Chematals Corporation.

· · · · ·
ODDS: 100%
ETA: 1990
PRICE: $11 PER PINT
FOR ROPEL
· · · · ·

Denatonium saccharide is a chemical compound that even when diluted to 1 part per 100 million retains its distinctive flavor. "It's vile. It has a lingering, terrible taste," according to Mel Blum, one of its inventors.

Why would anyone set out to create such a bad taste? "There was a definite need for a very bitter, low-toxicity flavor," says Mal Hollander, who, along with his brother Gary and Blum, invented the stuff. Its main use will be in certain poisonous compounds to signal people to stay clear of them. Analagous to the rotten-egg smell placed in normally odorless natural gas, the compound will also deter children from ingesting toxic household chemicals.

The company has also formulated an animal, rodent and bird repellent using "the vilest taste" as an ingredient. Called Ropel, when spread on trash it deters even the hungriest foraging animal for quite some time. "To taste Ropel is to know how it works," says Mel Hollander. "It lingers for several hours, and only a mouthwash or stiff whiskey can make it go away."

· · · · ·

PHONE SHIELDS

If you've ever tried to conduct a conversation over a slimy public phone while holding it six inches from your ear, Anthony Oliver may have the product for you. His OliverShield is a paper guard that adheres to the mouthpiece or earpiece

• • • • •
ODDS: 100%
ETA: 1990
PRICE: $3 FOR 30
• • • • •

of the phone you're using, to block out infectious viruses and bacteria.

Oliver came up with the idea for this germ barrier after years of "constant disgust at the condition of public phones at lovely places like LaGuardia Airport," and the decision to do something about it has resulted in his becoming a full-time entrepreneur.

The OliverShield is mounted on a Band-Aid–type, non-toxic adhesive that sticks to the phone before use and can be peeled off when you're ready to hang up. The shields can be ordered through OliverShields, 124 Mount Auburn St., Suite 200, Cambridge, MA 02138.

BEAR REPELLENT

Who knows? Maybe Ben was really a gentle bear and Grizzly Adams enjoyed breaking bread with his large, hairy, four-legged pal. But for most of us, the thought of a face-to-face encounter with a grizzly or any other type of bear turns our insides cold as the Alaskan tundra.

• • • • •
ODDS: 100%
ETA: 1990
PRICE: $12.95 & $29.95
• • • • •

251

That's why Bill Pounds, an outdoorsman from Missoula, Montana, who'd had his fill of stories about bear maulings, invented a powerful bear repellent known as Counter Assault. The spray's active ingredient—a derivative of cayenne pepper—is propelled up to 30 feet by two inert gases. "This way you can get the bear before he's right next to you," explained Ron Rennick, president of Missoula's Bushwacker Backpack and Supply Company, the only outlet selling the 13-ounce can of orange aerosol spray.

Using Counter Assault, University of Montana researchers have conducted 300 tests on bears. The effectiveness rate: 100 percent. Why does this product succeed when others, including skunk odors, rubber bullets, and tear gas, fail? The chemical irritates nerves in the animal's eyes and nose and temporarily impairs its respiratory system. The EPA has told Pounds and Rennick that they can't yet claim outright that Counter Assault works on bears until the required paperwork is completed.

Plans are under way to make a 7-ounce can for use on smaller animals. This can will have a 12-to-15-foot range and be more potent than Mace, said Rennick, because of the higher pepper concentration and the extended shooting range. "With Counter Assault, you're not maiming things with a bullet, but you are letting them know you mean business," he added.

HOMING DEVICE IMPLANT

An implantable homing device for humans! Daniel Man, a plastic and reconstructive surgeon from Boca Raton, Florida, first thought of the idea ten years ago during his hospital residency in Kentucky, where he became fascinated by unsolved kidnapping cases. He has since developed and patented a tiny transmitter sealed in plastic that can be surgically implanted behind a person's ear.

ODDS: 75%

ETA: 1992

PRICE: N/A

"It's a simple twenty-minute operation, requiring a very small incision," says Dr. Man. The battery-operated device, which can be recharged through the skin, is about the size of a quarter and can send a signal several miles. Each device is programmed to give off a unique signal at preset intervals. The signal would be picked up by cellular telephone antennae. When three towers detect the signal, the person's location can be pinpointed by determining the angle of the signal received by each tower. Three helicopters equipped with receivers could serve the same purpose in the absence of cellular telephone towers.

Dr. Man cites many potential uses for the homing device, from monitoring the movements of prisoners on release programs to locating Alzheimer's patients and kidnap victims.

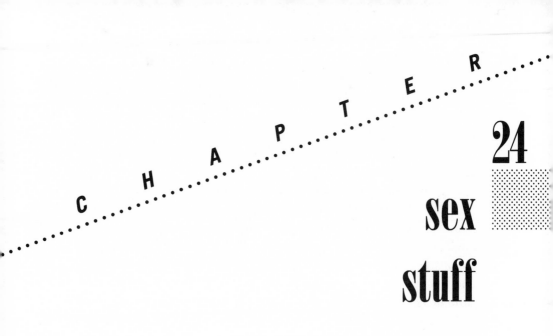

24

sex
stuff

THE FEMALE CONDOM

What do you get when you cross a prophylactic with a diaphragm? You get the next rage in birth control: the female condom. It's disposable, designed for one use only, and is inserted much like a diaphragm, but requires no fitting— one size fits all!

• • • • •
ODDS: 99%
ETA: 1991
PRICE: $5 FOR 6
CONDOMS
• • • • •

Bente Gregerson and her husband, Erik, a gynecologist in Denmark, headed an international group of gynecologists and obstetricians that developed the idea for a female barrier contraceptive. Concerned about sexually transmitted diseases, Bente came up with the concept. The rest is history—or herstory—in the making. The condom consists of a soft, loose-fitting polyurethane sheath and two flexible rings at either end. A domed surface of polyurethane encloses one ring. This

255

end is inserted into the vagina, fitting over the cervix much like a diaphragm, and serves as an internal anchor. The penis enters through the outer ring, which opens over the labia outside the vagina. The penis is able to move freely inside the female condom without dislodging the device.

The advantages are many: Unlike the male condom, this version gives the woman control over her own safety. Its looser fit provides more comfort for the man and since no aroused state is required for application, spontaneity is increased. With the entry ring extending slightly beyond the opening of the vagina, both the entry to the vagina and the base of the penis are better protected. These condoms have little or no risk of tearing or ripping due to the superior strength of the polyurethane. Some critics are concerned that the outer ring of the condom could get pushed up into the vagina and reduce protection, but those who have tested it say the female condom works like a charm.

The U.S. manufacturer, Wisconsin Pharmacal Company, has temporarily named the device WPC-333. Clinical trials for safety, comfort, and effectiveness are under way in the United States, United Kingdom, Denmark, Germany, and Sweden. The World Health Organization is conducting studies in fifteen other countries as well.

ELECTRIFIED BIRTH CONTROL

While driving to work one day, New York gynecologist Steven Kaali was thinking about the battery that needed changing in his watch. His thoughts wandered, and Dr. Kaali, a family-planning researcher, suddenly wondered if a small battery inserted in a diaphragm might not kill sperm.

• • • • •
ODDS: 75%
ETA: 1992
PRICE: $60–$80
• • • • •

256

He now has a patent on such a device. The tiny battery is cylindrical, a quarter-inch long, and the same width as the stick on a cotton swab. It is built into the rim of the diaphragm and sends its signal out across the dome. It kills sperm by zapping them when they cross the low-level electrical field.

The battery, which lasts six months, produces only 50 microamps at 2.8 volts—the identical current created by a pacemaker and even less than the battery in an electric watch. "No one would feel anything from the current, except the sperm," Dr. Kaali explained. And so far, he adds, it has proven 100 percent effective in lab studies and animal experiments.

The electrical birth control device has also shown that it can kill bacteria and fungus as well as sperm. According to Dr. Kaali, it should cure yeast infections, and research is being conducted to determine if it could even kill the AIDS virus at the moment of transaction.

Although several pharmaceutical companies have expressed interest in the electrical diaphragm, there are no concrete marketing plans yet. Dr. Kaali believes that the diaphragm could be in drugstores within two years after a company purchases the patent rights.

IMPOTENCY PILLS

Every year erectile insufficiency, or impotency, leaves an estimated 20 million men feeling sexually and emotionally inadequate. To date, injections and psychological treatment have been the tools used to combat this most private

· · · · ·
ODDS: 50%
ETA: 1992
PRICE: N/A
· · · · ·

of problems—not always with success. And if the condition is traced to purely physical causes, doctors often prescribe an injection to be administered just before intercourse. Naturally, this limits spontaneity and can be, well, awkward. But Grant Gwinup, an M.D. and professor of medicine at the University of California at Irvine Medical Center, offers new hope to these unhappy men—and their partners.

257

It's a pill called phentolamine, and in initial tests it helped eight of sixteen impotent men maintain erections long enough to complete intercourse. The pill is safer and easier to take than the injection, which can cause infection in rare instances or, more commonly, a condition known as priapism—continuous, non-sexual erection.

Ciba-Geigy, an international pharmaceuticals firm whose U.S. operations are based in Ardsley, New York, manufactured phentolamine for use in counteracting hypertension. But when an improvement in its product came along, the company discontinued production. Dr. Gwinup knew that phentolamine was the same ingredient commonly injected into the penis to treat impotency. "I figured an oral dose would be more comfortable and convenient," he says. One drawback: When injected, the drug goes directly into the bloodstream, therefore reaching effectiveness in minutes; the oral dose takes up to an hour.

"Ciba needs to be convinced that there's a market for this," says Dr. Gwinup, who notes that the company manufactured the drug on machinery that is now obsolete. He adds that phentolamine in oral form would need additional FDA approval before it could be marketed.

The doses used in the case study were obtained before Ciba stopped production. Dr. Gwinup asks that anyone interested in seeing the medication made available again write to Ciba-Geigy.

TIME-RELEASE BIRTH CONTROL

258

The trouble with birth-control pills is that you have to remember to take them! Now, thanks to research conducted by the Population Council, a non-profit international organization, there's a new method that's more convenient and needs no reminders.

• • • • •
ODDS: 95%
ETA: 1992
PRICE: N/A
• • • • •

Researchers have developed a time-release implant method using six thin match-size, hormone-filled capsules. The implants are inserted surgically, in a fan shape, on the inside of a woman's upper arm. They're flexible and comfortable. Proper doses of a progestin hormone are released at a slow, steady rate, preventing pregnancy within hours of insertion and lasting up to five years.

So far studies show less than one pregnancy in every one hundred users per year, yet NORPLANT, the registered trademark, is totally reversible and can be removed surgically at any time.

NORPLANT has already been approved in twelve countries, including China, Sweden, and Finland. Clinical tests have been completed in the United States and are under way in forty other countries.

SEXUAL RISK GAME

There may soon be a new way for young people to learn about the pleasures and pitfalls of human sexuality. The folks in the Office of Student Affairs at the University of Guelph in Ontario, Canada, figure there is no better way to make students of the nineties sexually aware than by making a game of it all.

ODDS: 85%
ETA: 1991
PRICE: $30

Sexual Risk is chockful of questions and answers. For example:

People over a certain age do not like to and should not have sex. True or false?
False. A person is a sexual being from womb to tomb and need never stop having sex.

The game has been greeted enthusiastically on the Guelph campus, where it is used as an introduction to sex discussions with trained counselors. The university's Industrial and Innovation Services office feels that with a little refinement the game could catch on with youth organizations and the public at large.

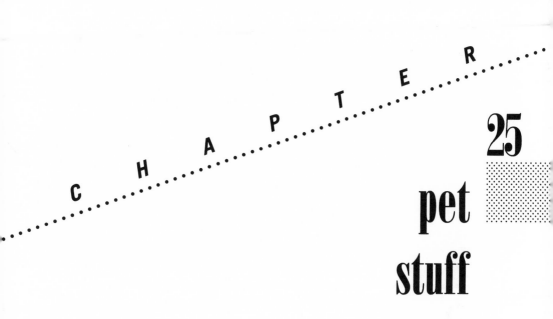

pet stuff

EDIBLE PET SPOON

The idea was wonderfully simple. No one—especially a six-year-old—likes taking the spoon that fed the cat, gooky with canned food, and washing it off. So Suzanna Goodin, whose chore it was to do just that, complained to her mother, "Why can't there be a spoon that the cats can eat?"

• • • • •
ODDS: 50%
ETA: 1992
PRICE: N/A
• • • • •

That idea won Suzanna first price in the *Weekly Reader* magazine's annual inventing contest for kids. In the kindergarten-to-grade-4 category, the edible pet spoon beat out over a hundred thousand other bright ideas.

Suzanna, now nine, and her mom, Jennifer, baked up a batch of hard biscuits, added a little garlic, "because it enhances an animal's

261

appetite," and scooped out the food for their twin Siamese cats. Then they broke the spoon into pieces and "lo and behold, it worked!"

Suzanna and her mom have had a few nibbles, but so far no takers to market the edible pet spoon. But cats around their home in Hydro, Oklahoma, are eating them up.

PET VACUUM GROOMING DEVICE

Dog and cat owners know that shedding can be a real nuisance. Now one owner, Gregory Santana, a California lighting-studio technician, has done something about it. When his son, whose job it was to brush the family dog, got

ODDS: 100%

ETA: 1992

PRICE: $35

tired of removing hair from the dog, as well as the carpet, clothing, and furniture, Santana and his son, Alexander, turned inventors.

The result is the Pet-Vac, a grooming device that efficiently collects loose hair while you brush your pet. Pet-Vac will come with a variety of attachments, so you can choose the brush or comb best suited for your pet. Powered by rechargeable batteries, it operates quietly . . . so Fido won't be frightened.

NON-CHOKING DOG COLLAR

I f you find walking your rambunctious dog to be a pain in your neck, imagine how the dog feels. Every time you pull on the leash, poor Rover gets choked! Not very humane.

· · · · ·
ODDS: 100%
ETA: 1990
PRICE: $12–$18
· · · · ·

"We train horses, cattle, sheep, goats, and calves with halters, yet it is accepted practice to train dogs by choking," says Dr. Robert Anderson, veterinarian and director emeritus of the Animal Behavior Clinic at the University of Minnesota. Dr. Anderson and co-inventor, Ruth Foster, developed the Gentle Leader, a dog "halter" which takes into consideration a dog's natural instincts.

Gentle Leader consists of a strap that fits around the dog's nose and lower jaw, and another strap that runs behind the ears and joins under the jaw. "By controlling the animal's head and nose," Dr. Anderson explains, "you are better able to control the whole dog." The halter-type collar removes the pressure from the dog's throat and applies it to the nose and large muscles at the back of the neck. "Female dogs take their puppies by the scruff of the neck to control them," observes Dr. Anderson. "Older dogs remember this and recognize pressure to the back of the neck as control, and respond accordingly." When you pull and tighten the nose strap, the dog's mouth is forced closed, inhibiting barking or biting. But unlike a muzzle, which can cause a dog to panic, the strap loosens as soon as you slacken the leash. Rover learns that with good behavior he's going to be more comfortable.

Anyone, no matter how weak, can control any dog, no matter how big, and inflict no pain on the animal. It's Dr. Anderson's hope that Gentle Leader will reduce the number of dogs put to sleep by owners who can't control them.

Gentle Leader comes in three sizes and is available now at some pet shops and from veterinarians.

263

"BARK STOPPER" DOG COLLAR

I f your dog is considered the neighborhood nuisance—making you unpopular and your dog a prime target for a hit-and-run accident—your troubles are over. Veterinarians at Texas A & M University have developed a dog collar that will transform your canine from a miserable mutt back into man's best friend.

ODDS: 100%
ETA: 1990
PRICE: $60

The collar looks very similar to a standard dog collar but has a small speaker attached. When the dog begins to bark, the collar responds by emitting a high-frequency sound that is inaudible to humans, yet frightening to the dog. Once the dog has been exposed to the sound enough times, he begins to realize that it occurs only when he barks. Result: He stops barking and you stop receiving calls from angry neighbors. Even chronic barkers can be cured within a few hours, say the veterinarians.

The collar, however, will not turn your dog into a wimp. If he is barking because an intruder has entered your home or a person is being threatened, his natural instincts will take precedence over fear of the collar. Loyalty will overcome discomfort.

The collars are manufactured and at present sold only by Humane Technology at Texas A & M University.

REFRIGERATOR KITTY BOWL

I t was a sad day for William Crowell when his first cat, Squirt, died of feline urologic syndrome (FUS), a condition that causes crystals to form in a cat's bladder. Crowell was told that FUS and Squirt's death could have been prevented had the cat simply drunk more fresh water.

• • • • •

ODDS: 100%

ETA: 1992

PRICE: $20

• • • • •

So when his second cat died of the same disease, Crowell knew he had to do something. He started by consulting a number of pet professionals about FUS. The consensus of opinion was that cats will only drink cool water, yet the average pet bowl leaves water at room temperature within an hour.

One Sunday morning, when Crowell and his wife were packing for a church picnic, he had the notion to put one of those frozen blue ice packages underneath the kitty bowl to keep the water cool. A short time later, the world's first non-electric refrigerator bowl was patented. The professionals reported that water was kept cool for as long as twelve hours and that cats were drinking more water as a result. The bowl also kept food fresh for a longer time.

Kitty-Fridge, as the new bowl was named, is made of high-impact polystyrene. The bowl stands 3½ inches off the floor. A space in the base holds the reusable ice pack. Two packs come with every Kitty-Fridge, which is now available by mail order only. Crowell employs a local workshop for the handicapped and retarded to make the bowls.

Why only for kitties and not for dogs? "A large number of cats are picky eaters, unlike dogs, which gobble up everything you put in their bowl," says Crowell. The bowls are available now from The Cool

265

Water Co., Dept. CS, 811 West 5th St., Lansdale, PA 19446; 1-800-548-8706.

THE NAILLESS HORSESHOE

At long last, a new line of footwear for the stylish horse.

· · · · ·
ODDS: 100%
ETA: 1990
PRICE: $43.97 FOR 4
· · · · ·

The fashion—a bold departure from the traditional nail-on, steel horseshoe—involves a lighter look, in plastic. No nails bind shoe to hoof, only an adhesive for maximum comfort. The plastic shoe—durable, high-impact, and flexible—is heated and molded to the hoof for a custom fit.

The shoe was designed by two Massachusetts dentists, M. John Pautienis and Richard Shakalis. The partners had a horse-breeding patient who complained bitterly about the detrimental effects of old-style steel shoes: The shoes were ungiving and didn't allow the hooves to expand as they should. The nails, meanwhile, dried out the hoof, cracking and weakening it. The two dentists decided to apply the principles of dental bonding to this sole-full matter, reasoning that a hoof isn't all that different from a tooth. Both need the same protective care to last and perform well.

The idea made horse sense: "We came up with a shoe—the world's first nailless horseshoe—that would ensure the integrity of the hoof, even strengthen the hoof wall and protect it from premature wear," says Dr. Pautienis. The horseshoe, made from a durable General Electric plastic, is one-third the weight of conventional horseshoes. This means less wear and tear on the horses' tendons and ligaments. The dentists say the nailless shoe is not meant to replace steel shoes entirely, but rather is to be used every third time to allow nail holes to grow out for the next steel shoeing.

The horseshoes sell under the name SBS 100 System, retailing at $43.97 for four shoes. The price may go down as more sets are sold.

266

Shoe Bond Systems, the manufacturer, hopes to have "a sizable chunk of the horseshoe market by 1992," says Dr. Pautienis.

For information, contact Shoe Bond Systems Inc., 429 South St., Hyannis, MA 02601.

TWO-WAY-MIRROR BIRDFEEDER

Y ou never thought there would be a revolution in bird feeders, did you? Well, Tim Lundquist of Hudson, New York, the president of Meta Birdfeeders, is causing more of a ruckus than a flock of blue jays. How come? He added a two-

ODDS: 100%

ETA: 1990

PRICE: $100

way mirror! Now you can watch the birds from your kitchen window, without them watching you.

Shaped like a two-dimensional country home, the Meta Birdfeeder (patent pending) has three levels, a 45-degree roof—with chimney—and two outer walls. Besides offering easier viewing, it delivers birdseed better than conventional feeders.

Lundquist's invention uses clear polycarbonate tubes that are easily assembled and disassembled for cleaning. Fill the tubes with seeds, and birds can feast from any place on the feeder—from one of the three stories, the pitched roof, the chimney, or even from either of the two sides. Several openings along each tube allow for some 30 inches of feeding area. The tubes can each be filled with a different type of seed to attract the widest variety of birds.

267

The mirror is made of a metallic gold finish rather than silver, which seems to attract more birds, according to Lundquist. "Children can get a more connected relationship with the birds," he says. And everyone can enjoy watching the birds in their last-minute aerobatics before landing.

The Meta Birdfeeder attaches to your window by means of special struts that come with it. And when the seeds get wet and gucky inside, just disassemble the tubes and put them through the dishwasher.

26

future

cars

COLLISION-AVOIDANCE SYSTEM

T he idea of a collision-avoidance system is something that's bounced around the auto industry for years. After all, planes and boats use radar to avoid collisions. Why not cars? The problem with automobiles is that they travel so close together, there's little time to react once you're alerted to danger.

ODDS: 55%

ETA: 1999

PRICE: $600

Well, the Nissan Motor Company of Japan is now working on a system that does more than warn you of an impending collision, pedestrian, or obstacle on the road. It acts. Nissan's system projects a pulsating laser beam in front of the car. The beam is reflected by any object in its path to an optical head mounted on the front bumper. A computer then calculates the distance by measuring the time re-

269

quired for the beam to return to the sensor. The computer almost instantaneously measures the hazard level. If you're traveling too fast, it will instruct the throttle to back off. And if you're about to hit something or someone, it will slam on the brakes.

There's still work to be done on this system. But experts believe the odds are better than even that this type of collision-avoidance system will be standard equipment by the year 2000.

DRIVER PERSONALITY KEY

The push by car makers to build "user-friendly" vehicles will get a serious boost in the coming decade, thanks to the memory storage capabilities of onboard computer systems. The preferences of each driver who uses the car will be stored

ODDS: 60%

ETA: 1996

PRICE: $300

in the memory section and then activated by his or her specially coded Driver Personality Key.

When the driver slides his key into the ignition, electric motors will whir to life, setting the various adjustments to preselected positions. The system shown on Ford's HFX Ghia Aerostar concept van goes far beyond the seating memory feature available on some of today's luxury sedans. The rearview mirrors swivel to just the right angle and the safety belt shoulder strap is positioned where the driver feels most comfortable. The brake and accelerator pedals adjust up to 4 inches, allowing every driver to find just the right spot. According to Charles A. White, Ford Motor Company's chief of light truck chassis engineering, this system "vividly demonstrates what we might see in family vehicles of the future. These advanced components are special, but certainly within reach."

The Driver Personality Key is also a built-in security system. When it is removed, the vehicle is electronically disabled. It is safe from

jimmying and hot-wiring, as the computer, which controls all electronic functions, cannot be activated without the key.

CAR VIDEO NAVIGATION SYSTEM

I f we can land men on the moon and airliners can find their way to Des Moines on the foggiest of nights, how come we're still using antiquated paper maps to find our way in unfamiliar neighborhoods?

ODDS: 100%

ETA: 1990

PRICE: $1,500

Not necessary anymore; electronics has taken us far beyond the need to rely on such maps or a dimestore compass stuck to the dashboard with a suction cup. Video display route charting is here, in the form of the Etak Navigator, the first of a new generation of "smart maps."

Etak uses a cassette-tape data source to put an electronic road map up on a dashboard video monitor. Your car's location is indicated by a stationary arrow, while the map moves accordingly. A star on the display notes the destination. Motion sensors and an electronic compass update the location and reorient the map as you make turns. Map scale can be zoomed in from a 40-mile overview to a precise street address location. And, of course, the Etak will show you the best route if you punch in the destination before leaving home.

Also available soon will be navigational systems based on compact disc storage systems.

Of course, the big, time-consuming job is converting the information on paper maps to these electronic storage systems. The Etak Corporation of Santa Clara, California, is working on it.

271

SATELLITE NAVIGATION

The video navigation system (see page 271), which we'll see introduced early in the decade, should be passé by the end of the decade. It will be replaced by satellite navigation, an amazing system that will be able to pinpoint your car's location anyplace in the world, alert you to an upcoming traffic jam and show you all alternate routes, warn you of approaching bad weather, and so on. Your car will be bouncing signals off satellites in space just like the most advanced communications systems.

· · · · ·
ODDS: 70%
ETA: 1998
PRICE: $2,500
· · · · ·

Japan's Nissan Motor Company is spearheading the technology with its Satellite Drive Information device. Your location will be shown on your car's computer display screen, using Nissan's Global Positioning System. Forget video road maps and memory banks. The picture on your screen will be the real thing transmitted via satellite. The display screen will even tell you where to make turns and also measure distances (to the next intersection or to your final destination).

Satellite navigation is going to make it difficult for someone even with the worst sense of direction to get lost.

· · · · ·

TURBINE ENGINES

Turbine engines are coming to cars. That was the word from Chrysler Corporation twenty-five years ago. If you're still waiting for them, don't give up, but don't rush to your car dealer either. They're coming—when the cost of making them can be cut enough to make them affordable.

• • • • •

ODDS: 20%

ETA: 1999

PRICE: OUT OF THIS
WORLD

• • • • •

Similar to the kind used in jet planes, turbine engines are light; they have fewer parts and therefore have fewer mechanical problems. They can use a variety of fuels and they last a *long*, long time.

The costly, specialized materials make the turbine engine okay for use in a $1-million plane, but, despite the advantages, out of the price range for a family car.

The bottom line? A revolutionary breakthrough in ceramics and other high-temperature materials could unite the turbine and the automobile by the turn of the century. Otherwise, turbine engines might find their way into only the most exotic high-speed sports cars.

273

• • • • •

ANTI-NOISE CONTROLS

I t's like fighting fire with fire: cutting down all the whistles and drones inside a moving car by broadcasting sounds that cancel out unwanted noises. The engineers at Lotus Engineering in Norfolk, England, have given it the official name

ODDS: 25%
ETA: 1995
PRICE: $200

Adaptive Noise Control. Your dealer will probably just call it "anti-noise."

In the Lotus system, microphones are positioned in the seat headrests. These are tuned to register the pressure and frequency of annoying noises that originate from the engine. A microprocessor analyzes the signal and creates a sound that is similar but has its wave staggered so that the existing peaks are counteracted by new lows. The result is a neutral, quiet environment inside the car.

According to Malcolm McDonald of Lotus, "Our anti-noise will work for all models, at all positions in the cabin." The elimination of engine and wind noise will not only make car trips more pleasant, it will reduce driver fatigue.

The best news, however, is that this leading-edge technology won't be restricted to luxury cars. It's the less refined automobiles that need anti-noise most, and with such a low projected cost, it's likely to be applied to economy cars first.

274

AUTOMATIC TIRE CHECK AND FILL

I f you've ever had a blowout on a high-way (and who hasn't), you're going to really appreciate this latest bit of auto technology. It will not only alert you to a low tire, it will actually fill the tire while you're on the go.

ODDS: 90%

ETA: 1992

PRICE: $400

The device, called entireControl, produced by techni Guidance of California, uses sensors mounted on each wheel to detect any change in tire pressure. This information is then relayed to the car's central computer. "If the pressure decreases to 15 psi [pounds per square inch] a CHECK TIRE warning will begin to flash on the dash and an audible beeper will warn you to get the car off the road," explains inventor Shrikant Gandhi.

This is the system Gandhi and techni Guidance use now, and it's already available on a few luxury cars. Their latest advance, however, takes it one step further. By means of a reservoir mounted on the inside of the wheel rim, carbon dioxide can be added to the tire. The system monitors the tire pressure in all four tires and automatically adjusts the pressure to maintain it at the preset, driver-programmed level to provide better road handling, improved fuel economy, and peace of mind. Proper inflation pressure can not only prevent blowouts and save lives, it can also save your tires.

And with a premium set of four tires costing up to $1,000, the automatic tire check and fill can't get here soon enough.

MULTIFUEL VEHICLES

The fuel shortages of the 1970s showed car owners and manufacturers just how dependent we are on the volatile petroleum market. That lesson led to experiments with other fuels and other kinds of automobile engines.

ODDS: 40%
ETA: 1997
PRICE: $750

At General Motors, a giant step has been taken with the development of an experimental multifuel model of the Chevrolet Corsica. The car can be fed a diet of gasoline or methanol, or a combination of the two. Future models may be able to burn other alcohol blends, or even propane.

The problem with building such a vehicle has been that different fuels burn at faster or slower rates. So the challenge was to create an engine that could be tuned for acceptable performance no matter what the fuel. Chevrolet's solution is a sensing unit which measures the power potential of the fuel. It then electronically adjusts the ignition timing and fuel-injection settings to match the speed at which the fuel burns.

If and when multifuel vehicles hit the American road will depend as much on world politics as on technology. A serious gasoline shortage would no doubt speed the development of these versatile cars.

HEADS UP DISPLAY

F rom the beginning of automotive history a century ago, the task of keeping a driver informed of operating
conditions such as speed and fuel has
been vital. Yet presenting that information has always required that the driver

ODDS: 100%
ETA: 1990
PRICE: N/A

divert his attention from the road ahead and search his dashboard for
the appropriate gauge or meter. No more, thanks to technology adapted
from the leading-edge information display systems of military fighter
jets.

With Heads Up Display, a device mounted on your dashboard
projects an image 8 feet ahead of the vehicle into the driver's field
of vision. The system, developed by Hughes Aircraft for General
Motors, projects speed, low fuel level, high beam headlight indicator,
and turn signal. The obvious advantage is that the driver no longer
has to take his eyes off the road for a quick update of instrument
readings. But more than that, he'll avoid eyestrain by not having to
adjust for the change in focus distances and outside/inside light levels.

THE NO-FLAT SPARE TIRE

T his is an innovation that seems long
overdue: a tire that won't go flat.
The Uniroyal Goodrich Corporation has
developed a spare made of a polyurethane
elastomer, a material that's both tough and
flexible. It's these properties that give the

ODDS: 85%
ETA: 1992
PRICE: $100

277

"no air" spare the ability to provide a smooth ride while at the same time resisting the kind of road hazards that make pneumatic tires go flat.

The new tire has a paddle wheel design that's light yet durable. Its rubber tread is similar to that of its "air" counterpart and should be good for 3,000 miles of driving.

The new spare is 20 to 25 percent lighter than pneumatic spares and occupies about 35 percent less trunk space, according to Uniroyal Goodrich spokesman Leonard Stokes. And most important, because the new tire is not pressurized, it won't deflate with time while it sits in the trunk.

The Department of Transportation began testing the polyurethane tire in mid-1988, but Stokes warns that it won't be available until late 1991 at the earliest, since Uniroyal Goodrich has yet to even choose a production site.

REMOTE-CONTROL CAR STARTER

W hen it's cold outside you can start your car from more than a football field away with Auto-Command Remote-Control Car Starter.

• • • • •
ODDS: 100%
ETA: 1990
PRICE: $320
• • • • •

From inside your home or office, a touch of the transmitter button on your keychain will turn on your engine, as well as the heater, defroster, windshield wipers—and in summer, the air conditioner. It will operate from as far away as 400 feet. The starter consists of a small box hooked up inside your car with fifteen wires that serve as sensors to turn on the appropriate functions. The box is activated by a radio transmitter system. "The system actually monitors the vehicle," says Mike Stern of Design Tech International Inc., which makes Auto-Command.

For example, if you start your car but no key is inserted into the ignition within ten minutes, the car shuts off. Or if a thief tries to steal the car without the key, the engine shuts off when the brake or the accelerator is activated. Also, if someone, say a child, gets into the car and takes it out of PARK without inserting the key, the engine turns off.

Auto-Command is available now in a few specialty catalogues or from Design Tech, 7401 Fullerton Rd., Building I, Springfield, VA 22153.

LIGHT-SENSITIVE CAR WINDOWS AND MIRRORS

T he idea of car windows which adjust their tinting to the brightness level outside seems straightforward enough: after all, haven't those eyeglasses been available for years?

ODDS: 75%

ETA: 1994

PRICE: $650

Ford Motor Company's Glass Division has taken the concept a step further. They call it Switchable Privacy Glass, and use LCD technology, the same mechanism found in the display faces of digital wristwatches. Basically it adjusts the transparency of the glass from fully transparent to nearly opaque.

A slight variation of this feature will be used in rearview mirrors. Depending on the illumination falling on the mirror from the headlights of cars behind, the mirrors will vary their reflection to offer glare-free rear vision. Additionally, an electroluminescent halo surrounding the mirrors will help the driver to locate them quickly in the dark.

Over at General Motors, Charles M. Jordan, head of the corporate design staff, acknowledges GM is working on the same technology. "I expect to see glass roofs, the kind where you dial in opaque or clear depending on how hot the sun is. It's likely that the whole upper part of the car will be glass."

279

SMART SUSPENSION

Before too long, cars will be coming with no springs attached. Shocked? Don't be, because cars won't have any shocks either!

ODDS: 90%
ETA: 1993
PRICE: $2,000

Replacing coil springs and shock absorbers will be active suspensions—systems that adjust automatically to bumps and potholes. With hydraulic rams supporting the chassis, active suspensions will smooth the car's ride before the tire can rise out of the pothole. Built-in sensors will let a central computer know exactly what is happening at each corner of the car. The driver can program this system for a ride that's "soft," yet still as responsive as a sports car. Michael Kimberley, chief executive at Lotus Engineering in Hethel, England, where the system originates, put it this way: "The old days of compromise have gone. You can literally program whatever ride and handling behavior you want."

At present, active suspensions are being used only in Grand Prix racing cars. The high cost is keeping them out of mass production for the time being. But the technology is here, and someday you'll have an active suspension in your car.

PLASTIC ENGINES

I t's the automotive engineer's dream: to replace an engine's complex heavyweight iron castings with a single extrusion of plastic. That fantasy, as the new decade begins, is close to reality thanks to fiberglass-reinforced composites.

ODDS: 25%
ETA: 1997
PRICE: $500 EXTRA

The major car manufacturers have already seen running prototypes of plastic engines that show real promise. They're light and they're strong, and according to their inventor, Matty Holtzberg, an engineer from Franklin Lakes, New Jersey, they are destined to be the engines of the future.

Still, the automotive giants are slow to jump on a new technology when it means a major change in production. As a result, American motorists are likely to see advanced plastic composites used inside engines—connecting rods, pushrods, and the like—before the entire casting goes plastic.

But don't be surprised if new ultralight economy cars appear before the year 2000, with hearts of plastic under their hoods. The technology is here now.

NIGHT-VISION DISPLAY SCREEN

T his bit of useful technology will come to us care of the military. It's a night-vision system that will let us see through darkness, fog, and rain far better than with the most powerful headlights.

ODDS: 20%
ETA: 1999
PRICE: $1,500

Presently under development at the

281

General Motors Technical Center in Warren, Michigan, the system uses a special receiver sensitive to infrared rays that projects onto a dashboard-mounted TV screen an image of what's in front of the car. The picture is actually formed by heat values emitted from objects in the car's path. "The road, the grass beside the road, the light pole alongside the road will all look different," says Harvey Burley, a GM advanced-product engineer.

GM has a prototype infrared night-vision system, but it's large and must be mounted on the car's roof. Furthermore, the infrared receiver requires cooling by liquid nitrogen. Producing a smaller unit and solving the heat problem are the challenges that must be overcome before this system makes it to your Chevrolet.

TWO-CYCLE AUTO ENGINES

Car makers all over the world, including Detroit's Ford Motor Company, are taking a hard look at a two-cycle engine developed by Australia's Orbital Engine Company.

ODDS: 65%
ETA: 1995
PRICE: SAVINGS OF $300–$500

The incentives are there. With far fewer pieces inside, the engine is inexpensive to build. And it's lighter, too, which means it consumes less gasoline. Two-cycle engines operate without valves or camshafts, producing power with each complete turn of the crankshaft. Standard four-cycle auto engines generate power on just half of their revolutions. The result is that Orbital's 90-pound engine can better the output of four-cycle engines even though it is one-third the weight.

Further, this more efficient combustion process makes it easier for the car to meet federal exhaust-emission regulations, according to the engine's inventor, Ralph Sarich of Perth, Australia. Sarich's engine offers considerable refinements over the old two-cycle engines used in outboard motors and in the Saab cars of the early sixties. There's no need to premix the oil with the gasoline, and modern noise controls have almost eliminated the raspy ring-a-ding sound of those earlier engines.

According to automotive experts, how soon two-cycle engines end up in showrooms depends on the politics of royalties, patent rights, and the resistance of car makers to retool their production lines. If Detroit dallies, says one automotive writer, look for Tokyo to leap at the chance to go two-cycle.

FOUR-WHEEL STEERING

Sure, four-wheel steering is already here. But so far it's a flashy novelty on sports models rather than an important safety and driving feature. By the mid-nineties, four-wheel steering should be as common as front-wheel drive.

ODDS: 100%

ETA: 1994

PRICE: $900

The strength of four-wheel drive is maneuverability. In low-speed situations the back wheels turn about 5 degrees in the opposite direction of the front wheels. And although 5 degrees doesn't sound like a lot, it makes a huge difference when you're trying to park your car in a tight space. At high speeds, four-wheel steering greatly improves stability, particularly when making fast lane changes on the freeway.

So, four-wheel steering is not just for speed demons and car nuts. It's for every driver. Right now, only the high cost is holding it back. But four-wheel steering is coming in the nineties. Greater mass production should bring the price down and put it on every car except the lowest-priced models.

283

DRIVE BY WIRE

It sounds almost a bit scary: a car's steering and speed controlled by sensors connected only by thin wires rather than by all those heavy mechanical links still found in the cars of the eighties. But drive by wire is almost certainly in the automobile's future.

· · · · ·
ODDS: 99%
ETA: 1995
PRICE: NO INCREASE
· · · · ·

Basically, all the bulky tubes and rods and other mechanical stuff on present-day cars will be trashed in favor of a system that operates on sleek, little (the size of a half dollar) electronic sensors connected by skinny wires. The sensors will detect when you put your foot on the pedal, or the brake, or which way you turn the wheel and how much. They will transmit what they "sense" to a central system, which will then issue the right command.

The advantages are many. Driving precision is increased, for starters. And with all the bulky stuff replaced by thin wires, the car will not only be lighter but it will be quieter, since the gaps in the car's bulkhead will only have to be big enough to pass a small wire through.

For $70,000, BMW will sell you their model 750iL, the only car currently available that runs on drive-by-wire linkage. And although it's all new to the automobile, airplanes have been flying by wire for quite some time. So, if this talk about little wires operating your car still scares you, remember that the system has proved safe for air travel. Soon it will be on your car.

284

· · · · ·

AUTOMOTIVE TV-MONITOR SYSTEM

Maybe you've seen this TV-monitor system on those small airport buses that take you to your rent-a-car. A video camera is mounted on the rear of the vehicle and a small black-and-white TV monitor is mounted on the dashboard. The result is a clear, wide view with no blind spots.

• • • • •

ODDS: 75%

ETA: 1995

PRICE: $1,350

• • • • •

The device should prevent accidents and save lives. But it will be the mid-nineties before it goes on sale to the general public. The Automotive WatchCam is manufactured and marketed by Sony Security Systems in Paramus, New Jersey. Right now it's being marketed only to the truck, bus, boat, and recreational-vehicle industries.

Says John Garrison, division president, "The WatchCam provides a more complete view when the driver is maneuvering, especially when backing up. With full audio capability, the system is particularly helpful for drivers being guided into especially tight parking spots." As you can imagine, the bigger the vehicle, the more helpful the WatchCam, as looming back ends can obstruct views for as far as 30 feet.

The systems are small, as space is at a premium in most vehicles. The monitors are either 4.4 inches or 5.5 inches. The larger unit comes with day/night switches for picture adjustment. The camera has water-resistant housing and cable capable of withstanding temperatures from -22 degrees Fahrenheit to $+167$ degrees.

Although automobiles have only a small blind spot, William Yan, director of sales and marketing for Sony's automotive WatchCam, believes the monitor system can be a viable product for car drivers. It will "instill confidence in drivers," he says.

27

and still
to come . .

DO-IT-ALL COMPUTER NOTEPAD

This is the computer of the future. It will do a ton of stuff, yet be light enough to carry around. And the things it will do will amaze you.

• • • • •
ODDS: 75%
ETA: 1999
PRICE: $2,000
• • • • •

The instrument is the brainchild of five students and two faculty members at the University of Illinois. They won a contest sponsored by the Apple Computer Company to come up with a personal computer for the year 2000.

Their invention is called the Tablet. There's no prototype yet, but most of the technology is here and the rest is on the drawing board. Bartlett Mel, one of the student contestants, explains that the Tablet is nothing like present-day PCs—a box with a keyboard. "Our machine is completely portable. It's the size of a standard notebook pad

287

and weighs one to two pounds." There are no buttons, knobs, or keys. Now, here's what the Tablet will do:

1. Using a no-ink stylus, you'll be able to write and receive written messages.
2. You'll watch television on it. Actually, you'll be able to watch sixteen squares of different programming simultaneously.
3. Around the edges of the Tablet will be infrared sensors—like your TV remote control. These will enable the Tablet to talk to other Tablets in the same room, or to any other compatible electronic equipment—including full-size computers.
4. The Tablet will come with an optional wall-size screen so that you can enlarge anything you display on the small screen.
5. You will be able to insert optical laser cards—the floppy disks of the future—which are the size of credit cards. Each will be able to store four hours of video or two thousand books. So you'll be able to read or watch prerecorded videos on your handy computer.
6. The Tablet will double as a cellular phone. Touch the phone icon, give the computer the number, and you can communicate with anyone anywhere in the world. Your voice will be transmitted by a built-in microphone. And using the optional lapel-size camera accessory, you'll even be able to send video images.

Had enough? Well, there's one more bit of magic. Using the government's Global Positioning System, Tablet will tell you exactly where you are and give directions to any place you want to be.

And should you lose your precious computer, Tablet can phone home to tell you where to find it!

· · · · ·

SELF-CLEANING HOUSE

If it's true that cleanliness is next to godliness, then Frances Gabe of Newberg, Oregon, should be ready for sainthood.

· · · · ·

ODDS: 50%

ETA: 1995

PRICE: $30,000–
$40,000

· · · · ·

Twenty-seven years ago, Ms. Gabe had a husband, a houseful of children, and a growing construction business. She had little patience for cleaning chores and resented the time they required. Thus the idea for a house that cleaned itself was born.

Today, at the age of seventy-three, Ms. Gabe lives in a prototype of the self-cleaning house, which she built herself for $15,000. She spends her days perfecting the various cleaning, drying, heating, and cooling apparatuses in her cinder-block home, which "cannot be injured by water and ammonia."

The idea is that each room in the house will contain a two-part washing apparatus. One part is a small, rotating fixture located on the ceiling that sprays water and ammonia onto the walls and central part of the room. The second part, which looks like a baseboard, shoots out the cleaning solution to wash the floor. When you're tired of the dust and dirt, just turn on the control valve and close the door behind you. Ammonia and water pour forth, followed by a clean water rinse and blow-dry. Indeed, the process resembles an automatic car wash. Total cleaning time: five minutes.

The thing is, cars don't contain valuable books, works of art, and furniture. No problem, says Ms. Gabe, who adds, "It's amazing how many things can be made waterproof." Wooden furniture and floors are liberally varnished. Casters assure that furniture is lifted out of harm's way. Upholstery is waterproofed. Books, art, and electrical appliances are either inserted in canisters with waterproof lids or into protective, sealable sleeves. All shelves are mesh, thus allowing water to flow right through.

Related time-saving devices for the house include the organic, automatically-operated self-cleaning toilet and a kitchen cupboard

289

that is really a dishwasher. Once the dishes are cleaned, they stay where they are: no unloading.

Ms. Gabe is in the process of writing a how-to-build-your-own-self-cleaning-house book and seeking financial support for the project. She keeps at it because "over the years I've talked to literally thousands of women about cleaning. Only four said they actually enjoyed housework. Cleaning is backbreaking work. It involves stooping, and I say, 'Stoop, stoop, stooping is *stupid!*' "

Guided tours of her house are available for a minimum group of five people at a cost of $5 per person. The Goldstein Gallery of Design, Housing and Apparel at the University of Minnesota in Minneapolis has on display a two-story model of the self-cleaning house.

ELECTRIC CAR

B uilding a practical electric car has never really been the problem. The hard part is developing a battery that can make it go fast enough and far enough to make it worthwhile.

· · · · ·
ODDS: 70%
ETA: 1997
PRICE: $20,000
· · · · ·

But there are three major forces that could propel electric cars onto the road before century's end. First, pollution. Electric cars don't produce carbon monoxide, a key ingredient in smog. Second, another oil crisis. It hasn't happened yet, but depleted reserves around the world hint that an oil shortage might not be far away. Nothing like necessity to spur invention. And third, superconductivity—the ability to generate electricity without resistance. Scientists have been able to achieve superconductivity only in temperatures that are hundreds of degrees below zero. But recent developments have raised those numbers, and the possibility of reaching normal temperature levels is growing less and less remote. Success would make electric-car performance a breeze.

The first consumer design to hit the road, however, could be a so-called hybrid vehicle from Volkswagen. The car's driver would alternate between gasoline and electric power, depending on driving conditions. In slow, stop-and-go traffic, for example, electricity is ideal. Less power is necessary, and less fuel is wasted. For normal and highway speeds, the driver simply switches to gasoline.

A lithium/iron/sulphide battery is currently showing promise as a viable power source. Experimental delivery vans have run up to 200 miles on a single charge. So someday, some way, it figures that you'll be saying, "juice 'er up" instead of "fill 'er up."

THE GUERRILLA INFORMATION NETWORK

The communal spirit of the sixties will find a voice in the communications revolution of the nineties. That's the vision of Fen Labalme, who created NewsPeek (see Electronic Newspaper, page 155) while studying at the Massachusetts Institute of Technology. If information is indeed power, then that power should be with the people, reasons Labalme. Which is what his Guerrilla Information Network (GIN) is all about.

ODDS: 80%
ETA: 1999
PRICE: FREE

First, it is a customized news service. Tell your computer what you want to know and it will spend the day gathering that information. Second, and most important, GIN will contain data from an infinite number of sources—newspapers, magazines, radical writers, grassroots organizations, manufacturers, politicians, and individuals . . . even you. Anyone who has something to say can write for GIN. And anyone who wants to know anything can find it out from GIN.

"Computers that can access GIN," Labalme predicts, "will be in bus stations, grocery stores, libraries, as well as in homes." The equipment will plug into fiber-optic phone lines, which will be commonplace by the late nineties.

Could an individual, company, or government agency control the data in GIN? No, says Labalme, because you could access information not just by subject but by source. For example, if you wanted to know about nuclear missile tests, you could get the government's opinion and you could also get the opinion of the environmental organization Greenpeace. You could also obtain the additional information that people like you have added to the files.

Labalme has been working on GIN for several years. His motivation? He wants people to be educated, and he believes that the publishing establishment has a monopoly on information. "I'm certainly not in this for the money," he says, "I just want it to happen."

The spirit of the sixties lives on!

NON-CONTACT PEN

Did you ever try to write your name on a T-shirt with a ballpoint pen? The nib of the pen keeps jabbing the threads and you're sure you're going to rip the cloth before you get your message across it.

. . . . .
ODDS: 25%
ETA: 1995
PRICE: UNDER $125
. . . . .

Well, Michael Piatt and Harry March of Eastman Kodak Company's ink-jet operations in Dayton, Ohio, have a solution. They had already designed an airbrush with twelve nozzles, so the thought of a miniature airbrush with just one nozzle— and eventually with exchangeable cartridges for different colors— didn't seem like a bad idea.

March sketched out the necessary components and now he and Piatt have been granted a patent for Kodak. The pen is an intricate device composed of resistors, its own drive circuitry, a battery, and an ink cartridge. Ink is squirted directly onto a writing surface out of a nib that is one one-thousandth of an inch in diameter. The ink spray is highly controlled and therefore doesn't blotch or skip or create other problems often associated with regular pens. Raise it from the surface a bit and you can create different effects, such as misting. "It's clearly not for everybody," says Piatt, "and it's not a replacement for a ballpoint, but if you have an artistic flair and like to doodle, this could be a cool addition to your pen collection."

Are we talking about the felt-tip of the nineties here? We'll just have to wait and see!

DOME HOMES

A man's home may be his castle, but a man's dome is his energy saver as well as his political and aesthetic statement.

ODDS: 40%

ETA: 1996

PRICE: $5,000–$15,000

The geodesic dome-shaped home is not for everyone, concedes Michael Busick, president of American Ingenuity, Inc., of Melbourne, Florida. If you're concerned with looking like the Joneses, then a dome home, no matter how efficient, probably isn't for you. However, Busick and wife, Glenda, have convincing reasons for their belief that the dome is the home of the future.

First and foremost is the matter of energy. The Busicks have patented a non-toxic insulation process that they say makes their dome homes three to four times more energy efficient. Instead of using 11 to 14 inches of porous fiberglass padding stuffed into traditional wooden, "block-style" homes, American Ingenuity utilizes 7 inches of polystyrene-foam triangles, which are chemically stable, will not rot or deteriorate, and are non-toxic even if burnt.

Polystyrene is not often utilized in the construction of traditional

293

homes because it is more expensive than commonly used fiberglass. But because the surface of a geodesic home is less than that of a square-shaped house, less polystyrene is needed. The combination of polystyrene insulation and the concrete exterior keeps homes warmer in winter and cooler in summer. In 1986, for example, the Busicks spent only $110 to heat and air-condition their 2,000-square-foot Florida home. The dome is just as efficient in colder climates.

Currently, there are sixty American Ingenuity homes in the United States. Six different dome home kits, which include only the exterior shell, are available, in sizes from 470 to 3,000 square feet. For information call 407-254-4220.

FLYING SAUCER

ODDS: 50%

ETA: 1999

PRICE: GOOD QUESTION!

Bet you've always wondered why no one has ever come up with a real flying saucer. The reason is that no one could make an engine that could move a vehicle from any point on a 360-degree circumference. In other words, all engines move forward or backward. A real flying saucer should have the ability to move in any direction and do it smoothly, without losing balance.

Peter Hsing figured out what to do. His ten-page patent text describes an aircraft that uses four hundred mini-engines and a gyro stabilizer that keeps the aircraft level. The nozzle of each tiny engine can be aimed to direct the aircraft. By firing different clusters of engines at different times, the pilot can steer the craft and regulate speed. "NASA says it could work. They are studying my plans. The question is whether it can be fuel-efficient and not cost too much," says Hsing.

Hsing, who has sixteen patents and another six on the way, says the flying saucer will be easier to maneuver than a helicopter.

FREEZING HUMANS

Freezing humans for the purpose of preservation is a medical advance that will almost certainly become reality someday. However, whether it happens before the end of the century will depend more on money than on science.

ODDS: 35%
ETA: 1999
PRICE: $125,000

"The technology is not far away," contends Hal Sternberg, a leading cryonics researcher at the University of California at Berkeley. "But some say, 'It's farfetched, so why invest?' In reality, cryonics technology may be simple compared to the biological realities of curing cancer or AIDS." And of course, the main reason for freezing is to keep people "alive" until cures for such deadly diseases and aging can be found.

This is how far scientists have progressed: A beagle named Miles (after Woody Allen's character in *Sleeper*) was anesthetized, laid on a bed of ice until his temperature fell to 68 degrees Fahrenheit, emptied of his own blood, filled back up with a synthetic blood that wouldn't clot in the cold, and then almost frozen. For the hour he spent at or below 50 degrees, Miles was legally dead. "Thawed" and reinjected with his own blood, Miles "came back" and proceeded to lead a normal life, "in perfect health," says Sternberg.

The next step is monkeys. And ultimately, people. But there are still obstacles to overcome. Experiments are now being conducted to determine how to minimize the microscopic damage to tissues that takes place during the freezing process.

Though there are people who have great reservations about cryonics, others view it with tremendous hope. "Someone who has a disease may choose to be frozen until the disease can be cured," says Sternberg, "or maybe somebody just wants to live in the future." The repercussions boggle the mind.

295

ALPHABETICAL LIST OF PRODUCTS

299

FOR THE BEST IN PAPERBACKS, LOOK FOR THE

In every corner of the world, on every subject under the sun, Penguin represents quality and variety—the very best in publishing today.

For complete information about books available from Penguin—including Pelicans, Puffins, Peregrines, and Penguin Classics—and how to order them, write to us at the appropriate address below. Please note that for copyright reasons the selection of books varies from country to country.

In the United Kingdom: For a complete list of books available from Penguin in the U.K., please write to *Dept E.P., Penguin Books Ltd, Harmondsworth, Middlesex, UB7 0DA.*

In the United States: For a complete list of books available from Penguin in the U.S., please write to *Dept BA, Penguin,* Box 120, Bergenfield, New Jersey 07621-0120.

In Canada: For a complete list of books available from Penguin in Canada, please write to *Penguin Books Ltd, 2801 John Street, Markham, Ontario L3R 1B4.*

In Australia: For a complete list of books available from Penguin in Australia, please write to the *Marketing Department, Penguin Books Ltd, P.O. Box 257, Ringwood, Victoria 3134.*

In New Zealand: For a complete list of books available from Penguin in New Zealand, please write to the *Marketing Department, Penguin Books (NZ) Ltd, Private Bag, Takapuna, Auckland 9.*

In India: For a complete list of books available from Penguin, please write to *Penguin Overseas Ltd, 706 Eros Apartments, 56 Nehru Place, New Delhi, 110019.*

In Holland: For a complete list of books available from Penguin in Holland, please write to *Penguin Books Nederland B.V., Postbus 195, NL-1380AD Weesp, Netherlands.*

In Germany: For a complete list of books available from Penguin, please write to *Penguin Books Ltd, Friedrichstrasse 10-12, D-6000 Frankfurt Main 1, Federal Republic of Germany.*

In Spain: For a complete list of books available from Penguin in Spain, please write to *Longman, Penguin España, Calle San Nicolas 15, E-28013 Madrid, Spain.*

In Japan: For a complete list of books available from Penguin in Japan, please write to *Longman Penguin Japan Co Ltd, Yamaguchi Building, 2-12-9 Kanda Jimbocho, Chiyoda-Ku, Tokyo 101, Japan.*